Offshore lending and financing

a practical and legal handbook for lenders, borrowers, investors and their professional advisers

Vaumini Amin, BA (Hons), FCIB, FRSA

GRESHAM BOOKS

WOODHEAD
PUBLISHING
LIMITED
IN ASSOCIATION WITH
THE CHARTERED
INSTITUTE OF
BANKERS

Edited by Paul B Sugden, BA (Hons), ACIB, Advocate of the Royal Court of Jersey, Barrister of Lincoln's Inn.

Published by Gresham Books, an imprint of Woodhead Publishing Limited, Abington Hall, Abington, Cambridge CB1 6AH, England

First published 1998

British Library Cataloguing in Publication Data
A catalogue record for this book is available from the British Library.

ISBN 1 85573 329 3

Typeset by Euroset, Hampshire, England.
Printed by St Edmundsbury Press, Suffolk, England.

To my husband Mahendra Amin, my mother Hirnaxi Patel
and to my late father, Chimanbhai Dahyabhai Patel,
who is greatly missed.

Contents

Preface

This is a book intended to identify the key dos and don'ts of lending with an offshore element; it aims to serve as a source of practical guidance for bankers and others concerned in lending transactions involving a connection with a foreign law. It is not the intention that the book will provide a full comparative legal reference work, but it is intended to provide sufficient information as to the issues that arise for lenders so as to identify relevant issues of concern. The inclusion of consideration of tax treatment is intended to be a basic guide only and to assist the lender in identifying the types of tax-based uses for lending that involve the use of international offshore financial centres.

The book has been prepared in two parts, with an intended emphasis on practical guidance in the context of relevant law. The first part serves as a general introduction to the selection, usage and language of international offshore financial centres. Although the focus of attention is the use of such centres in lending structures, many of the issues highlighted (for example, choice of applicable or governing law) are relevant to lending with any foreign law connection. The second part focuses on the law and practices of some of the most frequently encountered international offshore financial centres. The chapters dealing with each chosen international offshore financial centre are, so far as possible, set out in the same order and manner in order to facilitate easy cross-reference and comparison.

This book has been prepared on the basis of the issues relevant to a lender operating from an 'onshore' jurisdiction, the law of which is familiar to the lender. For most purposes it is assumed that the United Kingdom is the onshore jurisdiction. In this context, and for most purposes, references to 'the lender' may concern matters that are of equal significance for an investor. Similarly, references to 'the borrower' should be read as including a third-party guarantor, surety or other provider of security.

Every effort has been made to ensure accuracy in the text, but it is recognised that there may yet remain an occasional error. Likewise, every effort has been made to trace relevant copyright owners, but if any have been inadvertently omitted, an appropriate acknowledgement will be made at the earliest opportunity.

The law is stated up to date as at January 1997 but it should be recognised that the competitive nature of international offshore financial centres raises the prospect of unanticipated change. This work is not intended to be an exhaustive reference work and no attempt has been made to consider complex transactional issues arising, for example, on syndications.

The author's thanks are due to the editorial staff of Woodhead Publishing, the Chartered Institute of Bankers and its library and, especially, to Chris Moon and to Geoffrey Reeday for their help. Thanks are also due to the editor, Advocate Paul Sugden, and to his wife Carol who typed the complete text. Finally, and most importantly, personal thanks are due to my husband Mahendra for his support, encouragement, general forbearance and practical help in proof-reading.

Table of cases

Table of statutes

United Kingdom

Bermuda

Treaties

Conventions

Acknowledgements

Appleby, Spurling & Kempe
Cedar House, Hamilton HM 12, Bermuda
Tel 809 295 2244

Eidgenossisches Amt für das Handels Register
Office Federal du Registre du Commerce,
3003 Berne
Tel 031 322 4191

Euromoney Publications Plc
57 North Hill, Colchester, Essex CO1 1QD
Tel (01206) 579591

Financial Supervision Commission (Isle of Man)
PO Box 58, 1–4 Goldie Terrace, Upper Church Street,
Douglas, Isle of Man IM99 1DT
Tel (01624) 624487

Government of the British Virgin Islands
PO Box 418, Road Town, Tortola, British Virgin Islands
Tel (809) 49 45355/6

Guernsey Financial Services Commission
Valley House, Hirzel Street,
St Peter Port, Guernsey GY1 2NP

J A Hassan & Partners
57–63 Line Wall Road
Gibraltar
Tel 350 79000

Jersey Financial Services Department
Cyril Le Marquand House, PO Box 267, The Parade,
St Helier, Jersey JE4 8TP
Tel 01534 603000

The Law School (Cayman Islands)
Tower Building, George Town, Cayman Islands, British West Indies
Myers & Alberga
PO Box 472, Grand Cayman, Cayman Islands, West Indies
Tel 809 949 0699

Ogier & Le Masurier
PO Box 404, Pirouet House, Union Street,
St Helier, Jersey JE4 9WG
Tel 01534 504000

Ozannes
PO Box 186, 1 Le Marchant Street,
St Peter Port, Guernsey GY1 4HP
Tel 0 1481 723466

Part II

1 ‖ Offshore centres: an introduction

Introduction

This chapter identifies and considers those features which lead to the treatment of a country, state or other geographical or political unit as an *international offshore financial centre*. Such an exercise is of significance to the lender in a transaction which is in some manner connected to an international offshore financial centre because each such feature (and the borrower's or lender's reason for selecting them) forms part of the lender's exposure to risk.

1.1 Definition

What is meant by the term 'international offshore financial centre'? An abstract definition serves no purpose. An offshore centre exists by usage: it is recognised by an amalgam of features which, taken together, offer particular advantages for investment by non-residents through, but not in, the jurisdiction concerned. It has a separate system of fiscal law but need not be a separate nation state. Usually, its status is a product of history or of geography which has been exploited over time to create a financial centre.

Today, international offshore financial centres (*offshore centres*) play a vital role in facilitating investment worldwide. In a global economy, offshore centres are a focal point for the collection and channelling of wealth into onshore financial centres.

It is a common perception that an offshore centre is used exclusively because it brings tax advantages to the investment or financing structure. It is certainly true that most, if not all, offshore centres:

- have no relevant incidence of income or capital gains tax (i.e. do not tax the proposed activity or entity); and/or
- have a tax regime which is neutral; and/or
- provide access to double taxation arrangements; and/or
- impose no withholdings on distributions and other payments.

It is important, however, not to overlook the significance of other issues relevant to the choice of offshore centre, including:

- the absence of foreign exchange restrictions;
- political stability;
- geographical location, including time zone;
- communication links;
- internal skills infrastructure;
- regulatory infrastructure;
- banking secrecy and professional confidentiality generally;
- investor perception; and
- political affiliation.

1.2 Should a lender be concerned by a borrower's choice of offshore centre?

The answer is yes. What follows will highlight the manner in which characteristics of an offshore centre (or the characteristics of a borrower or investment vehicle whose incorporation or existence is exclusive to a particular offshore centre) will affect analysis of (i) credit risk (which includes country or sovereign risk), (ii) the ability to secure such credit risk and (iii) the ability to achieve and retain the intended return to the lender. Before considering, by way of introduction, the significance to the lender of the features which drive the borrower's choice, note should be made that today's offshore environment is dynamic and competitive, bringing rapid change and a trend of continuous innovation.

1.3 The borrower's criteria for choice

No two offshore centres should be regarded as the same. Some have similarities, but no assumptions should be made. The lender must be mindful that the borrower's criteria for selection may be based on priorities very different from those of the lender. For example, the borrower may put tax efficiency and banking or jurisdictional confidentiality above the need for political stability or the soundness of the regulatory regime. Although the chapters that follow will deal, in more detail, with issues that arise from the selection either of a particular offshore centre or of the type of borrower particular to that offshore centre, the lender should always have in mind the interaction of (and relative weight to be given to) each of the following factors which may or may not have formed part of the consideration of the borrower and to the issues discussed in further detail in this chapter.

1.3.1 Political stability

Political stability allows for clearer assessment of risk. Political instability increases risk through the possibility of change. Initial reasons for selection (for example, tax efficiency) may disappear. In a worst case, change in political regime may lead to the seizure of assets (*expropriation*), change in law or imposition of foreign exchange restrictions, all of which may have dire consequences for the viability of an investment or financing structure.

1.3.2 Geographic location and communication

Remote offshore centres with problems of communication will hinder efficiency in both the setting up and running of investment and financing structures. While air and other travel links may not be as significant in an age of electronic communication, their practical significance should not, in appropriate circumstances, be overlooked. Telecommunications, postal and courier services must be viable and efficient.

1.3.3 Professional and financial infrastructure

Well developed financial and professional infrastructure may, of itself, provide evidence of political and economic stability. The presence of international financial institutions and representatives of recognised law and accountancy firms will reflect general confidence in the stability and competence of the offshore centre. The competence and choice of local or expatriate professionals, for example in the accountancy and legal fields, may impact on the lender's ability to rely on opinions and financial statements.

1.3.4 Regulatory and legal framework

In some offshore jurisdictions the regulatory or legal framework may provide the sole rationale for its choice. For example, a high net worth individual may choose a structure in which *asset protection* (see below, para 4.4.7.2) is viable and sustainable against creditors. The competition between offshore centres ensures that many seek to create opportunities particular to that jurisdiction or not otherwise widely available. Such opportunities may be based on either tax efficiency or other commercial advantage. A recent example is found in the adoption by the island of Jersey of legislation enabling the incorporation of limited liability partnerships.

While the regulatory or legal framework may be a significant criterion in the borrower's selection of an offshore centre, it may have equal significance to the lender on an ongoing basis. It will be important to the lender that the authorities and courts of the offshore centre are familiar with, and sympathetic to, features of lending practice and enforcement of the lender's rights. For example, will a judgment taken against the borrower in the lender's jurisdiction be enforced in the offshore jurisdiction without a further court hearing? The regulatory framework may be of particular significance in establishing the reputation of the offshore centre. Significant protection may be afforded to the lender where reliance can be placed on the efficiency of local regulators in applying appropriate standards to the incorporation or other formation of borrowers and conduct of business in areas such as collective investment funds, provision of investment advice, and banking and insurance.

1.3.5 Reputation

In large measure, the reputation of an offshore centre will reflect all of the issues discussed above. In today's regulatory environment, however, it is important to lenders that their reputations should not be damaged by association. By their nature, offshore centres may be a target for use by criminals for money laundering or other illegal purposes. An understanding of why the borrower has selected an offshore centre may save the lender from subsequent adverse or damaging comment, even if misplaced. The borrower's choice and use of an offshore centre, particularly one of sound reputation, should not of itself cause concern as to the probity of the borrower or its transaction, but the absence of a proper and under-standable basis for selection may be a real cause for concern and further enquiry.

1.3.6 Banking secrecy and confidentiality

A legitimate interest in the preservation of confidentiality may have a place in the borrower's selection of offshore centre. High net worth individuals may wish their financial affairs to enjoy a degree of confidentiality which may not be achievable in their country of residence or domicile. An unexplained or disproportionate search for confidentiality should, however, be cause for concern and further enquiry.

1.3.7 Costs

Where two or more offshore jurisdictions offer the same facilities to the borrower (for example, tax exempt corporations) the cost of formation and ongoing administration of those incorporations may be a determinative factor in the borrower's choice.

1.4 The legal personality of the borrower

Opportunities offered by offshore centres are often based on the characteristics of corporate or other entities peculiar to the law of a particular offshore centre. In dealing with a borrowing or an investment vehicle, it is important for the lender to understand and be comfortable with the nature and qualities of the borrower or investment vehicle. If it is a corporation, is its capacity limited in any way? Should the lender be concerned by issues of *ultra vires*, either in relation to the corporation or its officers? What information is available about the corporation and its officers, either on public registries or at its registered office or otherwise? More generally, and whether the borrower or other party is a natural person, corporation, partnership, trustee or other entity, does the law of a jurisdiction to which they are subject provide it with legal personality and capacity to enter into a proposed transaction in a relevant way? As will appear in later chapters, the nature or legal personality of the borrower is of crucial significance to the lender involved in a transaction with an offshore or foreign law element.

1.5 The system of law

In the definition of an offshore centre (see above, para 1.1) reference is made to the requirement that an offshore centre may have its own legal system and a separate system of fiscal law. An offshore centre need not be a separate nation state: Jersey, Guernsey and the Isle of Man form part of the British Isles (as dependent territories) and are not nation states but each has a separate system of law. In the main, history will have determined the source of a relevant system of law but it should not be overlooked that some modern offshore centres are a deliberate creation of a parent nation state – for example Labuan, created as a *federal territory* by the state of Malaysia. By contrast Liechtenstein, Luxembourg and Switzerland have systems of law as separate nation states. In very general terms, and historically, most offshore centres can be divided between those which have systems of law based on an English *common* law model, and those which are based upon a European *civil* law model. It is important, however, not to overlook a third system of law, which may generically be described as *Muslim or Shari'a law*, and which, although it may not be of direct application in the offshore centre concerned, may, because of its effect on a party to the transaction, play a part in the selection by such party of an offshore centre.

1.5.1 The common law model

Those offshore centre jurisdictions which possess legal systems based upon or influenced by English common law are both geographically and culturally diverse. Two principal groupings can be identified in the Caribbean jurisdictions of Anguilla, the Bahamas, Barbados, Belize, the British Virgin Islands, Cayman Islands, Nevis, St Kitts and the Turks and Caicos Islands. A second major grouping is that of the British Channel Islands and the Isle of Man. There are then others (some of them new as offshore centres) such as Western Samoa, Labuan, Mauritius and the Cook Islands. While some jurisdictions with common law derived legal systems have remained British Crown dependencies or territories, others have gained independence and have systems of law materially modified by statutory provision and cultural practice. Of significance, however, most common law jurisdictions share a common approach to corporate legal personality, do not recognise a partnership or firm as having a separate legal identity and do recognise the concept of a trust.

1.5.2 The civil law model

Those jurisdictions which trace their legal systems back to mainland European jurisdictions, such as France, Germany and the Netherlands, tend to draw upon a legal system described as a *civil law* system. Historically such legal systems all have their roots in the Roman codified system of law. For the purposes of this work it is perhaps sufficient to note that of the principal offshore centres, the Netherlands Antilles are perhaps the best known offshore centre with a civil system of law. More curiously, however, it is relevant to note that the Channel Island jurisdictions of Jersey and Guernsey have legal systems which draw their customary law from the civil Norman French customary law, although their companies laws and trusts laws are now based on legislation drawn from English models.

1.6 Constitutional affiliation

Few true offshore centres are sovereign nation states. Even those that are (for example, Switzerland, Luxembourg and Mauritius) are not immune from external political influence and pressure. Most offshore centres have constitutional ties to a nation state, most frequently the historic colonial powers such as Britain, France, the Netherlands, Portugal and Spain. The range of constitutional relationships is broad but it is right to note that as a matter of international law it is invariably only nation states which have power to enter into true *treaty* relationships. In consequence, an offshore centre may have the right to internal self-governance (for example, the exclusive right to administer its internal legal system and raise and apply taxes within its territory) yet remain subject to outside forces in relation to the international treaties to which it is bound as a party. At the present time there are two areas in which international treaty obligations are having, and are likely to continue to have, a significant effect, being:

- the international resolve to combat money laundering, reflected for example in early form by the United Nations Convention against Illicit Traffic in Narcotic Drugs and Psychotropic Substances 1988, and in current bilateral assistance treaties such as that between the United Kingdom and the United States of America; and
- the development of the European Union.

We shall now look at the second of these two areas.

1.6.1 The European Union (EU): a question of influence

Reference has already been made to the constitutional links between many well known offshore centres and those European nations with a colonial past. The degree of connection between offshore centres and the EU is complex, with many variations, but some principal groupings are as follows.

1.6.1.1 Member States
Luxembourg and Ireland are, as sovereign states, parties to and are bound by the EU Treaty.

1.6.1.2 Non-European territories
This is a description of the status of certain territories or dependencies of Member States and, in the case of the United Kingdom, includes the British Virgin Islands, the Cayman Islands and the Turks and Caicos Islands.

1.6.1.3 European territories
This is a description of offshore centres which, although not Member States, have a degree of connection with the EU, either as:

- a dependent territory of a Member State within or close to the European mainland, for example Gibraltar (which is subject to all rules except those in *Article 28 of the UK Treaty of Accession*), Jersey, Guernsey and the Isle of Man (which are dealt with as a special case by the provisions of *Protocol 3 of the UK Act of Accession*) and Monaco (which is part of a Customs Union with France); or
- European territories or states with a relationship with the EU or a Member State, for example Malta (which is part of a customs union), Cyprus (which has an association agreement with the EU and has applied for full membership) and San Marino (which is in a customs union with Italy).

1.6.2 EU Treaty obligations and directives

EU Treaty obligations and directives apply in general only to Member States and (with exceptions such as those for Jersey, Guernsey and the Isle of Man) to those European territories for which a Member State has responsibility for external relations. The extent of application of EU Treaty obligations to other territories which are 'associated' with the EU such as Cyprus and the Netherlands Antilles is the subject of the particular arrangements concerned.

For full Member States (such as Luxembourg and Ireland) the benefit of access to the so called 'freedoms' (the free movement of persons and the freedom to provide services) is available to persons who are citizens of or who are domiciled in a Member State. For practical purposes this means that such persons are able to take advantage of or are subject to the internal legislation of Member States giving effect to specific EU directives, examples of which are given in the following sub-paragraphs.

1.6.2.1 UCITS
The UCITS directive gives a right to market collective investment funds regulated in one Member State in each other Member State.

1.6.2.2 Bank harmonisation
The harmonisation of banking in the EU is effected through freedom of establishment, own funds, solvency and adequacy of supervision of financial institutions.

1.6.2.3 Companies
Harmonised rules relating to reporting, distributions to shareholders, standardised accounting standards, off balance sheet accounting and listing requirements, are to lead to common standards.

1.6.2.4 Investor protection
Harmonised rules relating to minimum compensation for investors, by a home country regulator of an investment business.

1.6.2.5 Free flow of capital

Harmonised rules relating to the free transfer of moneys between Member States for the purpose of investment.

1.6.2.6 Taxation

The development of rules relating to (i) mutual assistance of the enforcement of direct taxation, (ii) the elimination of double taxation provisions relating to adjustment of profits of related enterprises, (iii) the elimination of withholding on dividends between subsidiaries and holding companies with a 25% interest in the subsidiary, and (iv) the harmonisation of taxation on mergers and reorganisations.

1.6.3 European territories

Offshore centres that are European territories (see above, para 1.6.1), although not subject to direct application of EU Treaty obligations and directives, may nevertheless be indirectly affected by, for example:

1.6.3.1 Article 85

Article 85 of the EU Treaty prohibits agreements and arrangements which are intended to prevent, restrict or distort trade and competition between businesses of Member States. It is possible, however, that if a person in an offshore centre (for example, a Jersey company) enters into a prohibited arrangement with a person in a Member State, the person in the offshore centre may be subject to sanctions sought by the EU Commission within the EU and civil proceeding brought in the offshore centre.

1.6.3.2 VAT

Not all non-Member States are outside the EU for VAT purposes (Monaco and the Isle of Man are within the EU for VAT purposes), and while others are outside for VAT purposes (Jersey, Guernsey, Gibraltar and San Marino) the supply of services to persons in such offshore centres (for example 'management services') may attract VAT chargeable by the EU-based supplier. The UK has by the *Finance Act 1996* closed a VAT avoidance loophole which allowed persons who are unable to recover VAT to obtain provision of telecommunication services and other services from persons in a non-EU centre net of VAT.

1.6.3.3 The Rome Convention

The EEC Convention on the law applicable to contractual obligations of 1980 ('the Rome Convention') regulates the harmonisation of choice of law rules (see below, para 2.1) relating to commercial arrangements and came into force in relation to Belgium, Denmark, France, Germany, Italy, Luxembourg and the United Kingdom on 1 April 1991 and subsequently in Greece, the Netherlands and Ireland. Importantly, by virtue of Article 1(1) of the Convention, Member States to which it applies will implement its terms through their courts in relation to any contractual obligations where a choice between the laws of different countries arises. This means that the Convention will apply wherever the relevant court has jurisdiction, even if the contract involves parties from a non-EU Member State. *Article 27(2)(b)* of the Convention and the *Contracts (Applicable Law) Act 1990 s.8* provide that it may be extended directly to the Channel Islands and Isle of Man.

1.7 The lender's overview

The use by a borrower of an offshore centre, and the borrower's criteria for choice may increase the lender's credit risk, through the operation of factors with which the lender may not be familiar. To reduce the degree of risk the lender should:

- identify the offshore centre concerned;
- identify and understand the borrower's purpose in using an offshore centre within the transaction;
- identify and understand the borrower's reason for choosing the offshore centre concerned;
- identify the issues of foreign law involved; and
- identify the compliance and practical consequences for the lender and for the transaction of the borrower's use and choice of an offshore centre.

Each of Chapters 2 to 9 addresses issues which raise issues of risk for the lender where the proposed transaction has a connection with an offshore centre or otherwise with a foreign law. To identify problems, create certainty and thereby reduce risk, the lender should, wherever an offshore centre's use is contemplated, consider the need for a legal opinion to be given by reputable lawyers competent to advise on the law of the offshore centre concerned. Chapter 10 discusses the use of foreign law legal opinions in more detail and provides an example of general form and content. In the intervening chapters attention will be drawn to particular issues which will, usually, form the subject matter of a foreign law legal opinion.

2 | Offshore centres: foreign law concepts and terms

Introduction

This chapter will attempt to identify and explain concepts, and within those concepts terms commonly used in connection with offshore centres or otherwise in connection with a foreign law.

2.1 Applicable law and jurisdiction

The rules of law governing the application of more than one system of law to relationships between parties and as applied by the courts of a particular territory are referred to as rules of *private international law* or *conflict of laws*. The grant of a loan, credit or other facility is an arrangement intended to form a binding agreement between the parties to it. As such, it falls within that part of the law described as the *law of obligations* or *contract*. The law which governs the agreement or contracts made between parties is described variously as the *proper law, governing law,* or *applicable law* (this book will use the term 'applicable law' which should be read as including a reference to the proper or governing law).

The applicable law may apply to the whole or to part only of a contract. In lending transactions which involve connection with a foreign law the lender should seek to increase certainty and thereby reduce risk through the selection of an applicable law, a process referred to as the *choice of law*. The ability of the parties to a contract to freely select the applicable law (whether applying to the whole or part of the contract or to change the applicable law subsequent to the formation of the contract) is described as *party autonomy*. English common law has historically recognised a broad party autonomy, and in the case of *Vita Food Products Inc v Unus Shipping Co* [1939] A.C.277, Lord Wright said:

> *Where there is an express statement by the parties of their intention to select the law of the contract, it is difficult to see what qualifications are possible provided the intention expressed is bona fides and legal and provided there is no reason for avoiding the choice on the ground of public policy.*

The Rome Convention (see above, para 1.6.3.3) provides in Article 3(1) that: 'By their choice the parties can select the law applicable to the whole or part only of the contract.' It should be noted that the freedom accorded to the parties to choose the applicable law extends to the ability to sever one part of the contract or arrangement from another and to apply a different applicable law to each (referred to as *dépecage*). It has already been observed that the Rome Convention and its application to choice of law issues may apply wherever the courts of a Member State to which the Convention applies has jurisdiction over a relevant issue. It should, likewise, be noted that not all legal systems accord the same degree of freedom of choice to the parties to select the applicable law. Historically, many states of the United States of America have applied objective, inflexible tests using either the place of contracting or the place of performance to fix the applicable law.

2.2 Limitations on the lender's ability to select an applicable law

In *Vita Food Products Inc v Unus Shipping Co* (see above, para 2.1) reference was made by Lord Wright to the requirement that the choice must be made in the absence of a reason for avoiding the choice on the ground of *public policy* and must be *bona fide* and legal. The Rome Convention provides in Article 3(3) that:

> *The fact that the parties have chosen a foreign law, whether or not accompanied by the choice of a foreign tribunal, shall not, where all other elements relevant to the situation at the time of choice are connected with one country only, prejudice the application of rules of the law of that country which cannot be derogated from by contract, hereinafter called 'mandatory rules'.*

The reference to *mandatory rules* is a reference to the rules of a domestic system of law which cannot be the subject of derogation by contract, for example the rules providing controls on exemption clauses contained in the *Unfair Contract Terms Act 1977.* This provision in the Rome Convention restates a limitation generally held to apply under the common law, that the choice of applicable law should not have a predominant evasive intent.

2.3 Factors influencing selection of applicable law

The lender should select the applicable law having regard to the following factors.

2.3.1 The competence of the legal system

It is important that the chosen system of law recognises and is capable of regulating the substance of the proposed transaction. The existence of relevant legislation need not necessarily indicate the existence of a body of case law or other precedent necessary to provide certainty in the construction or application of the relevant laws.

2.3.2 The stability of the legal system

The legal system should demonstrate evolutionary rather than revolutionary change. Stability in the legal system is likely to be a reflection of political stability.

2.3.3 The convenience of the legal system

It may be advantageous to have a legal system which, in its application, practice and procedure, is familiar to the lender and borrower. This may lead to a selection of the applicable law of the jurisdiction in which the credit or lending assessment is made rather than, for example, that of the lending or booking office, although in such a case it is necessary to consider the impact of the law of the place where the account is maintained with the possibility that a legal opinion will be required.

2.3.4 The place where assets are located

It will almost always be appropriate to create a security over assets in accordance with the law of the jurisdiction in which the asset is located (see below, Chapter 9).

2.3.5 A requirement to 'insulate' the transaction

It is very often desirable that a system of law is chosen which is different to that to which a counterparty is subject and under which a counterparty might have rights and remedies which are undesirable in the context of the transaction.

2.4 Jurisdiction

In the context of this chapter, a reference to *jurisdiction* is a reference to the extent to which a court has or may assume responsibility for determining issues in a dispute between the parties. Although it is beyond the scope of this book, the lender should note that the courts of some jurisdictions, particularly the Federal and State courts of the United States, purport to act with a jurisdiction appearing to extend beyond their territorial borders (for example in relation to US dollar-denominated transactions), a process sometimes termed *extraterritorial* or *long arm* jurisdiction. As a general rule, a lender should ensure that the courts of the territory whose law has been chosen as the applicable law will have the relevant jurisdiction to hear and determine any dispute between the lender, the borrower and any other relevant party as this will increase certainty as to the interpretation of the chosen applicable law and is likely to reduce costs in any necessary proceedings. The question of whether the courts of a particular territory have jurisdiction is generally determined by rules of private international law as applied by the courts of the territory to which the issue of jurisdiction has been referred (the *lex fori*). English law now applies the different sets of rules, depending upon the prevailing facts and in accordance with the rules and treaties set out below.

2.4.1 The traditional rules

In cases where the Conventions (see below) and the *Civil Jurisdiction and Judgments Acts 1982 and 1991* do not apply, the English courts apply procedural tests based on 'presence' (*in personam* jurisdiction) where the parties to a dispute are present within the territory and can be duly served with the originating process (for example writ or originating summons). The English courts assert a narrow jurisdiction as against the whole world (*in rem*) in relation to some admiralty actions. Although the English court has jurisdiction based on presence, it may, nevertheless, agree to *stay* the proceedings:

- where it is demonstrated that the courts of another legal system are seized of the same matter between the same parties (*lis alibi pendens*); and
- where the English courts may be seen as the least convenient in which to try the issues (referred to as the doctrine of *forum non conveniens*).

In a further case, the English courts may decline jurisdiction on the basis of some supervening limitation, for example where the subject matter of the proceedings involves foreign land.

2.4.2 The Brussels Convention

Originally entered into between the six members of the European Economic Community, the *Convention on Jurisdiction and the Enforcement of Judgments in Civil and Commercial Matters* was signed in 1968, and came into force in 1973. It was acceded to by the United Kingdom in 1978 in amended form and was given effect in the United Kingdom through the *Civil Jurisdiction and Judgments Act 1982*. It applies in relation to those EU Member States which are a party to it (*Contracting State*) and only to civil and commercial matters where the defendant is domiciled in the EU or, if not, where the dispute involves title to real property in a Member State or where the agreement confers jurisdiction on the courts of the Member State.

2.4.3 The modified Convention

When the United Kingdom gave effect to the *Brussels Convention* through the *Civil Jurisdiction and Judgments Act 1982* it applied a modified version of the *Brussels Convention* to civil and commercial matters where the defendant is domiciled in the United Kingdom or where the proceedings concerned are of a type which attributes jurisdiction regardless of domicile, for example in disputes involving title to real property in the United Kingdom.

2.4.4 The Lugano Convention

The *Lugano Convention*, agreed in 1988, is a convention on jurisdiction and the recognition of enforcement of judgments, intended to provide a parallel to the *Brussels Convention* but applicable to the EFTA bloc and allowing accession by the present members of the EU and the EFTA bloc. In the United Kingdom the Lugano Convention has been implemented by the *Civil Jurisdiction and Judgments Act 1991* which came into force on 1 May 1992. It applies in the United Kingdom and in other EU Contracting States where the matter is a civil and commercial matter and the defendant is domiciled in an EFTA Contracting State or where, if the defendant is not so domiciled, the case involves title to land in an EFTA Contracting State or where there is a submission to jurisdiction over the courts of an EFTA Contracting State.

The modified Convention and the Lugano Convention are designed to facilitate international commerce by the mutual recognition of judgments and a restriction on the ability of a plaintiff to bring proceedings in a multiplicity of jurisdictions (*forum shopping*).

2.5 Submission to jurisdiction

The lender should wherever possible ensure that transaction documents contain a selection agreed between the parties of the court which is to have jurisdiction to determine disputes. This agreed selection is accomplished through a *submission to jurisdiction* in an express contractual provision (a *jurisdiction clause*). Submission to jurisdiction in a lender's documentation is normally sought on a non-exclusive basis: that is, the borrower agrees irrevocably to submit the resolution of disputes to the courts of a jurisdiction, but allows the lender to bring proceedings in any other competent jurisdiction. The operation of so-called non-exclusive jurisdiction clauses must now be viewed in the context of the application of *Article 17* of the *Brussels Convention* (see above, para 2.4.2) which (in relation to an agreement in writing involving international trade or commerce) provides that:

- in the case of parties to a contract who are domiciled in a Contracting State, the courts of a chosen Contracting State or States shall have *exclusive jurisdiction* (i.e. the chosen courts must accept jurisdiction to the exclusion of the courts of any other Contracting State); and
- in the case of parties none of which is domiciled in a Contracting State, provides that where the courts of a Contracting State are chosen, they may accept jurisdiction based on their application of private international law rules, and if, but only if they accept jurisdiction, will have exclusive jurisdiction as against the courts of any other Contracting State.

2.6 Applicable law and jurisdiction, checklist and summary

In summary, where the lender is asked to enter into a transaction with a person having a connection (as to which see below) with an offshore centre having a different system of law (a *foreign law*) the lender must ensure that:

- the lender has chosen (and all relevant parties have agreed to and are bound by) the lender's preferred system of law (the *applicable law*) to govern the rights of the parties between themselves relating to the loan and any security;
- there is a selection of jurisdiction and that the chosen courts will have jurisdiction because all of the relevant parties have submitted to the jurisdiction of such courts; and
- a judgment given by the courts to whose jurisdiction the parties have submitted will be enforced by the courts of any relevant offshore centre by reciprocal enforcement without the need for a rehearing of the entire case.

2.7 Domicile

The concepts of domicile, residence and nationality are used to identify the system of law applicable to a person (the *personal law* or *lex domicilii*).

The concept of *domicile* is a creation of the law. Every person has a domicile and can have no more than one domicile at any one time. Domicile connects a person to a system of *municipal* law (*Henderson v Henderson* [1967] P.77). Determination of domicile by reference to municipal or territorial law means that a person who is a national or citizen of a federation of states will have a domicile which connects that person with a particular state, for example of the United States. The function of domicile in identifying the applicable personal law is the determination of:

- capacity to marry;
- capacity to make a will;
- intestate succession to moveables;
- formalities for the creation of a will of moveables;
- legitimacy;
- formalities for adoption;
- formalities for and capacity to divorce.

2.7.1 Definition of domicile

In English law, domicile has been defined as the place which a person has voluntarily fixed as a permanent and not merely a temporary home (*Wicker v Hume* (1858) H.L.Cas.124). In those jurisdictions following the civil law model, the concept of permanence is replaced by a reference to a concept of *habitual* residence. Although it is fundamental that each person has a domicile (and only one domicile at any single point in time) there are, in fact, three types of domicile which the person may have, as follows.

2.7.1.1 Domicile of origin

A domicile of origin is the domicile which a person acquires at birth, as being that of his father as at the time of birth. Where the person is illegitimate or where the father is not alive at the time of the child's birth, the child may acquire the domicile of its mother as its domicile of origin (*Re Dulip Singh* [1890] 6 T.L.R.). In most jurisdictions, the domicile of origin may be changed but it can never be lost (*Bell v Kennedy* (1868) L.R.1 Sc. & Div. 307, H.L.). It is, in effect, perpetual and will reinstate itself as the domicile of a person, in the absence of any other form of domicile (in English law, referred to as the doctrine of abeyance and revival) (*Udny v Udny* (1969), L.R.1 Sc. & Div. 441, H.L.).

2.7.1.2 Domicile of choice

A domicile of choice is the domicile which a person acquires through (i) the contemporaneous existence of an intention to reside permanently in a particular place, and (ii) the fact of that person's residence in such place. Where these two factors exist, and where the person has full legal capacity (i.e. is of full age and has full mental capacity), a domicile of choice will supercede a domicile of origin applicable to that person; such domicile of origin, as is stated above, is then in abeyance. As both the intention to reside in the relevant place and the fact of residence must exist together, it is possible that such domicile of choice may be abandoned without a subsequent domicile of choice being established.

2.7.1.3 Domicile of dependence

A domicile of dependence is the domicile which a person who is not of full legal capacity may acquire, as distinct from that person's domicile of origin, because such person's domicile is deemed by law to follow that of a parent or other person. A person so dependent cannot by his own act change his domicile but a change may be effected by the person on whom he is dependent. The domicile of a legitimate child may, therefore, change with that of his father and the domicile of an illegitimate child (whose father is dead) may change with that of his mother. Adopted children may acquire the domicile of their adopting parents.

2.7.2 Special applications of domicile

Domicile is from time to time adopted as the concept by which a particular legislative provision is to apply and then made the subject of a particular definition. In English law examples are to be found of its use in the *Civil Jurisdiction and Judgments Act 1991* and the *Inheritance Tax Act 1984.*

2.7.3 The domicile of a company

The domicile of a company is usually that of its place of incorporation or registration and of its proper law. Chapter 6 considers the implications for a lender arising from the domicile of a company and from the possibility that a company may change its domicile, and looks in more detail at the significance of 'residence' for companies.

2.7.4 English reform of domicile

Following recommendations of the Law Commission in 1987, radical changes to the English concept of domicile have been under consideration which would:

● introduce a single type of domicile, being that acquired by a person being a non-domiciliary present in a new country in which he intends to settle for an indefinite period; and
● introduce a domicile for children being that of the country with which a person under 16 years has the closest connection.

Although it was suggested that these changes would be introduced in legislation brought forward in early 1994, to date the changes have not been effected.

2.8 Nationality

The concept of *nationality* is used to describe an individual's allegiance to a nation state. While common law jurisdictions have tended to retain domicile as the connecting factor to a system of personal law, civil law jurisdictions (for example, France since 1803, Italy, Austria, Sweden, Spain, Portugal, Germany, Belgium, the Netherlands, many Eastern European countries, many South American countries, Japan and many other Asian countries) use the concept of nationality to determine the relevant system of personal law.

2.9 Residence

The concept of *residence* does not, of itself, determine a person's relevant system of *personal law*, although to acquire a domicile of choice there must be residence in the territory concerned. It is, however, an important concept in determination of the application of a relevant system of *fiscal law* to a person. Residence may also be important as a basis upon which a person is subject to the jurisdiction of the courts of a relevant territory and, in particular for the purposes of a lender, as a basis for jurisdiction in relation to that person's insolvency. Further considerations of the concepts of *residence* and *ordinary residence* are referred to below at para 2.10.4.

2.10 Fiscal law

The *fiscal* law of a jurisdiction is the law of that jurisdiction relating to the public revenues and the taxes, duties and imposts by which such revenues are raised. Attention has been drawn to the significance that tax planning may have in the choice and role of an offshore centre in a lending or investment structure. As the *fiscal* law may extend to all nature of taxes and duties accruing in respect of a lending or investment transaction, it is necessary to question whether any aspect of the transaction gives rise to a liability to a relevant tax or duty in a relevant offshore centre. So, for example, it is important for a lender to determine that neither the lending of the proposed moneys, nor the securing of such lending, gives rise to the payment of any stamp or other duty, including any court or other registration fees.

2.10.1 Tax avoidance and tax evasion

In so far as the borrower's concern may be to identify and use an offshore centre which is a low tax jurisdiction, the lender may, not least for the purposes of the *all crimes* money laundering issues discussed in the next chapter, require to determine that the transaction to which the lender is to be a party is one that does not offend against any of the systems of *fiscal law* to which the parties are subject. In this context, it is important, in the first instance, to draw a distinction between tax evasion and tax avoidance.

2.10.1.1 Tax evasion
Tax evasion is generally held to involve the avoidance of payment of taxes without the avoidance of the liability to pay such tax. In short, *tax evasion* involves breaking the relevant fiscal law, with the consequent imposition of criminal sanction. Unlawful actions may, most frequently, involve the making of false or incomplete returns and it may, therefore, be important to the lender to ensure that he is being asked to do nothing in which he

might be deemed to have assisted a person in the commission of an offence under a relevant fiscal law. In this context, it is not unusual for lenders to be asked to omit references to the existence of offshore security or guarantors from loan agreements and facility letters. Not only does such omission weaken the lender's documentation, it may in future expose the lender to criminal sanction.

2.10.1.2 Tax avoidance
Tax avoidance is generally used to describe the legitimate avoidance of liability to pay tax, through so-called *avoidance schemes*.

2.10.2 Anti-avoidance measures

In an increasingly sophisticated world, state revenue authorities have progressively sought and obtained legislative powers intended to ensure that they have available a range of measures to counteract *avoidance schemes*, such measures generally being referred to as *anti-avoidance measures*. It is important to recognise that while it is invariably legitimate for a person to seek to organise his affairs so as to minimise liability to taxes, he may choose to do so by schemes which, although not covered by specific legislative provisions, give rise to such a prospective loss of public revenue that the relevant revenue authorities will wish to curtail the extent of such loss to the maximum extent possible. In general, avoidance schemes are likely to involve the following issues.

2.10.2.1 Residence
By changing residence, a person may seek to migrate from a high tax to low tax jurisdiction.

2.10.2.2 Source
A person may seek to migrate to a territory which does not tax income or gains drawing from a source outside of the territory on a worldwide basis.

2.10.2.3 Classification of profit or gain
A person may seek to exploit difficulties in distinguishing between 'income' and 'capital', in order to reclassify that which would otherwise be income, or to defer the receipt of such income so that, in either case, it may be classified as a capital gain on which a lower liability to tax may arise.

2.10.2.4 Ownership or control
A person may transfer assets or rights so as to provide the accrual of an income or gain to a party (whether an individual, trust or corporation) in whose hands the accrual is not liable to tax.

These issues are commonly the subject of complex *anti-avoidance* provisions. The most frequently met anti-avoidance provisions are those which, (i) in the case of migration, seek to control liability to tax on change of residence, by deeming a disposal to crystallise a gain, (ii) deem moneys accruing to a person assessable to tax as income, thereby defeating attempts to reclassify them as a capital gain, or (iii) otherwise defer receipt of such income by *rolling up*. In the case of *anti-avoidance* based on ownership or control (usually situated in a low tax offshore centre) a person may be subject (i) to deemed ownership or distribution (for example, in the case of moneys received by a trust in respect of which such person is a settlor or beneficiary) or (ii) be taxed on moneys in a holding company or corporation in respect of income or gain received by a subsidiary in a low tax jurisdiction because such subsidiary is a *controlled foreign company* (often referred to as *CFC legislation*, as to which see Chapter 6).

2.10.3 Liability for assessment to tax

Most systems of fiscal law seek to make persons liable to tax by reference to the concepts of *domicile, residence* or *ordinary residence*, so that in relation to residence:

- persons resident are liable to assessment to tax on all of their income, profit or gain on a worldwide basis; and
- persons who are non-resident are liable to assessment for income, profit or gain arising or sourced within the territory concerned.

2.10.4 Residence

The English courts have stated that residence is an issue of fact. The House of Lords have stated that to reside is to 'dwell permanently or for a considerable time, to have one's settled or usual abode in or at a particular place' (*I.R.C. v Lysaght* [1928] A.C. 234). Where the test is that of residence, mere presence without ownership of property may be sufficient to give rise to assessment to tax. A taxing authority may regard a person as resident by reference to physical presence alone. Usually, this objective approach is applied by reference to stated periods of physical presence in any given fiscal year (for example, 183 days in the year of assessment, for United Kingdom purposes) but such tests simply deem residence, they do not necessarily mean that residence can never be established through presence for a lesser period.

2.10.5 Ordinary residence

In the English case of *Levene v I.R.C.* [1928] A.C. 217, Viscount Cave stated: 'Ordinary residence denotes residence with some degree of continuity and apart from accidental or temporary absence.' References to ordinary residence as a basis for assessment to tax tend to be a reference to evidence of permanence or a quality of habitual residence which will override temporary absence during any year of assessment. Frequently the availability of accommodation to a person will deem such person to be resident in the fiscal jurisdiction irrespective of the period for which the accommodation is used during the year of assessment. In this context ownership of property is not necessary, it is only necessary that property is available for occupation although this is not now the case in the United Kingdom. The manner in which the tests of residence are applied means that a person may be resident for tax purposes in more than one fiscal jurisdiction: he may be resident in one and ordinarily resident in another.

2.10.6 Companies' residence

As with individuals the liability of a company for assessment to tax will arise because the company is, or is deemed to be, resident. In the case of companies there is, however, no distinction between residence and ordinary residence. The treatment of residence of a company was considered by the House of Lords in *De Beers Consolidated Mines Ltd v Howe* [1906] A.C. 455, where Lord Loreburn LC said:

> *In applying the conception of residence to a company, we ought, I think to proceed as nearly as we can upon the analogy of an individual. A company cannot eat or sleep, but it can keep house and do business. We ought, therefore, to see where it really keeps house and does business.*

From the words of Lord Loreburn has come the widely applied test of determining the place at which the *control* and *management* of the company is carried out. These issues are considered in more detail in Chapter 6.

2.10.7 The lender's tax position

In most cases, it will be the borrower's tax planning which has dictated the proposed lending structure and the use of an offshore centre. In such case it remains important that the lender ensures that the structure does not, for any reason, give rise to adverse tax consequences for the lender.

2.10.8 Withholding

The most frequently encountered adverse tax consequence for lenders in transactions with a foreign law element is *withholding* tax, a method of tax collection used by revenue authorities. It requires that the borrower deduct from sums payable to the lender sums deemed to represent tax which may be payable by the lender in the borrower's fiscal jurisdiction. Where the lender has no liability to tax in the borrower's jurisdiction, tax withheld may be capable of being reclaimed.

2.10.9 Grossing-up provisions

A lender should always seek to determine that no withholding will apply to payments due under or in connection with the lending, particularly in relation to payments representing, or deemed to represent, interest or a gain. In addition, however, the lender must ensure that all lending documentation which contains payment covenants also contains so-called *grossing-up* provisions. These are provisions which are intended to ensure that the amount actually due to the lender is the amount required to fully discharge the borrower's obligations under the law of the contract.

2.10.10 Double taxation treaties

Double taxation treaties are treaties entered into between jurisdictions with separate systems of fiscal law intended to ensure that a person assessable to tax in both jurisdictions on the same profit or gain does not, in fact, pay tax twice. Further consideration of their use and importance is set out in Chapter 8.

3 | Due diligence: know your customer

3.1 The need for due diligence

Due diligence effectively carried out reduces the lender's exposure to risk. A foreign law element in a lending transaction means that the lender is exposed to a higher degree of risk than is the case where the lender's relationship with the borrower is regulated pursuant to a single system of law and a single jurisdiction. Putting to one side issues of credit risk which may be of a pure balance sheet nature, compliance with a soundly based *know your customer* procedure will reduce exposure to:

- potential criminal liability on the part of the lender;
- loss through fraud on the part of the borrower; and
- risk of damage to the reputation of the lender.

Risk is increased where:

- the borrower or provider of security is domiciled, resident or constituted under a foreign law; and/or
- assets comprising the security for the lending are held offshore (possibly in a 'back to back' arrangement in which, most frequently, a loan is taken in a jurisdiction in which tax relief or other advantage is available in relation to the interest payable and security is provided offshore, usually against cash and/or securities, the income or capital gains on which can be received in the low tax jurisdiction); and/or
- loan proceeds and repayments are received from outside the jurisdiction in which the loan is made.

Any one or more of these elements may mean that it is more difficult to establish from a verifiable source (i) the true identity of the party and/or true ultimate beneficial ownership of a corporate party, (ii) the legitimate purpose for the involvement of the foreign law element, and (iii) the source of funds and/or assets to be received or held by the lender, or to his order.

Moreover, the lender may be subject to the civil and criminal laws of more than one jurisdiction, with the consequence that, in default, the lender's assets and reputation are at risk.

3.2 Criminal liability

International recognition has increasingly been given to the fact that crime is no respecter of the territorial limitation of national criminal justice systems. To the contrary, sophisticated commercial frauds and money laundering schemes have, more often than not, exploited the territorial limitation on the ability of courts to enable the victim or law enforcement agencies to pursue the wrongdoer and his proceeds of crime across international borders. The recognition that multinational financial institutions, and in particular sophisticated money transfer and settlement systems, are increasingly a tool of the international criminal and money launderer, has prompted the development of a web of mutual and bilateral assistance treaties binding nation states:

- to criminalise money laundering (in relation to all serious crimes including in some cases fiscal and foreign exchange evasion); and
- to provide to each other the assistance of their respective law enforcement agencies and courts in co-operation to investigate serious crime and its proceeds, to gather evidence and to seize (and ultimately confiscate) the proceeds of serious crime.

Insofar as international treaty obligations have imposed on the United Kingdom the need to adopt new domestic legislation, this has been undertaken in the form of offences created in relation to drugs trafficking, terrorism and other serious crime (so-called 'all crimes' legislation).

3.3 The Basle Statement of Principles

The resolve of bank regulators to signal mutual resolve in adherence to measures intended to combat the use of the financial system for the laundering of the proceeds of crime was manifested by the *Basle Committee on Banking Regulations and Supervisory Practices* when, in 1988, it issued a Statement of Practice in which it was stated:

> *Whatever the legal position in different countries, the Committee considers that the first and most important safeguard against money*

laundering is the integrity of banks' own managements and their vigilant determination to prevent their institutions becoming associated with criminals or being used as a channel for money laundering.

It is suggested that the reference to *vigilant determination* translates for practical purposes as *due diligence*. The Statement further highlighted the requirement for:

- customer identification (*know your customer*), requiring that a bank should make reasonable efforts to determine the true identity of all customers requesting the institution's services and that it should be the institution's clear policy that it will not conduct business with customers who fail to provide evidence of identity;
- compliance with laws, in that a financial institution should ensure that its business is conducted in conformity with high ethical standards and that the laws and regulations of relevant jurisdictions are adhered to; and
- co-operation with law enforcement authorities, in that an institution should provide full co-operation within the limits of the laws governing customer confidentiality so that where there is an awareness of facts which lead to the reasonable presumption that moneys derived from a criminal activity, appropriate measures, consistent with the law, should be taken to deny assistance, sever relations with the customer and close or freeze relevant accounts.

3.4 United Kingdom domestic legislation

The *Drug Trafficking Offences Act 1994* provides for powers to assist the law enforcement agencies in the investigation of drug trafficking and drugs money laundering, the seizure of the proceeds of drug trafficking and the confiscation of such proceeds. The predecessor of the Act in the form of the *Drug Trafficking Offences Act 1986* forms the model for legislation since adopted in Jersey, Guernsey, the Isle of Man, Gibraltar and Hong Kong. Section 50 of the Act creates an offence of assisting another to retain the benefit of drug trafficking, knowing or suspecting that such other is a person who carries on or has carried on drug trafficking, or has benefited from drug trafficking. It is a defence to show that a person has disclosed to a constable (a police or customs officer) his *suspicion or belief* that funds or investments are derived from or used in connection with drug trafficking or any matter on which suspicion or belief is based. Importantly, section 50 further provides that any such disclosure shall not be a breach of any restriction upon the disclosure of information *imposed by contract.* Finally, section 50 provides that if a person commits any act in contravention of the section but makes a disclosure before he does the act concerned, or does the act with the consent of the constable, or, after the commission of the relevant act on his own initiative and as soon as is reasonable, makes disclosure he shall not be guilty of an offence. Section 52 of the *Drug Trafficking Offences Act 1994* provides that it is an offence to fail to report *knowledge or suspicion* of drug money laundering which a person gains in the course of a trade, profession, business or employment. The report is required to be made to a constable (a police or customs officer) or to a supervisor (the reporting officer) in accordance with the established procedures of that person's employer. Section 52 provides that such a report does not constitute a breach of any restriction on the disclosure of confidential information. Section 53 provides that it is an offence to prejudice an investigation by disclosing information or any other matter likely to be prejudicial knowing or suspecting that there is or is to be an investigation into drug money laundering, or a disclosure to a constable or supervisor under sections 50, 51 or 52.

3.4.1 The Prevention of Terrorism (Temporary Provisions) Act 1989 as amended

Section 11 of the *Prevention of Terrorism (Temporary Provisions) Act 1989* created an offence of assisting another to retain the proceeds of terrorist crime materially similar, but not identical, to the terms of section 24 of the *Drug Trafficking Offences Act 1986.* The *Criminal Justice Act 1993* inserted a new section 18A imposing a duty to disclose (in default of which an offence is committed) *knowledge or suspicion* that another person is providing financial assistance for terrorism on those who gain such knowledge or suspicion in the course of a trade, profession, business or employment. As with the scheme under the *Drug Trafficking Offences Act 1994*, a person making disclosure is saved harmless for any breach of a contractual duty of confidence.

3.4.2 The Money Laundering Regulations 1993 (SI 1993 No 1933)

The *Money Laundering Regulations* give effect in the UK to the *Money Laundering Directive (91/308/EEC)* and extend to banking, investment and insurance business. Persons engaged in such business are required to have systems in place to prevent money laundering. The Regulations define money laundering by reference to drug trafficking and financial assistance to acts of terrorism, together with those offences introduced by the *Criminal Justice Act 1988.* The Regulations are supplemented by the Guidance Notes issued by the Joint Money Laundering Steering Group. The scheme of the Regulations requires, among other things, that banks and building societies within the UK:

- adopt and implement internal controls, policies and procedures to deter criminals from using their facilities for money laundering and establish clear responsibilities and accountabilities in respect of such policies, procedures and controls;
- introduce procedures for the prompt validation of suspicions and subsequent reporting to the National Criminal Intelligence Service (NCIS);
- provide an 'appropriate person' (referred to in the Guidance Notes as the Money Laundering Reporting Officer) as a central point of contact with NCIS in order to deal with and report suspicions from staff regarding money laundering and provide such officer with necessary access to systems and records to fulfil such role; and
- establish and maintain close co-operation and liaison with the Law Enforcement Agencies, including NCIS. The Guidance Notes suggest that as good practice, banks and building societies should make arrangements to verify, on a regular basis, compliance with policies, procedures and controls relating to money laundering activities so that management may be satisfied that the Regulations are being complied with. The Guidance Notes suggest that larger banks and building societies will wish to use internal audit or compliance functions to undertake the verification role.

3.4.3 Identification procedures

The Regulations (regulations 7 and 9) require that banks and building societies seek satisfactory evidence of identity of a prospective customer (the Guidance Notes refer to 'verification of identity'). Verification of identity is required at the time of opening of an account or of entry into a business relationship; in the absence of such verification as soon as reasonably practicable, the business should not proceed. The Regulations do not specify what may or may not represent adequate evidence of identity; however, the Guidance Notes (at paragraphs 51–59) set out *what might reasonably be expected of banks and building societies with effect from 1 April 1994*. The Guidance Notes state that:

- records of supporting evidence and methods used to verify identity must be retained for five years after the account is closed or the business relationship is ended;
- the bank or building society should establish to its satisfaction that it is dealing with a real person (natural, corporate or legal) and verify the identity of those persons who have power to operate any bank or investment account (see also Chapter 4);

- the best identification documents possible should be obtained from a prospective customer and it should be assumed that no single form of identification should be relied upon as representing correct identity, so that an appropriate verification procedure should involve a cumulative process in which a person's address should be separately verified as the current permanent address; and
- in connection with joint accounts where the account holders have different surnames and/or addresses, the bank's records and procedures should include and verify the name and address of all account holders.

3.5 Money laundering and the European Union

The influence of the EU, through connection with Member States, on major offshore centres has been highlighted in Chapter 1. The EU's influence (notwithstanding the fact that directives may not be directly applicable to such offshore centres) is no less important as a stimulant to the adoption of anti-money laundering measures in many offshore centres. Reference has already been made to the adoption by the British offshore dependent islands of legislation broadly similar to that introduced by the United Kingdom to meet its obligations under *EU Directive 91/308/EC.*

3.6 Mutual and bilateral treaties

The fight against criminal money laundering has seen the implementation of a large number of mutual assistance and bilateral treaties facilitating co-operation among judicial and law enforcement authorities for the exchange of information, the obtaining of evidence and the seizure, freezing and forfeiture of the proceeds of crime. In 1989 the United Kingdom and the United States entered into a bilateral treaty which in its terms extends to those territories the international relations of which the United Kingdom is responsible for, and provides for assistance in relation to:

- taking the testimony or statements of persons;
- providing documentary information, records and articles of evidence, including bank, financial, corporate and business records;
- executing requests for searches and seizures; and
- freezing and forfeiting the proceeds and instrumentalities of drug trafficking.

The *English Criminal Justice (International Co-operation) Act 1990* provides that the courts of the United Kingdom may give assistance for the obtaining of evidence in the United Kingdom in respect of any offence which is not a 'fiscal offence'. Fiscal offences may, however, be the subject of (i) a request from a country or territory which is a member of the Commonwealth, or (ii) is made pursuant to a treaty to which the United Kingdom is a party, or (iii) where the conduct constituting the offence would constitute an offence of the same or similar nature if it had occurred in the United Kingdom.

4 | The legal personality of the borrower

4.1 The significance of legal personality

A lender must be concerned to determine the legal status of a borrower. Legal status will, in accordance with the law of the relevant domicile or nationality (see Chapter 2), determine:

- that the borrower is validly existing and otherwise duly constituted;
- the extent of the borrower's capacity;
- the powers which the borrower has and how they are exercised;
- the ability or otherwise of the borrower to hold and deal with assets or incur liabilities;
- the extent to which and the manner by which the borrower incurs liability to taxation; and
- the extent to which and manner by which the borrower can be made subject to legal process by suing and being sued in its own name.

These fundamentals are a consequence of the legal *personality* of the borrower. This chapter will consider those types of borrower or counterparty most frequently encountered in connection with offshore centres.

4.1.1 Is the borrower a legal person?

As a starting point, the lender must be concerned to determine the extent to which, if at all, the borrower has a legal existence or personality in its own right. Where the borrower is not, for the purposes of a relevant law, a legal person, the lender must lend to one or more persons having capacity to contract and bind the party, i.e. to a trustee of a trust, the partners of a general partnership or the 'general partner' of a limited partnership.

4.1.2 Has the borrower been duly formed and maintained in existence?

Where it is determined that the borrower may have separate legal personality, the lender should confirm that:

- all steps necessary to constitute such legal personality have been completed (for example, the steps needed to form a company);
- no action has been taken or has been omitted to be taken which is necessary to maintain the borrower in existence (for example, that all necessary filing or registrations have been made, taxes or fees paid); and
- no resolution or other relevant event has occurred which will or may lead to the dissolution or winding-up of the borrower.

4.1.3 Capacity

A question which follows the existence of legal personality is that of whether the borrower has the *capacity* to enter into and discharge its obligations in relation to the transaction concerned. The issue of capacity has many possible applications to a borrower so that, by way of example:

- the capacity of an individual to enter into a transaction may be subject to age and mental capacity; or to rules affecting capacity to deal with matrimonial or heritable property (as to which, see Chapter 5);
- the capacity of a company may be determined by reference to the objects for which it has been constituted so that the *ultra vires* doctrine applies to make void acts of the company outside of or inconsistent with its stated objects (as to which, see Chapter 6).

The issue of capacity will be considered in more detail in relation to the ability of natural persons, corporations and trustees in Chapters 5, 6 and 7 respectively.

4.2 Companies

The company or corporate entity is the most frequently encountered form of legal personality. Corporate personality may come in a multitude of guises. Differences may be the result of the legal system from which the offshore centre has evolved, or may be more particularly attributed to the company by legislative or other provision. The latter is becoming increasingly frequent as offshore centres compete to provide ever more flexible legal personality to attract business. Generally, however, most companies or other corporate bodies will have two features which will then tend to be modified to a greater or lesser degree, being:

- separate legal personality (established in the English common law model by the House of Lords in *Salomon v Salomon & Co* [1897] A.C. 22); and
- the capacity for continuity of existence.

In most jurisdictions, and in the majority of individual cases, a company may also restrict the liability of its voters and contributors as members, shareholders or stockholders to the value of their capital subscribed, or to the value of their liability to subscribe. In an offshore context, these characteristics of corporate legal personality may be used:

- to enhance confidentiality;
- to hold real or moveable property other than through individual ownership, thereby possibly avoiding inheritance law applicable in the domicile of a relevant shareholder; and
- to the extent that controlled foreign company legislation is not applicable or is capable of mitigation, to maximise each of (i) the opportunity to accumulate dividends and other income on a tax-free or tax-advantageous basis, (ii) the opportunity to realise gains on the disposal of investments without suffering taxation, and (iii), in some jurisdictions, the opportunity to avoid or minimise withholding applicable to distributions, which might otherwise arise in the jurisdiction in which the investments are situated.

4.2.1 Classification of companies

In the later chapters dealing with particular offshore centres reference will be made to features of corporations and companies exclusive to those jurisdictions. In this section the intention is to identify by short description the principal characteristics which distinguish types of corporation or company one from another and which are likely to be material to a lender.

4.2.1.1 Registered or unregistered

In those systems of law based on English common law, references to a *corporation* are likely to mean a corporate legal personality existing by virtue of statutory or other provisions (for example, Crown prerogative order or charter). Such *corporations* may pose particular problems for lenders because they are exclusively the product of their mode of incorporation, in which there may be a limitation on the ability to hold and deal with particular types of asset (for example, derivatives). In addition, the constitution of such corporations may require particular forms of sanction for contractual and other obligations to be binding. By contrast, and again in those jurisdictions following English common law, references to a *company* are likely to be references to a corporate legal personality registered or *incorporated* pursuant to a statutory framework. In most such jurisdictions, it is likely that some form of central register exists. In those jurisdictions following a US-derived legal system, it is likely that a reference to a *corporation* is a reference not to an *unregistered* corporate entity but, rather, to a *registered* corporate entity.

4.2.1.2 Public or private

In the context of offshore centres, this distinction is likely to form part of a regime intended to provide investor protection. As such, the distinction lies in the fact that the description *public* is likely to denote that the corporation or company concerned is entitled to raise capital by the issue of shares, or otherwise raise money by the issue of securities, to the public. In turn, it is likely that a public corporation or company is subject to additional reporting requirements, for example a requirement (i) for the appointment of auditors, (ii) for the publishing of audited financial statements and (iii) a requirement for the consent to the circulation of offer documentation or a prospectus relating to shares or security. By contrast, a *private* corporate or company may be defined as a corporation or company whose shares or securities may not be issued to the public, and which has a specified maximum number of shareholders. It is likely that a private company will be subject to less rigorous ongoing supervision by central regulatory authorities and, for example, (i) may be entitled to be a single member company, (ii) may dispense (subject to conditions) with the regular holding of general meetings, and (iii) need not appoint auditors or publish or otherwise file financial statements with a central regulatory authority.

4.2.1.3 Unlimited companies or corporations

This denotes a corporation or company whose shareholders have unlimited liability for the debts of the company or corporation. Unlimited liability companies tend to have only a narrow usage (and will not ordinarily be encountered in the context of the conduct of trade) but may be encountered where the predominant concern of an investor is confidentiality, because such companies usually carry the least stringent reporting and regulatory requirements.

4.2.1.4 Companies limited by shares

In those jurisdictions with a common law legal system, this is the most common form of company. Here, the liability of shareholders is restricted to the value of their paid-up subscriptions and any amount unpaid or uncalled in respect of the shares subscribed.

4.2.1.5 Companies limited by guarantee

This denotes a company (known as a *hybrid*) which may or may not have a share capital, in which the liability of members on a winding-up of the company is limited to the value of the guarantee, where such value is normally stated in the company's memorandum of association. Historically, companies limited by guarantee have been used to incorporate charities and professional bodies, but they have more recently found use in certain offshore centres as a form of *quasi-trust*. The use of *guarantee companies* as a *quasi-trust* predominates in those offshore centres where the legal system does not recognise, or has difficulty in recognising, the concepts and features of a common law trust. Such use normally allows those individuals who would be beneficiaries to enjoy profit participation (a vested interest in income) as guarantee members of a hybrid.

4.2.1.6 Limited life or limited duration companies
Some offshore centres have sought to provide for the incorporation of so-called *limited duration* (the Cayman Islands) or *limited life* companies (the Isle of Man and Turks and Caicos Islands). In many other offshore centres, the characteristics of the newly available limited life or limited duration company are to a degree emulated through the use of a guarantee company (for example, in Hong Kong, Cyprus, the Isle of Man and Gibraltar).

4.2.1.7 Tax-exempt companies
So-called 'exempt' companies are those which under the law of an offshore centre are deemed to be non-resident or otherwise outside of assessment to tax in the offshore centre. Usually, exempt status is available not only for companies incorporated in the offshore centre but also for companies incorporated in another jurisdiction and notwithstanding that control and management is exercised within the offshore centre concerned.

4.2.1.8 International business companies
This denotes a treatment of the relevant company under the fiscal laws of the relevant offshore centre so as, usually, to make such company resident and assessable to tax in that jurisdiction, yet distinguishing between income or gains earned by the company outside of that jurisdiction and income or gains earned within the jurisdiction. In relation to income or gain from a source outside, a flexible lower tax rate is intended to allow the tax-paying company to enjoy favourable treatment under double taxation treaties. While it is unusual that an international business company will have income generated within the relevant offshore centre, it is usual that such income or gain will be taxable at the rate or rates applicable to a tax resident person in the ordinary course. In a similar way, many offshore centres allow both locally incorporated and offshore incorporated corporations and companies to acquire non-resident status for taxation purposes in the offshore centre, whether or not the control and management of the corporation or company is undertaken within that jurisdiction; such status is generally referred to as *exempt* status.

4.2.1.9 Collective investment fund and mutual fund companies
This designation denotes the usage of a corporation or company for the issue of shares, securities or units to the public as a form of investment allowing mutual participation and risk-sharing in the investment activities of the corporation or company. Collective investment or mutual fund activity tends to take place under a statutory or other regulatory regime intended to provide varying degrees of investor protection. Such investor protection may include the requirement for consents (in the jurisdiction of incorporation) for the issue of shares, securities or units, the circulation of offering documents or a prospectus and may, in addition, require that a third party 'custodian' hold the investment assets of the collective investment or mutual fund on trust for the relevant corporation or company. In the context of collective investment or mutual fund companies, reference will be made to the terms *closed-ended* and *open-ended* companies. The former description denotes a company whose shares are incapable of redemption or repurchase, whereas the latter description denotes a company whose shares, being capable of redemption or repurchase, allow investors to come into and exit the investment corporation or company.

4.3 Partnerships

At its most general, a partnership must be an association of two or more persons carrying on a business for the purpose of profit.

4.3.1 Classification of partnerships

The following are the more frequently encountered forms or usages of partnerships.

4.3.1.1 General partnerships
A *general* partnership denotes a partnership in which each partner is liable jointly for the debts of the partnership. Fundamental to the concept of partnership in the common law legal systems is the agent and principal relationship. In a general partnership each partner is responsible for the acts of his partners as agents. Following the usage of the *Partnership Act 1890*, a general partnership is referred to collectively as a *firm*. United States' usage may refer to a firm as a company or association (as distinct from a corporation). The application of the law of agency to general partnerships in common law legal systems means that, in the absence of express agreement to the contrary, death, insolvency or other incapacity of one

party brings to an end the relevant partnership. Unlike corporations, there is, therefore, no perpetual succession.

4.3.1.2 Limited partnerships

A *limited* partnership is constituted as an association of one or more *limited* partners and one or more *general* partners. Only the *general* partner is entitled to participate in the management of the limited partnership and thereby incurs unlimited liability for the debts of the limited partnership. Limited partners are not entitled to participate in the management, but are entitled to share in the profits of the limited partnership. Their liability is restricted to the value of their capital committed. A limited partner is not an agent of the limited partnership, and their death, bankruptcy or other mental incapacity will not terminate the limited partnership. As a general proposition, limited partnerships will be constituted for a prescribed period in accordance with the limited partnership agreement and the relevant law, and may under certain circumstances continue (so that the parties remain bound by the agreement), notwithstanding a change in general or limited partners. Reference has been made above to the usage of US limited liability companies, largely as a result of their favourable categorisation as 'partnerships' under the US Internal Revenue Code. English law has long recognised a limited partnership, under the provisions of the *Limited Partnership Act 1907*. Although it has been possible, for many years, to domicile a foreign limited partnership in an offshore centre, or conduct its control and management (through the general partner) in an offshore centre where the general partner is a corporate entity having exempt (non-resident) status, most leading offshore centres have now moved to provide for the registration of a limited partnership under local law (limited partnerships are now available in the Isle of Man, Jersey, Guernsey and Bermuda). They are increasingly being developed as an effective investment vehicle for US pension funds. Beyond the favourable treatment accorded to a partnership by the US Internal Revenue Code, the essential feature of most common law derived limited partnership structures is the fact that they are treated as transparent by taxation authorities, so that income or gain arising to limited partners is assessable to tax in the hands of the limited partner, providing for flexible use of the tax status of individual limited partners. In most offshore centres, for example Jersey, non-resident limited partners are not assessed to tax on income or gains arising from investment outside of the jurisdiction. Limited partnerships are also finding use in asset protection structures, particularly when used alongside a trust, which enables a settlor and/or beneficiary to manage what is, in effect, the trust fund through the limited partnership of which the trust is a limited partner.

4.3.1.3 Limited liability partnerships

A further variation of a limited partnership exists in the form of a 'limited liability partnership' which is capable of constitution under the laws of a limited number of jurisdictions and, most recently, in Jersey as an offshore centre. Limited liability partnerships are likely to be encountered only in relation to firms of accountants and lawyers who, because of professional restrictions, are prevented from providing services out of limited liability corporations and who wish to limit their personal liability. Permissive legislation, of the type enacted in Jersey, imposes conditions on the use of such structures' designed to ensure protection to general creditors. The issue which arises for the lender is that of determining the extent to which the 'partnership' and each of its partners are liable for the debt incurred as a contract (usually this will not be a problem) and, if reliance is placed on the ability to recover against individual partners other than on the basis of contract, whether the limitation on liability adversely affects the lender's rights. A much more restricted issue for lenders in this area concerns reliance placed on the work product of accountants (as, for example, auditors) or lawyers providing opinions, where they are practising as limited liability partnerships. The lender should ensure that there is tangible asset cover (possible in the form of insurance) where figures are significant.

4.4 Trusts

The existence of trusts (or, in some jurisdictions, concepts which may be used at least in part in substitution for a trust) has been fundamental to the development of many offshore centres. It is, perhaps, fair to observe that trusts were one of the earliest forms of tax-avoidance scheme in the English mainland, such usage being traceable back to the avoidance of feudal dues under the Magna Carta of 1215. The *Finance Act 1991* has materially restricted the effectiveness of an offshore trust by UK-domiciled persons for deferral of capital gains tax and otherwise materially limited the tax-mitigating uses of an offshore trust by UK domiciliaries or resident non-UK domiciliaries. In contrast, the usage of trusts and quasi-trusts (for example, charitable trusts, purpose trusts, hybrid companies and limited partnerships) has grown significantly in structured finance transactions and, particularly, those intended to provide an 'off-balance sheet' solution. Moreover, those responsible for the administration of trusts in offshore centres have applied considerable effort over recent years in marketing (and therefore in the process of explaining) the nature and use of trusts to residents and domiciliaries of legal systems which have not, historically, themselves recognised trusts as a method of effective tax avoidance and inheritance planning.

4.4.1 What is a trust?

A trust is not in itself a legal person, it is rather a description of those duties and obligations which a person, described as a *trustee*, has in relation to certain property held by him or under his control. It is fundamental to the concept of a trust (but see the description which follows of non-charitable purpose trusts) that the trustee can be compelled by a court to deal with the trust property for the benefit of one or more other persons, the *beneficiaries*. Trusts were able to develop as a product of the common law system because of the willingness of the Chancery Courts of England to recognise the right to hold property in both a proprietary and *equitable* capacity (sometimes described as the distinction between *legal* and *beneficial* ownership). It is important to recognise that a trust is a creation of a system of law applicable in a particular jurisdiction or offshore centre. A trust so created may or may not be recognised by the system of law of another jurisdiction, and in particular another offshore centre. Those jurisdictions having a civil law system have, with limited exceptions (most notably those of the Channel Islands), failed to provide for trusts. In particular, because many civil law jurisdictions base rights in property exclusively on possession, difficulties exist in establishing a basis for the beneficial ownership of property as separate to the rights of the person having title and possession during a particular period of time. Moreover, both civil law and Muslim/*Shari'a* law countries of the Middle and Far East, share an adherence to concepts which restrict the ability of individuals to dispose of property and in particular real property (in the main, land and buildings and the right thereto) otherwise than in accordance with laws which govern inheritance (so-called *forced heirship* rules). The importance to offshore centres of trusts has meant that even where the indigenous legal system has not provided for trusts, many jurisdictions (including those with a civil law legal system) have sought to introduce the concept of trust by statute. Many more jurisdictions with a common law legal system recognising trusts have sought to codify, amend or expand their trust law by statute in order to achieve objectives otherwise not provided for under the established trust law. In the case of the Channel Islands of Jersey and Guernsey, it is instructive to note that for many years it was argued by some that trusts set up under the laws of those islands were invalid because (as their customary law was civil law based) there was no recognition of the concept of a trust. Both islands have now enacted specific trust legislation and, indeed, in the case of Jersey, significant amendments have been made to the relevant statute in order to expand its use so as to enable the creation of valid trusts where they might otherwise offend against forced heirship rules applicable to a non-Jersey domiciled settlor and, most recently, to allow for the creation of 'purpose trusts' (as to which, see further below). This proactive creation of law so as to expand the concept of a trust has, in recent years, included legislation introduced by the Caymans, Bermuda, the Bahamas, the Turks and Caicos, Gibraltar, St Kitts and Nevis and Cook Islands to introduce recognition of so-called *asset protection trusts*, or *APTs*. The outcome of this wholesale growth in the concept of trusts is that a lender should make no assumption as to the nature of a trust encountered as part of a lending proposal. The lender's principal concern will be to ensure that he has recourse to the relevant property underlying the trust. This and other issues raised in lending to trusts are dealt with in Chapter 7.

4.4.2 Hague Convention on the law applicable to trusts (1984)

The ability of parties to obtain international recognition of trusts is, in part, determined by the *Hague Convention on the law applicable to trusts (1984)* which, to date, has been ratified by Australia, Italy and the United Kingdom and which came into force on 1 January 1992. Article 2 of the Convention states:

> *A trust has the following characteristics—*
> *(a) The assets constitute a separate fund and are not part of the trustee's own estate;*
> *(b) Title to the trust assets stands in the name of the trustee or in the name of another person on behalf of the trustee;*
> *(c) The trustee has the power and duty to manage, employ or dispose of the assets in accordance with the terms of the trust and special duties imposed upon him by law.*

4.4.3 The role of the trustee

Although the trust does not have a legal personality or existence of its own, the title or other right to the trust property vests, subject to the terms of the trusts, in the trustee. As will be described in greater detail in Chapter 7, it is the capacity of the trustee (and the restrictions on the ability of the trustee) to deal with the trust property which forms the primary concern for a lender. In the case of most trusts encountered in connection with an offshore centre, it is likely that the trustee will be a professional trust corporation, acting through its officers and employees, or a lawyer or an accountant. The terms of the trust deed or instrument will, subject to the applicable proper or governing law, determine both the 'trusts' (the duties and obligations of the trustee) and the trustee's powers.

4.4.4 The beneficiaries

For a trust to exist, it is necessary that there is one or more other person (or possibly a purpose) for whose benefit the trustee will hold the trust property, such persons being called the *beneficiaries*. In certain circumstances, the lender may be concerned with the rights and interests of the beneficiaries in or to the trust property.

4.4.5 Classification of trusts by mode of creation

It is sometimes easy to confuse a description of trusts by reference to the objective for which they are created with that description of a trust which is intended to reflect the nature of the trust and, in particular, the manner by which it has been created. As to the latter, the following classification is most usual.

4.4.5.1 Statutory trusts
A statutory trust is a trust created by statute. For example, under English law, sections 34 and 36 of the *Law of Property Act 1925* provide for forms of statutory trusts as a 'trust for sale' and section 33 of the *Administration of Estates Act 1925* provides that on the death intestate of a person, his property vests in his personal representatives upon 'trust for sale'.

4.4.5.2 Express trusts
An express trust is a trust created by intentional act of the parties, most frequently through one person, the *settlor*, declaring that he holds property on trust (or the settlor transferring property to another as trustee) to be applied for the benefit of predetermined or determinable beneficiaries in accordance with the relevant deed or instrument.

4.4.5.3 Implied trusts
An implied trust is a trust presumed to arise as the intention of a person as deemed settlor.

4.4.5.4 Constructive trusts
A constructive trust is a trust deemed to arise by operation of law, for example where a person receives property knowing it to be the property of another.

4.4.5.5 Resulting trusts
A resulting trust is a trust which is expressed or implied so that in default of property vesting in a manner anticipated by the parties, it is held by a designated person for the beneficiaries.

4.4.6 Classification by nature of interests

Trusts are, likewise, sometimes described by reference to the nature of the beneficiary's interests under two distinct types of trust interest as follows:

4.4.6.1 Fixed interest trust

A fixed interest trust is a trust under which one or more named beneficiaries (or members of an identifiable class of beneficiaries) have now, or may in the future have, a vested entitlement to the income or capital of the trust fund.

4.4.6.2 Discretionary trusts

A discretionary trust is a trust under which one or more beneficiaries are identified (or are capable of being identified) as a class in whose favour the trustee may exercise a discretionary to distribute the income or capital of the trust fund. It is important to recognise that a discretionary trust gives no present right or entitlement to its beneficiaries, except that they may have the right to force the trustee to consider the exercise of the relevant discretion. Importantly, the beneficiaries of a discretionary trust have no right in or title to the trust fund. In contrast, the beneficiaries under a fixed interest trust have a right enforceable against the trustee (and arguably an enforceable right to the trust property) in accordance with the terms of the trust. A single trust deed or instrument may constitute a trust which is, in its terms, both discretionary and fixed interest, so that, for example, trust property vests in beneficiaries on the happening of a certain event, for example the death of the settlor.

4.4.7 Classification by use

It is increasingly the case that trusts are described by trust professionals in terms that relate to the principal objective of the trust. In this context, the following descriptions are those most likely to be encountered, the objectives being those set out against the relevant description as follows.

4.4.7.1 Accumulation and maintenance trusts

An accumulation and maintenance trust is a form of trust most frequently constituted for the benefit of minor children and under which the minor child has no vested interest in the trust fund (i.e. it is not, at that point, a fixed interest trust) but under which the beneficiary will become entitled to the property or an interest in it on attaining a specified age, with the trustee being under a duty to accumulate interest in the interim. The trustee will, however, have a discretion to use income generated by the trust fund to maintain the beneficiaries pending their attaining the specified age.

4.4.7.2 Asset protection trusts

An asset protection trust is a form of trust used principally by professionals such as doctors, lawyers and accountants to protect their assets from prospective creditors. As all trusts require that the title to assets is transferred to a trustee and have as their purpose the protection of those assets for the benefit of beneficiaries, a specific reference to an APT tends to be a reference to a trust constituted under the law of a jurisdiction which has, through legislation, extended the validity of trusts in a way which assists the trustee in resisting claims by creditors. Examples of such jurisdictions are given above at para 4.4.1. It is a widely held view that, aside from those jurisdictions which have given extended recognition to asset protection as a purpose, asset protection can exist in other forms of trust, provided that the transfer of trust property to the trustee was validly undertaken by the settlor and was not, in particular, undertaken with the intention to defeat existing actual or contingent creditors, in short as a fraud on such creditors.

4.4.7.3 Charitable trusts

A charitable trust is a form of trust which has purposes which comply with a definition of 'charity' in accordance with their proper or governing law. English common law has, historically, recognised only those trusts which have beneficiaries and, save for the exception created in relation to non-charitable purpose trusts, it was not possible to constitute a trust for purposes which were other than 'charitable' in accordance with English law, these previously being those prescribed by the *Charitable Uses Act 1601*, or the preamble to it, and now the *Charities Act 1960*. The advantages of charitable trusts under the trust frameworks of many offshore centres include the fact that a charitable trust, while having charitable objects as beneficiaries, is nevertheless entitled to own as part of the trust fund many forms of asset, for example debt receivables. Accordingly, charitable trusts have been used creatively in so-called 'off-balance sheet structures' and 'securitisations'.

4.4.7.4 Secret trusts

A secret trust is a form of trust constituted during a person's lifetime in relation to property disposed under that person's will as testator, but so that the legatee receives as trustee pursuant to the secret trusts for the benefit of an undisclosed beneficiary. The use of a secret trust therefore overcomes the public nature of a will where that might cause the testator difficulty if there is somebody in respect of whom he owes an obligation such as an illegitimate child or mistress, but whose identity or existence he wishes to keep secret.

4.4.7.5 Purpose trusts

A purpose trust (or non-charitable purpose trust) is a form of trust validly constituted for a non-charitable purpose, as distinct for the benefit of persons as named or identifiable beneficiaries. In general, one advantage of a purpose trust is that it is usually unaffected by restrictions on the perpetuity or duration of trusts, although it should be noted that a purpose trust in Jersey is subject to the limitation on duration of 100 years contained in the *Trusts (Jersey) Law, 1984. The Hague Convention* (see above, para 4.4.2) defined a trust so as to include 'one for a specified purpose'. Since that time offshore centres, first in Bermuda and then in the British Virgin Islands, Belize, Mauritius, Cyprus, Nevis, Anguilla, the Seychelles, the Bahamas and Jersey, have passed legislation intended to modify their trust law so as to allow for non-charitable purpose trusts. The flexibility of non-charitable purpose trusts has allowed for their use in establishing offshore business structures. For example, a purpose trust might be used for a transactional purpose, such as the building of a ship, or the arranging of finance, including the promotion of a company or corporation by the issue of shares. Generally, the limited purposes for which a valid purpose trust can be constituted are those which are reasonable, possible to fulfil and not contrary to law or public policy.

4.4.7.6 Unit trusts

A unit trust is a form of trust constituted as a means by which a large number of people may invest their money through the pooling of subscriptions and through the investment of the pooled subscriptions in investment assets intended to constitute the trust fund. The assets will be held by a trustee in the usual way, with investment decisions being delegated to a professional investment manager. In such manner the risk of investment is spread between investors and the size of fund may enable the holding of diverse assets, also spreading and thereby reducing risk.

4.4.7.7 Trading trusts

A trading trust is a form of trust under which the trustees are empowered to undertake trading activity. As a general proposition, the risks involved in trading are risks that will be inconsistent with the inherent duties of a trustee, principally the duty to preserve and enhance the value of the trust fund pending distribution or application in accordance with the specified trusts. In some jurisdictions, trading trusts have, historically, provided fiscal advantage, in that their profits have attracted a lower rate of tax. Such advantage is now much reduced (for example in Australia) and such trusts hold little advantage over traditional limited liability corporations. Where the relevant proper or governing law allows, it may, nevertheless, be advantageous for trustees to have the power to undertake trading activity although it is likely that a trustee will exercise any such power with great caution.

Chapter

5 | Considerations when lending to individuals

Introduction

This chapter considers issues of particular concern arising in relation to lending to one or more individuals where the transaction involves a foreign law connection. Such a connection may arise (i) because the borrower or guarantor or other surety is non-resident, (ii) because assets to be held as security are located offshore, or (iii) because the facility or some element of the facility is made available offshore or is otherwise subject to a foreign law. Where the borrower is an individual (or more than one individual) and the lending transaction attracts the risks associated with a foreign law connection (see above, para 3.1), the lender should:

- ensure that the borrower has the capacity to enter into, be bound by and perform in accordance with, the transaction terms;
- ensure that there are no regulatory or other extraneous restrictions on the borrower's ability to perform in accordance with the transaction terms (for example, exchange control);
- ensure that the reasons for the foreign law connection are understood, it being insufficient to accept an explanation that the transaction is so structured for 'tax reasons';
- ensure that existing and probable charges to tax do not adversely affect the lending (for example, through application of withholding);
- ensure that viable and cost effective means of enforcement exist in all relevant jurisdictions and that there are no material impediments (for example, in the form of onerous personal service requirements) to enforcement; and
- ensure that the implications of an insolvency affecting the borrower in a relevant foreign jurisdiction are understood.

In addition to the issues specific to lending to individuals, the lender must have regard to the need, in all cases:

- to complete due diligence in relation to know your customer (see above, Chapter 3);
- to identify and select, by express provision, an appropriate applicable law for all transaction documents, to obtain the express submission to the courts of an appropriate jurisdiction by all relevant parties (see above, Chapter 2); and
- to require the appointment of an agent for service in relation to a relevant party resident outside of the chosen jurisdiction.

5.1 Capacity of natural persons

In Chapter 4, and in relation to borrowers that are not natural persons, it was suggested that it was necessary to ask the question: does the borrower have legal personality? In the case of a natural person who is at the time of the transaction living, legal personality can be assumed to exist, but the question becomes: can the individual borrower enter into an agreement for obligations (a *contract*) by which the borrower will be bound? In short, does the individual borrower have the relevant legal *capacity*? The consequence of an absence of capacity can make the contract capable of being declared void (*voidable*) or, worse still, a nullity (*void ab initio*).

5.1.1 A natural person of full age and of sound mind

The lender should check to establish that the borrower is:

- alive;
- of full age (if there is any cause for doubt, obtain a birth certificate or note age from a passport); and
- not subject to any apparent mental infirmity (most likely to be evidenced by forms of protectorship or receivership).

Satisfaction of know-your-customer due diligence should ensure that the borrower exists and has been properly identified. With that as a starting point, it is next necessary (i) to identify the system of law under which capacity will be determined and (ii) to identify those factors which might limit capacity. In this context, nearly all sophisticated jurisdictions recognise that minor children should not, without more, be fixed with contractual obligations, the implications of which they may not have fully understood. For the same reasons, a person who is deemed, or proven, not to be of sound mind at the time when a purported agreement is made may be held not to have entered into such agreement entirely understanding the consequences. In both cases there is a lack of capacity. The problem for a lender is the prospect that the rules determining capacity may, in a transaction with a foreign element, be set by a system of law, to which the natural person or the transaction is expressly, or deemed to be, connected and pursuant to which the borrower may lack the relevant capacity.

5.1.2 Capacity: domicile, applicable law and the place where the contract is made

It might be thought that the capacity of a natural person to enter into contractual obligations (in the same manner as their ability to make a will or contract a marriage) should in all cases be governed by the law of their domicile (*lex domicilii*) as the relevant personal law. The question of capacity to contract is expressly excluded from the *Brussels Convention* (see above, para 2.7.1) leaving national courts to apply traditional rules of private international law to the issue of capacity to contract. The exclusion of the issue of capacity from the *Brussels Convention* is subject to one limitation expressed in Article 11 which in relation to 'Incapacity' provides that:

> *In a contract concluded between persons who are in the same country, a natural person who would have capacity under the law of that country may invoke his incapacity resulting from another law only if the other party to the contract was aware of this incapacity at the time of the conclusion of the contract or was not aware thereof as a result of negligence.*

Article 11 will supplement the private international law rules of a Contracting State to the *Brussels Convention* where the defendant is domiciled in the EU, or the dispute involves title to real property in a Member State. The English courts, in applying private international law rules, have reached no clear decision as to whether capacity to contract should be determined under:

- the law of the domicile;
- the law of the place where the contract was made; or
- the applicable law of the contract objectively determined.

It is recognised that domicile provides an inappropriate test in commercial dealings, where it might lead to a party escaping liability through an undisclosed incapacity. It is likewise considered that although old English case law supports the view that the law of the place where the contract was made should govern the question of capacity, such a view is untenable if it enables a party to evade an incapacity by deliberately concluding the contract in a country where the law is more favourable. The modern view is that capacity should be determined by the applicable law objectively determined (that is, determined by a court as being the law with which the contract has its closest and most real connection). So, in the case of *Bodley Head Limited v Flegon* [1972] 1 W.L.R. 680 it was held that the capacity of the Russian author Alexander Solzhenitsyn to grant a power of attorney in favour of a Swiss lawyer was to be decided by Swiss law as the applicable law of the contract. Although it did not fall to be determined in the case, it was assumed that Alexander Solzhenitsyn did not have capacity under Russian law (his domicile) to enter into the power of attorney.

5.1.3 Capacity: how should the lender protect itself?

The issue of capacity requires that the lender focus upon:

- the domicile, residence or nationality of an individual borrower;
- the significance of the place at which a relevant contract is entered into, bearing in mind that with sophisticated high net worth individuals, the prospect exists that (for example) a contract governing a lending to be made by the lender's London branch is sent to the borrower's Swiss home, but is actually signed by the borrower's lawyer in New York;
- the implications that may flow from any document which contains no express choice of applicable law (so that it will fall to a court to determine the identity of the law with which the transaction contemplated by the document has its closest and most real connection objectively determined); and
- the necessity to determine an appropriate applicable law or laws by express provision for each relevant transaction document, ensuring that each such choice is valid in that it is not entered into merely to defeat a limitation to which one or other of the parties might be subject under the applicable law objectively determined.

5.2 Restrictions on dealing

The lender must be mindful of limitations on capacity which, while not generally affecting the ability of an individual to enter into binding contractual arrangements may, nevertheless, otherwise restrict the scope of an individual's ability to contract for liabilities, or deal with assets.

5.2.1 Bankruptcy or other insolvency proceeding

As a general rule, bankruptcy or an analogous insolvency or reorganisational procedure will restrict the debtor's ability to contract and deal with assets which may be vested in a trustee or other third party. Appropriate due diligence will address the existence of any bankruptcy or analogous insolvency proceeding to which an individual borrower is subject. It should not, however, be overlooked that both the effect of any such proceeding and its very existence may be much more difficult to ascertain in relation to an individual who has connections with a number of offshore jurisdictions. As will be seen later (in the context of enforcement) the concepts of domicile and residence, together with the existence of assets or business activity may, in any jurisdiction in respect of which such connection exists, provide an insolvency or bankruptcy jurisdiction. In appropriate cases and by way of supplementing contracting representations and warranties as to the absence of any bankruptcy or insolvency proceeding, a lender should consider making enquiries by:

- using established credit reference agencies with an international capability; and
- making enquiries in relevant jurisdictions (perhaps through local lawyers or other professionals able to conduct searches and/or make enquiries with court registries, etc), particularly in jurisdictions where the borrower is known to hold assets or conduct business.

5.2.2 Other restrictions on dealing

In addition to the restriction on dealing which bankruptcy or insolvency may impose on an individual, a foreign law to which the individual is subject may also impose restrictions of the following types.

5.2.2.1 Forced heirship rules

Forced heirship rules are restrictions on dealing with heritable property other than in accordance with the rules of devolution applicable to the individual or the property under the law of their domicile. Such rules have widespread application under *Shari'a* law in Muslim countries and in many European civil law jurisdictions. As a general rule, forced heirship will apply to the property of an individual pursuant to the law of their domicile and in respect of property (in particular real property) located within the jurisdiction of such domicile. The issue may be of significance to a lender where the apparent wealth of an individual is materially constituted by property in respect of which such individual does not have an unfettered right of disposal.

5.2.2.2 Matrimonial community property rules

Matrimonial community property rules are rules which, in most civil law jurisdictions and in many of the states of the United States, provide that a spouse is entitled to a proportion of the property acquired during the marriage. In addition to the significance that such interest may have on an assessment of the individual's disposable means, a lender must bear in mind that even where assets are apparently sheltered (perhaps deliberately) from the express jurisdiction of a particular territory's courts, significant bilateral and mutual assistance arrangements in the field of matrimonial law may mean that assets relied upon by the lender are materially affected by the enforcement of the rights of a spouse. It is not unheard of for individuals to seek assistance from their bank lenders in disclosed circumstances that assets are being held (and perhaps not disclosed) by the borrower offshore with the express intention of access being denied to them by an estranged spouse. Such circumstances are fraught with danger for the lender. A lender must also have regard to those rules which may grant to a spouse rights or interests in or to the property of the borrower which may affect its value and ease of realisation, particularly where relied upon by way of security – for example, the right of a spouse to occupy a matrimonial home or other property.

5.2.2.3 Restrictions on payment of interest or usury

Restrictions on payment of interest or usury are restrictions under *Shari'a* law on the rights of an individual to contract for and the rights of a counter-party to recover interest. While the effect of any such restriction on an individual in accordance with the law of his domicile or residence may be mitigated by a choice of applicable law under which the restriction does not apply, a lender must not overlook the problems that may arise on enforcement if the borrower has material assets within the *Shari'a* law jurisdiction.

5.3 Understanding the borrower's purpose

Where a borrower:

- contracts with a lender outside of the jurisdiction of his domicile or residence;
- relies upon a source of income arising outside of such jurisdiction; or
- provides or procures that security is available in an offshore jurisdiction,

a lender can only properly assess the existence or otherwise of the risks identified at para 5.2 above if the reasons for the involvement of a foreign law connection are fully understood. More often than not, an enquiry by the lender will produce the response that the borrowing is structured in a particular way for 'tax planning reasons'. Only by being satisfied as to the existence of a genuine and legitimate tax avoidance scheme will the lender be protected from the material risk that reference to tax saving is no more than a smokescreen for *criminal conduct* in the form of tax evasion or money laundering. In common with the approach adopted by most revenue authorities, a lender must be suspicious of any scheme which has no apparent commercial justification. Appropriate questions must be asked of any scheme which appears to involve an unnecessary 'back-to-back' arrangement. For example, why, without more, should a borrower be prepared to borrow onshore to acquire an asset, where cash or realisable securities are held offshore as security? It may be that simple justification exists, but the lender should never simply assume that the structure is dictated by unexplained and unverifiable tax purposes. A lender should, where tax planning is given as the reason for a cross-border structure, seek to obtain sufficient information to verify the absence of tax evasion and the existence of a viable tax avoidance structure. Although a lender may not be equipped to determine the ultimate viability of a complex tax avoidance scheme, real and practical comfort may be drawn from a confirmation of the basis of the scheme provided by reputable accountants and/or lawyers acting for the borrower.

5.4 The liability of the borrower to tax

The borrower, the borrower's assets and, ultimately, the borrower's estate will all, inevitably, be subject to tax. Whatever the identity and extent of other creditors, a lender can be sure that every non-resident borrower will have as his creditor the taxation authorities of one or more jurisdictions. What is more, it is likely that whichever taxing authority is or may be a creditor of the borrower is likely to enjoy preferential rights to recover taxes due against the borrower, his assets and estate within the territory concerned. Although the lender may not require a detailed knowledge of the borrower's tax status and affairs, a complete absence of knowledge may materially increase the risk of loss and may constitute a failure to comply with know-your-customer principles. Moreover, for the reasons that have been set out in Chapter 3 in the context of references to *all-crimes money laundering* legislation, the absence of an understanding of the borrower's tax status may lead to a failure to question a lending proposal the complexity of which is purportedly justified by reference to tax planning or tax avoidance.

As basic information relevant to the assessment of credit risk and know-your-customer, the lender should ascertain:

- the identity of all jurisdictions in which the borrower is or may be liable to income or gains during his lifetime and inheritance or other taxation on death;
- the source or place of generation of the borrower's taxable income or gains and the location of the borrower's principal fixed assets; and
- the identity of those jurisdictions in which the borrower receives or is deemed to receive (whether or not remitted) income or gains.

In looking, in more detail, at some of the principal tax-planning issues, the sections that follow will proceed primarily by reference to UK taxation law and practice, having regard to the position of a non-resident individual.

5.4.1 Basis of assessment to tax: residence, ordinary residence, domicile, nationality and citizenship

In Chapter 2, para 2.9 a brief introduction to the use of the concepts of residence and ordinary residence as the basis for liability to assessment to tax is set out. Reference has been made to the leading English case authority, *I.R.C. v Lysaght* [1928] A.C. 234 and to *Levene v I.R.C.* [1928] A.C. 217 as indicating that the test of residence is a test of fact in all the circumstances by reference to an individual's settled or usual abode and, in the case of ordinary residence, residence with some degree of continuity. For UK tax purposes, the concepts of residence and ordinary residence have the same meanings in relation to both income and capital gains taxes. Although the case authority suggests that the determination of the existence of residence and ordinary residence is a question of fact and degree, much of the day-to-day uncertainty as to the existence or otherwise of residence is for UK purposes avoided by reliance upon the statement of 'concession and practice' set out by the Inland Revenue in Part 1 of IR20. The principal features of the stated Inland Revenue practice are as follows.

5.4.1.1 Residence
In the case of presence for periods of between 1 and 183 days in a year of assessment, the existence or otherwise of residence will be determined by the application of tests to establish whether such visits involve an intention to reside *permanently or indefinitely* or merely as a *visitor.* If a person is, however, present in the UK for an aggregate period of 183 days in the year of assessment, such person will be resident for that year of assessment.

5.4.1.2 Ordinary residence
Ordinary residence will exist where residence continues year after year, so that residence determined in accordance with length of stay or otherwise may make a person resident but, where they normally live outside of the United Kingdom, not ordinarily resident. Conversely, if a person is

ordinarily resident but not resident for a tax year, they will remain ordinarily resident but will not be resident for that year of assessment.

5.4.2 Presence for less than 183 days in a tax year

Where a person is present within the UK for less than 183 days, residence, and in some cases ordinary residence, can nevertheless arise where:

1 such person comes to the United Kingdom to take up employment lasting two years or more, in which case he will be resident from the start of such period; or
2 such person has previously been abroad but takes up permanent residence in the United Kingdom with the intention of staying more than three years, in which case he will be resident and ordinarily resident from the beginning of such period; or
3 such person has previously been outside of the United Kingdom but spends an average of 91 days or more in the United Kingdom for four consecutive years, in which case he will be treated as resident from the end of the fourth year (or if the intention that such pattern of residence should exist from the outset, from 6 April in the first year that it is clear that such visits will be made); or
4 such person was previously ordinarily resident in the United Kingdom and continues to visit for periods which amount to an average of 91 days in each year, in which case he will be considered both resident and ordinarily resident.

5.4.3 Ceasing to be resident, or ordinarily resident

A person may cease to be resident where he was previously resident in the United Kingdom where, thereafter, all of the following apply:

1 such person is not resident in the United Kingdom;
2 such person is not ordinarily resident in the United Kingdom; and
3 the absence of such person from the United Kingdom is not merely temporary and in respect of an occasional residence abroad.

To be non-resident for a relevant year of assessment, each of the above conditions must exist throughout the relevant year of assessment except that, by concession, the Inland Revenue may allow non-residence from the date of departure in any case:

- where a person leaves the United Kingdom to reside permanently abroad; or
- the person goes abroad for the purpose of full-time employment under a contract of employment lasting in excess of one year and where the absence is in excess of one year.

5.5 United Kingdom resident non-domiciliaries

Special treatment (and therefore, special tax planning consideration) is accorded to individuals who, while resident in the United Kingdom, do not have a United Kingdom domicile. A person who is resident (and has a United Kingdom domicile) will be taxable in the United Kingdom on their worldwide income. If a person is resident but not United Kingdom domiciled, such person will be taxable only on non-UK source income actually remitted (in accordance with the so-called *remittance rules*). It is not unusual to find tax planning structures which involve offshore borrowing (secured on offshore-held assets and repaid by offshore source income) intended for application within the United Kingdom without giving rise to a taxable remittance. Because of the distinction capable of being drawn between the asset (for example a cash deposit) giving rise to the source of income (interest), it is not unusual for remittance-based tax planning to require segregation of those accounts to which interest (as income) is applied, maintaining as a separate fund (and on a separate account) the principal sum on which it is earned. In similar fashion, an individual resident but not domiciled in the United Kingdom is not chargeable to capital gains tax on the disposal of assets situated outside the United Kingdom except to the extent that amounts are 'received' in the United Kingdom in respect of the chargeable gain. In this context, and unlike the position in relation to income, section 12(2) of the *Taxation of Chargeable Gains Act 1992* provides that received extends to 'all amounts paid, used, or enjoyed in or in any manner or form transmitted or brought into the United Kingdom...'. Unlike the position in relation to income, no benefit exists in segregating between separate accounts, amounts as representing the cost or deemed cost of the asset disposed of from the gain or deemed gain on such disposal. Importantly, in this context, the *Taxation of Chargeable Gains Act 1992*, s. 21(1)(b) provides separately for gains arising through the holding of foreign currency bank accounts so that any withdrawal from such account is a disposal. A distinction must be drawn here between treatment of the 'gain' in the hands of an individual from the deemed treatment of such a 'gain' as income in the hands of a company, pursuant to the *Finance Act 1993*. In the case of an individual who is resident and domiciled in the United Kingdom, prescribed rules provide that a foreign currency bank account is situated in the United Kingdom if the creditor (customer) is resident in the United Kingdom. Where the creditor (customer) is a resident non-domiciliary, then pursuant to the *Taxation of Chargeable Gains Act 1992*, s. 275(1), such bank account is not situated in the United Kingdom unless the branch of the bank at which it is kept is within the United Kingdom. This facilitates treatment on a remittance basis where there is, over time, an accrual of gains in the foreign currency bank accounts (measured in sterling) so that such gains are only taxable if or when remitted to the United Kingdom.

5.6 Migration of individuals

The above brief explanation of the most frequently encountered elements in individual tax planning (and for the moment leaving aside the use of corporate vehicles and trusts) has focused on the liability to assessment to tax in the United Kingdom. The lender making facilities available to a high net worth individual must take account of the potential for change in the individual's taxable status, whether brought about intentionally or otherwise. The process by which a person removes or reduces a liability to assessment to tax in one jurisdiction (whether in respect of income, capital gains or on assets) so that such person (again whether in respect of income, gains or assets) becomes subject to tax in another jurisdiction is termed *migration*. On the basis that many jurisdictions may potentially assess a person to tax on their worldwide income (for example, as set out above in the UK based on residence and/or ordinary residence) but where some jurisdictions may assess a resident person to tax only on their domestic income, migration may be an option. Similarly, and perhaps more frequently, where a substantial gain realised within a particular jurisdiction will not be a taxable gain if, at the time of disposal, it accrues to a person who is non-resident, migration may be effected so as to avoid assessment to tax on the gain when it is realised.

5.6.1 Charge to tax based on citizenship

The consideration given above to the position of assessment to tax in the United Kingdom based on residence and ordinary residence (but distinguishing the position of a resident non-domiciliary) should not be taken as having universal application. By way of contrast, the United States taxes on, amongst other bases, citizenship. Accordingly, all United States citizens are liable to tax on worldwide income, gifts and estates, regardless of where they may live or be domiciled. An American citizen may not therefore migrate simply by changing residence, he must give up his US citizenship and, therefore, acquire another. Even so, if the US revenue authorities have reason to believe that a US citizen has renounced citizenship to avoid taxes, such person will remain subject to *anti-expatriation rules* for ten years.

5.6.2 Migration by UK resident taxpayers

The basis upon which a person resident or ordinarily resident for tax in the United Kingdom is able to cease being so resident is set out at para 5.4.3 above. Where, particularly in relation to a latent taxable gain, an individual who is presently resident or ordinarily resident in the United Kingdom wishes to avoid a tax liability on such gain, it is likely that the following will be necessary:

- the individual must be both non-resident and not ordinarily resident in the United Kingdom at the point in time at which the disposal occurs or is deemed to occur (para 5.4.1 above); and
- the disposal and gain must occur or be deemed to occur in a tax year in respect of which the person is non-resident, and is not ordinarily resident in the United Kingdom (in which respect such person is not entitled to rely upon the concession which allows for the splitting of a tax year if the purpose for seeking non-resident status is tax avoidance); and
- the actual disposal (and not merely the effective date of the disposal in accordance with the contract terms) must be in a year of assessment subsequent to which such person is non-resident or ordinarily resident – *Taxation of Chargeable Gains Act 1992*, s. 28; *J H & S Timber Ltd v Quirk* [1973] S.T.C. 111 and *Ayers v C & K (Construction) Ltd* [1975] S.T.C. 345.

5.6.3 Double taxation: unilateral relief for individuals

Chapter 8 sets out a general explanation of the operation of double taxation treaties and the consequent application of *treaty relief* and *unilateral relief.* For the purpose of this chapter, attention is drawn to the relief allowed by the United Kingdom Inland Revenue to individuals in the absence of a double taxation treaty or where an existing treaty does not cover particular tax. Such relief is available to a person resident in the United Kingdom in a relevant year of assessment and so that, in relation to income from offices and employments in an overseas country, the individual is permitted relief on tax paid as a credit against tax chargeable under Schedule E: *Income and Corporation Taxes Act 1988,* s. 794(2)(b). Moreover, if the income from offices and employments is sourced in the Channel Islands or the Isle of Man (s. 794(2)(a)), credit is given against any income.

5.7 Facilitating enforcement or realisation of security

The existence of a foreign law connection in a lending to an individual may introduce unfamiliar difficulties in the enforcement of the lender's rights and remedies against, or realisation of security held from, the borrower. In this context, the lender must ensure:

• that in relation to any court which is intended to have jurisdiction to determine disputes between the lender and borrower, the service of proceedings can be effected cost efficiently and without undue delay;
• that the borrower can be sued in his own name and is not entitled to claim any immunity from proceedings;
• that remedies which may be necessary to preserve the lender's claims pending judgment and enforcement will be available against the assets of the borrower in any offshore centre or jurisdiction in which they exist or are held (for example, through interim judicial attachment or freezing orders such as *Mareva*-type injunctions);
• that judgments or other orders obtained under the chosen applicable law and made by the courts of the jurisdiction to which the parties have submitted will be enforceable, ideally through *reciprocal enforcement provisions* not requiring reconsideration of the merits in any relevant offshore centre or jurisdiction;
• that there are no material stamp or other court fees likely to be incurred on enforcement of the lender's rights and, in particular, on realisation of security within an offshore centre or other foreign law jurisdiction; and
• that, in relation to security over assets held within an offshore centre or other foreign law jurisdiction, there are no untoward or onerous liabilities arising on the exercise of rights in connection with such assets or property. (As to taking of security in offshore jurisdictions generally, see Chapter 9 below.)

5.7.1 Service of proceedings

Service of process on an individual can be a greater problem than for a company or partnership, where the law of the relevant jurisdiction may provide for due service of process at the registered office or principal place of business. To avoid difficulty, the lender should ensure that all relevant transaction documents contain, in addition to the submission to jurisdiction, a contractual agreement as to the manner in which legal process (a writ, summons or order) may be properly served on the borrower. As a matter of private international law, the due service of legal process is a procedural issue determined by the *lex fori* of the courts having jurisdictions. The lender should, therefore, ensure that the contractual mode of service agreed to is valid and will be recognised by the courts of the relevant jurisdictions. As a matter of English procedure, and perhaps as a matter of general application, courts will not recognise as valid, service of legal process on a person outside of the territorial jurisdiction, without the prior approval of the courts (*leave to serve out of the jurisdiction*), a process which may involve expense and delay, and provide to the borrower an opportunity to contest the jurisdiction of the courts concerned. To allow valid service of legal process and avoid the problems associated with an application for leave to serve outside of the jurisdiction, a lender should ensure that the transaction documents incorporate, in all appropriate cases, the appointment of *an agent for service*. In transaction documents governed by a foreign law, care must be taken to ensure that a selected agent for service is qualified to act and that all appropriate formalities for the appointment have been undertaken in accordance with the applicable law and procedural rules of the jurisdiction. As the appointment of an agent for service generally involves payment of fees, it is not unusual for a lender to be asked to waive the requirement. It is suggested that the decision to waive the requirement should not, in the case of an individual not resident within the territory of the courts having jurisdiction, be lightly taken. At a practical level, the lender may be able to establish by enquiry the existence of lawyers or other professionals (suitably qualified) willing to act as agent for service on a relatively modest annual fee. It should be noted that the lender's own lawyers will be unable to act as, generally, they will be subject to a conflict of interest. Again, as a practical matter, it is usual for the contractual appointment of an agent for service contained within transaction documents to contain an undertaking that if, at any time, no agent for service is appointed then the borrower will forthwith be required to appoint such an agent.

5.7.2 Immunity

In the case of an individual borrower (as distinct from the difficulties which may relate to a state-owned entity or corporation), it ought to be possible, as part of the know-your-customer due diligence, to establish, as a question of fact, the existence or otherwise of a status attaching to the borrower giving rise to the prospect of *sovereign immunity*. The existence of sovereign immunity may mean that:

• without more, a relevant court may not have jurisdiction over the individual concerned;
• remedies or reliefs, such as specific performance, *Mareva* injunctions and the attachment of real property are not available; and
• if the lender is successful in obtaining a judgment or order in one jurisdiction, it may be unenforceable against the person or assets of the individual in another jurisdiction, particularly that in which they are resident, where it may be that the entitlement to sovereign immunity is more broadly based.

In the United Kingdom, the position of the English courts is, in relation to a party claiming sovereign immunity being other than the English Crown, governed by the provisions of the *State Immunity Act 1978* or, in default of the application of that Act, by common law rules. The lender must have regard to the English law position (and any rules applicable in the state in which the individual is resident or otherwise entitled to sovereign immunity) if the chosen applicable law is English law and if it is wished to bring disputes before the English courts. Similarly, in the United States, the position is governed by the *Foreign Sovereign Immunities Act 1976*, the provisions of which are broadly similar but not identical to the English Act. When dealing with a party having or likely to have an entitlement to sovereign immunity, and subject to the results of specific enquiry as to the nature, scope and effect of such entitlement within the state to which it relates, the lender should ensure that, in relation to a jurisdiction the courts of which have been selected to determine disputes between the parties, such immunity is waived or otherwise avoided by:

- an express contractual submission to the jurisdiction (in addition to operating as a waiver of any objection to jurisdiction on the basis of sovereign immunity, this will also provide general jurisdiction in accordance with common law principles – see Chapter 2); and
- ensuring express contractual waiver of any right to object to any relief or remedy available to the lender, including that required for enforcement or execution against any property and assets of the individual.

5.7.3 The availability of lender's rights, remedies and reliefs

It is important to recognise that if the lending is unsecured and the borrower's assets are outside of the jurisdiction under the laws of which the borrowing is made and to which the borrower has submitted, enforcement of any judgment or other rights and remedies available to the lender under the transaction documents may, for all practical purposes, be incapable of enforcement. Accordingly, much of the protection available to the lender must, in such circumstances, be considered, and if appropriate obtained, prior to the making available of facilities. It is of little comfort to know that a high net worth individual has substantial funds and securities under investment management in an offshore jurisdiction if the manner in which they have been held and their availability to the lender as a creditor has not been the subject of prior investigation. In the context of deciding whether or not the lender's position is only properly protected by the taking of appropriate security over the offshore assets, it will be relevant to determine whether the lender may have ready recourse to immediate relief in the form of court attachment or interim (*interlocutory*) injunctions such as that known as the *Mareva*-type injunction under English law. In this connection, it must not be assumed that the existence of assets within an offshore centre jurisdiction will, without more, mean that:

- the courts of such offshore centre jurisdiction will recognise an injunction or other order made by the courts having jurisdiction in relation to the lending; or
- the existence of the assets within the offshore centre jurisdiction concerned will give jurisdiction to the courts of such offshore centre to provide interim injunctions or other relief to the lender.

So, for example, the courts of the Island of Jersey have stated that they do not, without more, have jurisdiction to provide interlocutory relief where either there is no substantive cause of action over which they have jurisdiction, or the plaintiff has no proprietary or tracing claim to the assets concerned – see the Royal Court of Jersey judgment in *Abbott Industries v Warner*, unreported. It is further necessary to establish that the courts of the jurisdiction in which the assets are located have, in any event, reliefs and remedies equivalent to those available to the lender under the chosen jurisdiction and applicable law.

5.8 Reciprocal enforcement in the foreign territory

The lender should always seek to ensure that in the event of obtaining a judgment or order given by the courts of the jurisdiction to which the parties have submitted, such judgment or order will be enforceable without retrial of the merits in any jurisdiction in which the borrower may have material assets. In general terms, the lender should seek confirmation that either, as a matter of private international law, or, preferably, on the basis of mutual assistance arrangements, the courts of a jurisdiction to which the lender may require to have recourse will apply *reciprocal enforcement* of judgments or orders. In general terms, the application of private international law principles and/or reciprocal enforcement arrangements will generally apply to allow the enforcement only of a *final and conclusive judgment* given by a recognised superior court of the original jurisdiction. This requirement once again emphasises the need for the lender to ensure that there has been an enforceable submission to the jurisdiction of the original court and that process has been duly served, if necessary using an agent for service. A more difficult issue is whether a judgment or other order may be enforced if it is obtained in default of an appearance or defence (or otherwise as the product of some summary judgment process) in the original courts. For these purposes the lender should enquire as to any limitation on availability of reciprocal enforcement in a material foreign jurisdiction.

5.9 Court or other costs

The lender should enquire as to the existence or otherwise of stamp, court or other fees which may be payable in relation to any proceedings required to be brought against the borrower in a foreign jurisdiction. There may, for example, be material stamp duties or other fees payable in relation to the value of the underlying debt claim, irrespective of the assets available against which enforcement can be had.

5.10 Enforcement of security rights

The lender should ensure, prior to allowing draw-down under the facilities, that all appropriate steps have been taken to perfect security over assets held in an offshore jurisdiction or otherwise subject to a foreign law – see Chapter 9 below.

5.11 The issues raised by cross-border insolvency

A detailed consideration of the implications of insolvency affecting an individual in more than one jurisdiction is beyond the scope of this work, but the lender should note that where an individual is (i) resident in more than one jurisdiction, (ii) carries on an undertaking or business in more than one jurisdiction, (iii) has real property in more than one jurisdiction, or (iv) is domiciled in a jurisdiction other than that with which the lending transaction has its closest connection, a material risk arises of the borrower being subject to a foreign law bankruptcy or insolvency process. The issues which follow are the main headings under which concerns may arise for a lender where there is the prospect of a foreign bankruptcy or insolvency.

5.11.1 Can the lender commence or participate in a local bankruptcy?

Although bankruptcy of the borrower may be a last resort, particularly if the lender is unsecured, it may, not least because of the opportunity to pursue investigation, remain an important enforcement option. The jurisdiction of the English courts to entertain a bankruptcy at the instance of a creditor is provided in section 265 of the *Insolvency Act 1986* on the basis of five criteria, these being *domicile, presence, ordinary residence, place of residence* and the *carrying on of business.* It follows that the selection of English law as the applicable law, and the submission to the jurisdiction of the English courts in the transaction documents, is not determinative of the availability of an English court to receive a petition commencing bankruptcy. Even if the English court has prima facie jurisdiction to entertain a petition, it has a broad jurisdiction to stay the conduct of English bankruptcy proceedings. The exercise of this jurisdiction is governed by the same general considerations as apply to the existence or otherwise of general jurisdiction and will include:

- consideration of whether England is a convenient forum (*forum conveniens*);
- whether bankruptcy or other analogous proceedings have been commenced elsewhere (*lis alibi pendens*) – see *Spiliada Maritime Corp v Cansulex Ltd* [1987] A.C. 470;
- whether a majority of creditors are within or without the English jurisdiction (the existence of a majority of creditors outside of the jurisdiction may point to the existence of a more convenient forum); and
- the presence of assets (if there are no assets in England that may, again, point to the existence of a more convenient forum) – see *Re Robinson* [1883] 22 Ch. D. and *Re Behrends* [1865] 12 L.T. 149.

Where foreign bankruptcy proceedings have already been commenced, their existence alone will automatically allow a stay of English bankruptcy proceedings. If the English court has jurisdiction, the issue of an injunction in foreign bankruptcy proceedings seeking to restrain the commencement or conduct of other bankruptcy proceedings will not, of itself, determine whether or not the English court will grant a stay.

5.11.2 In which of two or more trustees in bankruptcy will the borrower's assets vest?

Where the courts of two or more territories have jurisdiction in relation to the bankruptcy of a borrower (and remembering, as is set out above, that the existence of foreign bankruptcy proceedings does not, of itself, preclude the conduct of English bankruptcy proceedings) an issue may arise as to the competing title to, or the benefit of, the property of the borrower. English authority relevant to these issues is related to, and a consequence of, the circumstances in which the English court will recognise and give effect to the foreign bankruptcy (para 5.11.3 below). As a starting point, it is important to determine the nature of the interest acquired or the capacity in which a relevant third party acts or purports to act on behalf of the bankrupt borrower's estate under the relevant foreign law. A distinction is drawn between (i) a trustee or officer who, by virtue of the foreign law, is automatically vested with title to property, and (ii) a person who has authority only to act as the representative, or *mandataire*, of creditors – see *Tenon v Mars* [1828] 3 Man & Ry. 38, where the English court ruled that a liquidator of a French form of partnership did not have authority to bring and defend proceedings in his own name. A distinction is also drawn between a purported automatic vesting under the relevant foreign law of *moveable property* (for example a debt, cash deposit and certain forms of securities) and *immoveable property* (land and buildings). Vesting of moveable property will be recognised by the English court following the making of a foreign order without confirmation or execution by the English court. In contrast, a foreign bankruptcy will not allow title to immoveable property in England to vest – *Waite v Bingley* [1882] 21 Ch. D. 674. Importantly for the lender, the vesting of moveable property situated in England in a trustee or other officer under a foreign bankruptcy will not preclude the operation of a prior attachment or security right (as to the proper law for the grant of security, see Chapter 9 below). Similarly, the existence of a foreign law bankruptcy will not preclude the jurisdiction of the English court to hear and grant relief in debt or other proceedings against the borrower, notwithstanding that any such proceedings may be precluded under the law of the foreign bankruptcy, although the English court may restrict the relief and orders that might otherwise be available to the creditor – see *Felixstowe Dock and Railway Co v United States Lines Inc* [1989] Q.B. This case concerned the operation of an insolvent reorganisation pursuant to Chapter 11 of the US Federal Bankruptcy Code where English creditors issued proceedings and obtained *Mareva* injunctions against the debtor after the commencing of the US reorganisation proceedings. In this case, the English court refused to discharge the English *Mareva* proceedings on the ground of the existence of the US insolvency proceedings. Importantly, however, Hirst J. held that although the *Mareva* injunctions would be maintained, the plaintiffs in the English proceedings would not be entitled to proceed to enforce, through attachment by garnishee, the assets of the insolvent defendant so as to place themselves in a preferred position as against the general body of creditors.

5.11.3 Mutual assistance

Reference has been made above to the narrow issue of the recognition by the English courts of the vesting of a bankrupt borrower's assets in a foreign trustee or other officer. More generally, it may be relevant to the lender to determine the extent to which mutual assistance is available in the conduct of bankruptcies which may affect the relevant borrower in one or more jurisdictions. As a matter of English law, the obligation of the English courts is now set out in section 426 of the *Insolvency Act 1986* (which replaces, in somewhat different terms, the provisions of section 122 of the *Bankruptcy Act 1914*). Section 426 of the *Insolvency Act 1986* requires that the courts having jurisdiction in relation to insolvency in any part of the United Kingdom shall assist the courts having corresponding jurisdiction in any other part of the United Kingdom or in any other relevant country or territory. At the present time the reference to *relevant country or territory* means any of the Channel Islands, the Isle of Man and those countries designated under the *Cooperation of Insolvency Courts (Designation of Relevant Countries and Territories) Order 1986* (SI 1986 No 2123) under which the following are designated relevant countries or territories: Antigua, Australia, Bermuda, Botswana, Canada, Falkland Islands, Gibraltar, Hong Kong, Ireland, Montserrat, New Zealand, St Helena, Turks and Caicos Islands, Tuvalu, and Virgin Islands. In the preceding paragraph, reference has been made to the recognition by the English courts of the vesting of moveable but not immoveable property in a trustee or other officer appointed under a foreign law bankruptcy. In contrast, the English *Insolvency Act 1986* provides in section 436 that 'property' (of the debtor) includes 'land ... wherever situated'. It is difficult to suggest with certainty the extent to which, if at all, extraterritorial recognition will be given to such automatic vesting of immoveable property in an English trustee in bankruptcy even in dependent territories such as the Channel Islands or other Commonwealth countries.

5.11.4 Can or must set-off be allowed in the foreign insolvency of the borrower?

Full consideration of insolvent cross-border set-off is beyond the scope of this work. The lender should, however, enquire and obtain foreign law legal opinion as to the existence or otherwise of insolvent set-off provisions where it may be material. For example, if a substantial cash deposit is to be held at a branch of the lender in an offshore centre as 'comfort' or formal security for facilities in another jurisdiction, the potential for an insolvency affecting the borrower in either one of the jurisdictions may give rise to inconsistent treatment of the right or obligation of the lender to set off credit balances against the borrowing.

6 | Considerations when lending to companies

Introduction

This chapter considers issues of particular concern arising in relation to lending to one or more companies where the transaction involves a foreign law connection. Such a connection may arise (i) because the borrower or guarantor company (or other corporate surety) is a 'foreign company' (meaning, for the purpose of this chapter, that it is incorporated and domiciled outside of the United Kingdom), (ii) because assets to be held as security are located offshore, or (iii) because the facility or some aspect of the facility is made available offshore or is otherwise subject to a foreign law. Where the borrower is a company (or more than one company) and the lending transaction attracts the risks associated with a foreign law connection (see above, para 3.1), the lender should ensure that:

- the borrower has been duly constituted and exists (i.e. has been formed and not dissolved) in good standing under the laws of the place of its incorporation and is not subject to any solvent or insolvent winding up proceeding;
- the borrower has complied with any special requirements in relation to its business, for example relating to banking, insurance, trustee or custodial services or gambling;
- the borrower has capacity to enter into, be bound by and perform in accordance with the transaction terms;
- in entering into the transaction, the borrower has undertaken all necessary acts of corporate governance and has complied with its own internal regulations for the approval and execution of the transaction documents and the performance of their terms;
- the borrower executes the relevant transaction documents in the appropriate manner;
- the performance of the transaction terms is lawful and that there are no regulatory or other extraneous restrictions on the borrower's ability to

perform in accordance with the transaction terms under the laws of the borrower's place of incorporation and elsewhere;

- the reasons for the foreign law connection are understood, it being insufficient to accept an explanation that the transaction is so structured for 'tax reasons';
- existing and probable charges to tax do not adversely affect the lending (for example through application of withholding);
- viable and cost effective means of enforcement exist in all relevant jurisdictions and that there are no material impediments to enforcement; and
- the implications of an insolvency affecting the borrower in a relevant foreign jurisdiction are understood.

In addition to the issues specific to lending to a company, the lender must have regard to the need, in all cases:

- to complete due diligence in relation to know-your-customer principles (see above, Chapter 3);
- to identify and select, by express provision, an appropriate applicable law for all transaction documents and obtain the express submission to the courts of an appropriate jurisdiction by the borrower and all other relevant parties (see above, Chapter 2); and
- in any case where a foreign company is not subject to fixed rules deeming presence within the jurisdiction (for example, through the carrying on of business at a principal office and/or through registration as an oversea company (see below, para 6.5.1) capable of service), the appointment of an agent for service within the jurisdiction.

6.1 Existence, capacity, due authorisation and execution

A company or corporation has a separate legal personality (see above, para 4.2) and has the opportunity for continuity of existence. Corporate legal personality is different from the legal personality of a natural person. Company or corporate legal personality is a creation of the legal system under which the company or corporation is created or constituted.

6.1.1 Corporate domicile and residence

Under English law the place of incorporation determines the nationality and the domicile of a company – *Gasque v I.R.C.* [1940] 2 K.B. 80 and *Kuenigl v Donnersmarck* [1955] 1 Q.B. 515. It follows that, prima facie, the domicile of a company is fixed at its incorporation and cannot be changed, although it has been suggested by Buckley J, in *Carl-Zeiss Stiftung v Rayner and Keeler (No 2)* [1970] Ch.D 506, that where the law of the place of incorporation allows for the substitution of another system of law as the proper law of the corporation, the possibility exists of re-domicile of a company. The *Civil Jurisdiction and Judgments Act 1982* (giving effect to the Brussels Convention (see above, para 2.4.2)) uses domicile to fix jurisdictional competence in civil and commercial matters by treating the *seat* of the company (*siège social*) as the domicile, so that in relation to the United Kingdom a company has its seat in the United Kingdom if, but only if:

> (a) *It was incorporated or formed under the law of a part of the United Kingdom and has its registered office or some other official address in the United Kingdom; or*
> (b) *its central management and control is exercised in the United Kingdom.*

The residence of a company or corporation is determined differently from that of domicile or nationality. The concept of residence in relation to a company or corporation is of particular relevance to the liability of the company to tax. A company is considered to be resident in the country in which it conducts its real business or where the central management and control is actually undertaken – *De Beers Consolidated Mines Ltd v Howe* [1906] A.C. 455. The determination of the place in which control and management is undertaken is a question of fact. The determination of residence for United Kingdom taxation purposes is further considered below (para 6.4.1).

6.1.2 Capacity

In the case of a company or corporation, a reference to *capacity* concerns the limitation on its legal personality. For the lender dealing with a foreign company, it is important to distinguish between:

- the extent to which the issue of capacity determines the rights between the borrower and the lender as a third party; and
- the extent to which capacity determines the rights between the directors, the company and its shareholders *inter se*.

As a matter of English law (it should not be overlooked that a number of offshore centres have company legislation based on the English Companies Acts) limitations on corporate capacity have existed through the operation of the *objects clause* contained within the *memorandum*. On this basis, English law has historically treated an act done by a company outside the scope of its objects clause as *ultra vires* and null and void, so that neither the company nor other parties to such a contract could sue or be sued on it – *Ashbury Railway Carriage and Iron Co v Riche* [1875] L.R. 7 H.L. 653. Today, as a matter of English law, the application of the doctrine of *ultra vires* has been materially modified by the substitution of a new section 35 in the *Companies Act 1985* pursuant to sections 108–112 of the *Companies Act 1989*. The effect of the reforms is to abolish the doctrine of *ultra vires* for the purposes of the relationship of a company with a third party. Nevertheless, the objects clause of the memorandum of an English company may still operate to effectively limit the capacity of the company as exercisable by the directors in the context of the relationships between the company, the directors and its shareholders. The directors owe a fiduciary duty to the company and the shareholders to exercise their powers *intra vires* the capacity of the company. In dealing with a foreign company, and in relation to its capacity to contract, the lender should be concerned to identify:

- the existence and, to the extent relevant, the operation of any residual doctrine of *ultra vires* under the law of incorporation;
- the absence in any event of any limitations on the capacity of the company imposed by the terms of the memorandum, articles, statutes, by-laws or similar documents constituting the company which may limit the power of the directors; and
- that there are no supervening limitations on corporate capacity imposed by statutes or other laws under which the company is incorporated.

The lender should ascertain (for example in the case of a corporation constituted to hold assets for the benefit of the public of a territory) that there are no limitations on the capacity of that company or corporation, for example to borrow money or provide security over its assets. To put the issue of capacity beyond doubt, the lender should:

- obtain a copy of any memorandum, statute, by-laws or other instrument setting out the capacity of the company or corporation under the relevant law; and
- obtain a foreign law legal opinion (see Chapter 10 below) confirming the capacity of the borrower to enter into the proposed transaction.

6.1.3 Due authorisation and execution

In order to establish that the transaction has been approved by the company (usually by the directors exercising the powers of the company) and that transaction documents are executed by a duly authorised signatory or under the seal of the company, the lender should, in relation to a foreign company borrower:

- establish whether any internal formalities are required to be completed by the borrower in order that it may approve entry into the arrangements contemplated by the transaction documents (assuming them to be within its capacity); and
- establish how the borrower should, as a matter of form, execute the transaction documents.

As to the first of these two issues, the lender is concerned to ensure that the directors or other officers of the company (or any other person) entitled and charged with the exercise of the powers of the borrower are:

- acting within any limitation on the exercise of such powers (for example contained within the *articles of association, statutes or by-laws*) (para 6.1.2 above); and
- that procedural steps required for the valid exercise of such powers have been followed.

Where appropriate, the lender should ensure that corporate resolutions of the directors or other officers have been made in an appropriate form at a meeting which is properly convened, quorate and otherwise held in accordance with the terms of the foreign company borrower's constitution. The absence of limitation on the powers of directors or other officers, the due authorisation of the company to enter into and be bound by the transaction arrangements and the proper extent of the consideration which should be evidenced by the records (for example, board minutes) of the directors or other officers' meetings should form the subject matter of issues to be addressed by an appropriate foreign law opinion (see Chapter 10 below). While it may be the case that the law of the jurisdiction of incorporation or domicile provides for a *presumption of regulatory* in favour of third parties dealing with the foreign company borrower, the lender may run the risk of being fixed with actual knowledge of a breach where it has complied with know-your-customer principles. Accordingly, the lender should ensure that it has determined, preferably by confirmation in a foreign law opinion, that any board or other meeting of relevant officers was convened and held in an appropriate manner, having regard to such issues as restrictions on the place at which meetings should be held, quorum for meetings, and the mode in which meetings are held. Because of the significance for tax purpose of residence determined by reference to the place in which directors' meetings are held (or, perhaps, the domicile of directors constituting a quorum) it is not unusual for the constitution of foreign companies to provide that meetings of its directors or other officers shall only be held, for example, outside of the United Kingdom or United States and that a meeting shall not be considered quorate if there is present a majority of directors domiciled in the excluded jurisdiction. Similarly, requirements for quorum should be addressed in the context of any limitation on the ability of interested directors to be counted as present and able to vote. Care should be taken where resolutions are those of a sole director, or are made in writing or by meeting covered by telephone, to ensure that such resolutions are within the powers of the borrower exercisable by the directors. As to the question of the manner in which the foreign company borrower may be required to execute transaction documents, the lender should have regard to:

- the requirements of form determined by the applicable law (if different to that of the foreign company borrower); and
- any requirements imposed on the foreign company borrower as to mode of execution of contracts.

Under English law, the formalities required of contracting parties have been much reduced, so that the distinction accorded to the execution of documents to be executed as a deed under seal (whether by an individual or a company) is now subject to the provisions of the *Law of Property (Miscellaneous Provisions) Act 1989*, s. 1(1)(b) which abolished the requirement for the execution of a deed by an individual under seal. The benefit of this provision is available to companies by the application of section 36A paragraph 3 of the *Companies Act 1989* which provides that a company may execute a document either under its common seal by a director and the secretary of the company, or by two directors of the company where the document is expressed to be executed by the company. The *Foreign Companies (Execution of Documents) Regulations 1994* applies the 1989 Act reforms to foreign companies. The lender must, nevertheless, establish whether there is any supervening mode of execution required by the foreign company borrower under the law of the place of its incorporation and, in particular, whether there are any prescribed forms of execution in accordance with the terms of its constitution (for example, any requirements that certain types of transaction documents be executed in a particular way).

6.2 Restrictions on dealing

The lender should ensure that:

- there is no supervening restriction on the borrower entering into the proposed transaction (for example, illegality as a matter of local law); and
- there are no consents, licences or registrations required in connection with the business of the borrower in its territory of incorporation or

elsewhere as a result of either (i) its business (for example, banking, insurance, the provision of trustee or custodial services or gambling), or (ii) arising from the nature of the intended transaction.

6.2.1 Illegality

The lender must ensure that the transactions contemplated by the lending arrangements are legal in the country of incorporation of the foreign company borrower. So, for example, regard must be had to the existence of relevant foreign exchange restrictions or the possibility that the transaction involves tax evasion. Notwithstanding that the terms of the contract may not give rise to the commission of any offence under the applicable law of the transaction documents, illegality may nevertheless mean that, on the basis of public policy, the courts of the jurisdiction of incorporation will refuse to enforce the contract under its applicable law.

6.2.2 Requirements for consents, licences and registrations

The lender should ascertain whether any element of the transaction gives rise to the requirement for a regulatory or other consent or licence. In the case of a foreign company borrower, this may arise in the context of the issue of any 'securities' (which may include a reference to shares, debentures, bonds, notes or other debt instruments or the circulation of any prospectus, or other offer, to the public). Care should also be taken to ensure that the form in which money is being raised does not constitute a *deposit-taking activity* regulated in relation to the conduct of banking business. Generally, registrations are likely to be required in relation to the grant by the foreign company borrower of security over its assets. This issue is dealt with in more detail in Chapter 9.

6.3 Understanding the borrower's purpose

Where a foreign company borrower:

1 contracts with a lender outside the jurisdiction of its place of incorporation or residence;
2 relies upon a source of income arising outside of such jurisdiction; or
3 provides or procures that security is available in an offshore jurisdiction,

the lender can only properly assess the existence or otherwise of additional risks to the transaction if the proper reasons for the involvement of a foreign law connection are fully understood. In the case of corporate borrowers, the variety of reasons for use of offshore incorporated entities may be broader in scope than those applicable in the case of an individual. It may, for example, be entirely appropriate that an international trading group operate a financing or captive insurance subsidiary in an offshore jurisdiction. Nevertheless, and in common with lending to individuals, it is incumbent upon the lender to ensure that an explanation given for an unduly complex structure involving an offshore entity is not a smokescreen for *criminal conduct*. The lender must recognise that the interposition of corporate entities can, in addition to tax evasion, facilitate complex fraud. Undue reliance on jurisdictional confidentiality and non-disclosure of beneficial interests are indicators which may give rise to a reportable suspicion. Where tax planning is given as the reason for a cross-border structure, the lender should seek to obtain sufficient information to verify the absence of tax evasion and the existence of a viable tax avoidance structure. Although a lender may not be equipped to determine the ultimate viability of a complex tax avoidance scheme, real and practical comfort may be drawn from a confirmation of the basis of the scheme provided by reputable accountants and/or lawyers acting for the borrower.

6.4 The liability of the foreign company borrower to tax

Reference has been made at para 6.1 above to the use of *residence* as the basis for determining the liability of a company to assessment to tax.

6.4.1 Central management and control test for residence

The United Kingdom Inland Revenue regard the determination of residence by reference to the place of central management and control as a question of fact, to be determined in accordance with available case authority as necessary. Nevertheless, the Inland Revenue provide practical guidance in a published Statement of Practice SP 1/90 which makes it clear that while the place at which meetings of directors are held may be indicative of the location of central management and control, it is only one of a number of factors to be considered. So, for example, the Statement of Practice makes clear that there may be circumstances pointing to the exercise of central management and control by a single person who is either the chairman or managing director and/or a majority shareholder, in which case residence may be consistent with the residence of such individual. Shareholder control is an issue in the case of a parent/subsidiary relationship, although the United Kingdom Inland Revenue will not question the independence of properly conducted corporate governance in the foreign company subsidiary. The conduct of meetings of directors outside of the United Kingdom may be overridden if the business undertaking is managed and directed wholly in the United Kingdom. If the location of meetings of the board of directors is to be determinative of the place of control and management, such fact will usually need to be consistent with (i) at least a majority of the directors making up a quorum being themselves non-resident, (ii) the proper exercise of all of the directors' powers by the directors, and (iii) evidence in the minutes of the board of directors and other company records.

6.4.2 Dual residence

As a matter of English law, a company or corporation may be resident in more than one jurisdiction in that, if it is a foreign company, it may be deemed resident in its place of incorporation (but note the possibility that, in the case of an offshore centre, it is an exempt company, i.e. non-resident (see above, para 4.2.1.7), and be resident in the United Kingdom pursuant to the central management and control test). At least as a matter of United Kingdom Inland Revenue practice, it would seem that a company may not have more than one centre of control and management: *Swedish Central Railway v Thompson* [1925] A.C. 495.

6.4.3 Charge to tax

If a foreign company borrower is resident in the United Kingdom on the basis of the central management and control test it will be chargeable to tax on all of its profits and gains at full corporation tax rate. As with an individual, however, the source of profit or gain is an important factor in the existence of liability of a charge to tax; although a company may be non-resident in the United Kingdom on the basis of the central control and management test it will, nevertheless, remain chargeable to tax on profits where it has a *permanent establishment* within the United Kingdom through a branch or agency. Moreover, a branch or agency constituting a permanent establishment for an otherwise non-resident company, may be assessed and charged in respect of the tax of the company in its own name.

6.4.4 United Kingdom controlled foreign companies legislation

In the case of individuals, the United Kingdom tax avoidance provisions address the transfers of assets abroad by an individual through Chapter III of Part XVII of the *Income and Corporation Taxes Act 1988*, s. 739. In any case where the shares of a non-resident foreign company are held by a United Kingdom resident company, it is necessary to determine whether the United Kingdom resident company will be chargeable to tax on the basis that the non-resident foreign company is a *controlled foreign company* (CFC) for the purpose of Chapter IV of Part XVII of the *Income and Corporation Taxes Act 1988*. The United Kingdom's CFC provisions enable the United Kingdom Inland Revenue to apportion to shareholders of a CFC taxable profits of the CFC as if they were the profits of a UK resident and so that the apportioned profits may be charged to United Kingdom corporation tax in the hands of the corporate resident shareholder. The CFC provisions are applied through the application of three tests:

1 determination that the non-resident foreign company is a CFC as defined;
2 if yes, determination that none of the statutory exceptions to the Inland Revenue making a direction to apply the CFC legislation is applicable; and
3 if no such exceptions are applicable, the positive decision by the Inland Revenue that there should be an apportionment of the CFC's profits.

As to the first limb, the foreign company (a) must be a 'company', (b) must be non-resident in the United Kingdom, (c) must be controlled by persons resident in the United Kingdom, and (d) must be subject to a lower level of taxation in the territory in which it is resident. The question of whether or not the non-resident foreign company is subject to a lower rate of taxation involves a notional computation of the tax it would pay in the United Kingdom and a comparison with the actual tax paid. Only if the actual tax paid is less than 75% of the notional United Kingdom computation is the condition satisfied. The manner in which this test operates means that provided the country of residence is not an *excluded country* for the purposes of the provisions, it may have a headline rate of corporation tax higher than the United Kingdom but nevertheless result in a lower amount of actual tax payable. Satisfaction of the second limb of the test involves the absence of application of five available statutory exceptions. The five tests are:

1 that the company operates an *acceptable distribution policy*, i.e. it distributes to its United Kingdom resident shareholders (directly or in-directly), in the case of a trading company not less than 50%, and in the case of a non-trading company not less than 90% of its available profits;
2 it engages in *exempt activities*, i.e. it is a specified class of overseas trading or offshore holding company;
3 it is a publicly quoted company, i.e. shares that carry not less than 35% of the voting power are held by the public and quoted and dealt in on a recognised stock exchange in the territory in which the company is resident;

4 it has notional United Kingdom profits not exceeding £20,000.00 per annum; and

5 its avoidance of United Kingdom taxation was not the main purpose, or one of the main purposes, for its activities or existence.

Finally, the third limb is that the Inland Revenue may, but is not required to, make a direction under the CFC legislation apportioning among the shareholders of the CFC the chargeable profits, that is the notional United Kingdom taxable profits. In this context, the Inland Revenue publish, from time to time, a revised list of *excluded countries* (generally those not regarded as tax havens) and with which country there may be a trading relationship. If the non-resident foreign company is resident in an excluded country, the Inland Revenue will not make a direction that chargeable profits be apportioned and assessed in the hands of the United Kingdom resident shareholders. For the lender, the existence or otherwise of taxation based on the CFC legislation may be of particular significance in a group lending situation.

6.4.5 Transfer pricing

Transfer pricing is a mechanism by which profit which would otherwise be generated in a high tax jurisdiction is generated in a lower tax jurisdiction either (i) by invoicing for supply of goods or services to the supplier in the high tax jurisdiction at a price which recovers for the invoicing company what would otherwise be profit, or (ii) by moving profit by a charge for 'management'. Anti-avoidance measures control transfer pricing by requiring evidence of pricing and recovery of management charges on a basis justifiable between arm's-length parties.

6.4.6 Migration of companies

At para 6.1.1, reference has been made to the fact that English law deems the place of incorporation as determining the nationality and domicile of a company. All companies incorporated in the United Kingdom prior to 15 March 1988 are, if trading, deemed to have become resident on 15 March 1993, and all companies incorporated after 15 March 1988 are deemed to be UK resident for tax purposes. As has been seen, a foreign company can be deemed tax resident on the basis of the existence of central management and control within the United Kingdom. In this context, the possibility of migration of companies begs the question of whether a United Kingdom registered company may change its place of incorporation, and thereby its domicile and proper law. It is clear that the *Companies Acts 1985–1989* make no provision for the alteration of the proper law or domicile of a company incorporated under those laws. While it has been argued by some that the freedom of establishment conferred by the Treaty of Rome permits the transfer of residence of companies between Member States of the European Union, it has nevertheless been held by the European Court of Justice that, as a company is a creature of national law it cannot re-domicile – *R. v H M Treasury and I.R.C., ex p. Daily Mail and General Trust Plc* [1988]. Moreover, the European Court of Justice held in the same case that the 'seat', or central control and management of a company could not likewise be transferred unless the national law permitted. As a matter of English law, a non-UK incorporated but resident company may migrate if (i) it becomes non-resident under the central management and control test, or (ii) it becomes dual resident. While, theoretically, the transfer of central control and management may appear straightforward, the lender should not overlook the possibility that central control and management is determined not by reference to the place at which the directors meet but by the place of residence of a controlling shareholder – *Unit Construct Co Ltd v Bullock* [1960] A.C. A foreign company may be dual resident in any case where there is a double tax treaty between the United Kingdom and another jurisdiction in which a foreign company resident in the United Kingdom is also resident pursuant to such other country's domestic laws. Prior to 1988, no company could migrate without Treasury consent. While such consent is now no longer required, there are two significant issues which arise on migration, as follows.

- *A deemed disposal:* for capital gains tax purposes, the migrating company is deemed, pursuant to the *Taxation of Capital Gains Act 1992*, s. 185, to have disposed of its assets immediately prior to the time at which it ceases to be resident, thereby crystallising any chargeable gain on the basis that the deemed disposal and re-acquisition take place at market value.
- *Obligation to notify the Inland Revenue:* the *Finance Act 1988*, s. 130, imposes an obligation on the migrating company to notify the Inland Revenue of the time at which it intends to migrate and of the tax outstanding or payable in respect of accounting periods before such time. The company is required to make arrangements for payment of all tax outstanding. Failure to comply with the notification requirements gives rise to a penalty in a sum equal to the tax outstanding at the time of migration which may be recovered, (i) from the migrating company itself, (ii) from any director of the migrating company or from any company which controls the migrating company, and (iii) from any person who has been instrumental in the breach by the directors of the notification requirements.

The Inland Revenue's practice in relation to corporate migration is set out in Statements of Practice 2/90 and 2/92.

6.5 Facilitating enforcement or realisation of security

The existence of a foreign law connection may introduce unfamiliar difficulties in the enforcement of the lender's rights and remedies against, or realisation of security held from, the borrower. In this context, the lender must ensure:

- that in relation to any court which is intended to have jurisdiction to determine disputes between the lender and the borrower, the service of proceedings can be effected cost efficiently and without undue delay;
- that the borrower can be sued in its own name and is not entitled to claim any immunity from proceedings;
- that remedies which may be necessary to preserve the lender's claims pending judgment and enforcement will be available against the assets of the borrower in any offshore centre or jurisdiction in which they exist or are held (for example, through interim judicial attachment or freezing orders such as *Mareva*-type injunctions);
- that judgments or other orders obtained under the chosen applicable law and made by the courts of the jurisdiction to which the parties have submitted will be enforceable, ideally through *reciprocal enforcement provisions* not requiring reconsideration of the merits in any relevant offshore centre or jurisdiction;
- that there are no material stamp or other court fees likely to be incurred on enforcement of the lender's rights and, in particular, on realisation of security within an offshore centre or other foreign law jurisdiction; and
- that, in relation to security over assets held within an offshore centre or other foreign law jurisdiction, there are no untoward or onerous liabilities arising on the exercise of rights in connection with such assets or property (as to the taking of security in offshore jurisdictions generally, see Chapter 9 below).

6.5.1 Service of proceedings

The observations made in relation to an individual at para 5.7.1 above, apply with equal merit to a foreign company. One exception is where the applicable law of the transaction documents is English law, the parties have submitted to the jurisdiction of the English courts and the foreign company is an *oversea company* for the purposes of section 744 of the *Companies Act 1985*, such that, in accordance with the provisions of section 695(1) it is required, *inter alia*, to register the name and address of at least one person resident in the United Kingdom who is authorised to accept service of process or notices on behalf of the company.

6.5.2 Immunity

In general terms, and once again, the matters set out in relation to the impact of sovereign immunity on the lender's position are those set out at para 5.7.2 above. The lender should, however, note that for the purposes of the *State Immunity Act 1978*, a distinction does exist between the State and 'separate entities'. Pursuant to section 14(1) of the Act, a separate entity is 'distinct from the executive organs of the government of the State and capable of suing or being sued'. Clearly, therefore, the lender must determine that, as a matter of English law, the foreign company is a separate entity for the purpose of the Act. In this context, it has been held that the Central Bank of Nigeria which was under government control and exercising the functions of a central bank was, as a question of Nigerian law, a separate entity – *Trendtex Trading Corporation v Bank of Nigeria* [1977] Q.B. 529. In the particular case of central banks, however, and following the provisions of section 14(4) of the *State Immunity Act 1978*, while there may be no immunity from proceedings, there will be immunity within the United Kingdom, from enforcement against the bank's property, which is regarded as being held not for commercial purposes but, rather, as the property of the relevant state. For the steps necessary to ensure waiver of sovereign immunity (whether in respect of proceedings or enforcement), the reader is directed to the provisions set out in para 5.7.2 above and, in particular, to the final three checklist points set out thereunder.

6.5.3 The availability of the lender's rights, remedies and reliefs

Under this heading, the reader is referred to the considerations set out at para 5.7.3 above. There are, however, additional difficulties associated with enforcement against corporate entities that do not exist in the case of an individual. In an offshore context, perhaps the most frequently encountered difficulty is that of obtaining information. While it may be the case that a company is resident and/or domiciled in an offshore centre because that is where it is incorporated, it may, nevertheless, be administered by professional corporate administrators in a quite separate jurisdiction and then have control and management (either in the form of the place at which directors' meetings are convened and held or in the form of a directing shareholder) in yet a third jurisdiction. So, for example a company incorporated in the British Virgin Islands may be administered by professional corporate administrators in Luxembourg (maintaining bank accounts subject to Luxembourg's banking secrecy laws) with a controlling shareholder (perhaps in the form of a Panamanian holding company operating through a power of attorney granted to an individual beneficial owner). In such circumstances, even the availability of the forms of relief referred to at para 5.7.3 above may not, for practical purposes, assist the lender. Of course, in the example given, know-your-customer due diligence ought to disclose the identity of the true beneficial owner (but that might not necessarily be so if the British Virgin Islands company is introduced to the lender through the Luxembourg manager as financial intermediary). In the example given, the lender may have the greatest difficulty in preventing dealings with the assets held by the British Virgin Islands company unless they have been identified in advance of the lending and are, perhaps, held through nominee or custodial arrangements over which the lender has actual control.

6.6 The opportunity for reciprocal enforcement, court or other costs and enforcement of security rights

In relation to foreign company borrowers, the reader is referred to the general considerations set out in the context of lending to individuals at paras 5.9–5.10 above.

6.7 The issues raised by cross-border insolvency

A company may only be the subject of *dissolution* (which must be distinguished from processes of *winding-up, liquidation* or analogous procedure) under the law of the place of its incorporation. It is equally almost certainly the case that a company incorporated within a jurisdiction is subject to the courts of that jurisdiction in relation to insolvency proceedings. For the lender, it is important, however, that in many jurisdictions (including the United Kingdom) the English courts have statutory jurisdiction to wind up a foreign company. The prospect that a corporate borrower may be the subject of insolvency proceedings in a multiplicity of jurisdictions gives rise to issues that are well beyond the scope of this book. Nevertheless, in assessing, at the outset, the risks associated with a lending structure involving a foreign company, the lender should have regard to the issues which follow.

6.7.1 Can the lender commence a bankruptcy in the jurisdiction of the lending?

For the purpose of the analysis that follows, it is assumed that the applicable law of the lender is English law and that the lending has been made to a foreign company which is not an *oversea company* (see above, para 6.5.1). In such a case, pursuant to Part V of the *Insolvency Act 1986* s. 221, the English courts have jurisdiction over foreign companies as falling within the category of *unregistered companies*. The *Insolvency Act 1986* defines *unregistered company* as including 'any association and any company which is not a railway company incorporated by Act of Parliament or a company registered in any part of the United Kingdom'. Section 221 provides that the English courts may have jurisdiction (i) if the company has been dissolved, (ii) if the company has ceased to carry on business, (iii) if the company is carrying on business only for the purposes of winding up its affairs, (iv) if the company is unable to pay its debts, or (v) if it is just and equitable that the company should be wound up. The English courts have applied the jurisdictional criteria set out under section 221 so as to assume jurisdiction where, for example, there is a branch office in England (*Re Matheson Brothers Ltd* [1884] 27 Ch. D. 225), where the foreign company has a place of business in England (*Tovarisbestvo Manufactur Liudvig Rabenek* [1885] 29 Ch. D. 219) and where there were assets within the jurisdiction (*Banque des Marchands de Moscou (Koupetschesky) v Kindersley* [1951] Ch. 112). In the case of *Derby & Co Ltd v Weldon (Nos. 3 and 4)* [1990] Ch. 65, the Court of Appeal ruled that it was not necessary for there to be assets within the jurisdiction in order that a receiver be appointed, and a *Mareva* injunction granted against the foreign company. In the case of a foreign company which is subject to a solvent winding-up, the *Civil Jurisdiction and Judgments Act 1982* (see above, para 2.4.2), s. 43 of which gives qualified effect to Article 16 of the *Brussels Convention*. The Act applies only in relation to a solvent company and only to foreign companies (with a seat in a Contracting State) in that (i) it was incorporated or formed under the law of that state, or (ii) its central management and control is exercised in that state.

It follows from the above brief analysis that the lender to a foreign company should, prior to making the loan available, be concerned with the issue of winding-up (whether solvent or insolvent) for the following reasons:

- the lender must determine that the foreign company is validly existing (i.e. that it has not been dissolved in its country of incorporation), that its assets remain vested in the company (i.e. they have not vested on the commencement of a winding-up or liquidation in some other person) and that the directors, other officers or agents on behalf of the foreign company, are entitled to contract on behalf of the company (i.e. the powers of the directors are exercisable by them and have not vested in some other person in the winding-up or liquidation of the foreign company); and

- that, should the lender wish to enforce its rights as against the borrower, winding-up or liquidation may be available as an appropriate remedy, not least because in the last resort a court-appointed receiver, special manager or liquidator may be the most effective manner through which to obtain access to the books and records of a foreign company and to investigate its affairs.

It follows that the lender's concern should be to establish, so far as possible, that a prospective borrower is not affected by any form of winding-up or liquidation prior to draw-down and that, in any event, the prospective borrower may be made subject to insolvency proceedings in a jurisdiction convenient to the lender, for example the United Kingdom.

6.7.2 Ancillary winding-up proceedings

In the foregoing paragraph, reference has been made to the jurisdiction of the English courts on the basis of section 221 of the *Insolvency Act 1986* and attention has been drawn to the prospect that a foreign company may be the subject of insolvency proceedings in more than one jurisdiction. Clearly, this prospect must be reflected in the terms of any contractual representation and warranty to be taken in the transaction documents from a foreign company borrower prior to draw-down and, to the extent reasonably practicable, in the terms of a foreign law legal opinion or opinions to be obtained. For the purpose of the potential application of English jurisdiction to winding-up proceedings, the lender should note that the existence of foreign winding-up proceedings (or indeed the dissolution of the company under the law of its place of incorporation) does not, of itself, preclude the jurisdiction of the English courts, as, in such circumstances, express provision for jurisdiction is made in section 225 of the *Insolvency Act 1986* in respect of an unregistered company (i.e. on the basis discussed above inclusive of a foreign company). For practical purposes, this provision operates as a modification of what otherwise would be the basis of an application to the English court for a stay of English insolvency proceedings where such proceedings were already on foot before the courts of another jurisdiction and allow, to a foreign liquidator or other relevant officer, an alternative to seeking recognition of his appointment in the foreign proceedings by the expedient of commencing further English insolvency proceedings.

6.7.3 Commencement of winding-up proceedings

The lender should note that, in relation to a foreign company, the method of commencement of winding-up proceedings in the jurisdiction of its incorporation (and in any other jurisdiction to which it may be subject to a winding-up or other insolvency proceeding) may be materially different from the procedure in the United Kingdom and may, for example, allow for a winding-up to be commenced by the company or a creditor by the commencement of proceedings without prior notice of a relevant court hearing to creditors (an *ex parte* application), or through the passing of a directors' and/or shareholders' resolution which may or may not require filing at a public registry or notice to creditors. In the United Kingdom the position is as follows.

- A *petition* in respect of an English company may be served at the company's registered office.
- A *petition* in respect of a foreign company registered in England as an oversea company may be served upon the person authorised to accept service on behalf of such company, or by service at the principal place of business of such company – section 695 of the *Companies Act 1985.*
- A *petition* may be served on a foreign company which is not an oversea company at its last known principal place of business, or at the place where the company has carried on business, or (and this assumes that the English court has accepted jurisdiction in the matter) in accordance with an order of the English court for substituted service.

6.7.4 Mutual assistance

It has been noted at para 6.7.2 above that the commencement of English insolvency proceedings provides to the liquidator appointed in foreign insolvency proceedings affecting a foreign company, an alternative to proceedings confirming recognition of his foreign appointment and, in particular, the vesting of the assets of the company in the foreign liquidator. It nevertheless remains the case that the courts of the United Kingdom have a well-established practice of recognising, in appropriate cases, the status of a liquidator appointed under the law of the place of incorporation of a foreign company – *Baden Delvaux and Lecuit v Société Générale pour Favoriser le Développement du Commerce et de l'Industrie en France S.A.* [1983] B.C.L.C. 325. Although, therefore, the recognition of foreign winding-up proceedings in accordance with the law of the place of incorporation may readily give rise to recognition by the English courts (who may then be called upon to distinguish between the authority of a liquidator to title to assets in his own name deemed to vest in accordance with the law of the place of incorporation and the right to administer assets title to which remains in the company), it is less certain that the English court will recognise a foreign winding-up proceeding commenced other than in accordance with the law of the place of incorporation of a foreign company and under the jurisdiction of that territory's courts. In the first instance, it may fall to the English court to determine whether the rules are those relating to bankruptcy or to liquidation or winding-up. Reference has been made at para 5.11.2 to the case of *Felixstowe Dock and Railway Co v United States Lines Inc* [1989] Q.B., which concerned a reorganisation process pursuant to Chapter XI of the US Federal Bankruptcy Code, but where, for the purpose of English proceedings, the English court ignored the title 'bankruptcy' and treated the procedure as that applicable in a winding-up. Moreover, the willingness of the English courts to recognise the appropriateness of a winding-up under the law of the place of incorporation does not, on the available authorities, mean that the English court gives exclusive jurisdiction to the law of the place of incorporation (to do so would, of course, prima facie, be inconsistent with the jurisdiction in fact adopted by the English courts under the *Insolvency Act 1986*). It is clear, however, that the English courts will not give recognition to a foreign liquidation merely on the basis of comity of law (i.e. on the basis that the English court would itself have jurisdiction to make a winding-up order) – *Re Trepca Mines Ltd* and *Felixstowe Dock and Railway Co v United States Lines Inc*, above. It is, however, clear that the English courts will, in appropriate circumstances, give recognition to a foreign law winding-up being other than the law of the place of incorporation, a proposition supported by the decision of the Court of Session in *Queensland Mercantile and Agency Co Ltd v Australasian Investment Co Ltd* [1888] 15 R.935. This case tends to suggest that where the foreign company has submitted to the law of the foreign jurisdiction in which the winding-up has been commenced, that is a factor which may provide a basis for recognition by the English court. The same case may equally support the view that the English court will recognise the foreign insolvency proceeding if the foreign company has carried on business within the jurisdiction of the relevant foreign court.

Considerations when lending to trustees

Introduction

This chapter considers issues of particular concern arising in relation to lending to, or obtaining security from, a trustee of a foreign trust. For the purposes of this chapter, a *foreign trust* is a trust which has a *proper law* or *applicable law* (see above, paras 2.1 to 2.3) which is a system of law different to that of the domestic law of the lender, or where, whatever the applicable law of the trust, it has trustees incorporated in a foreign jurisdiction (which may or may not be that of the territory of the applicable law of the trust). The nature of a trust has been described in Chapter 4, para 4.4. Accordingly, the focus of this chapter will be a short consideration of those issues which, in the context of a foreign law legal opinion (as to which see Chapter 10), and from a practical point of view, should be of concern in relation to a foreign law trust. In this context, the lender should ensure that:

- the trust has been duly constituted and that it validly exists under its applicable law;
- the trustee has had validly transferred to the trustee and holds (or has held to the trustee's order) the trust property (the *trust fund*);
- pursuant to the applicable law, the trustee has the capacity and power to enter into the loan or security transaction and has properly approved and executed the relevant transaction documents;
- where it is a company, the trustee is duly incorporated and validly existing under the law of its place of incorporation, and where it is a professional corporate trustee, that it holds all appropriate licences and consents and complies with all other relevant formalities, to undertake trust administration in the place of administration of the trust;

- the performance of the transaction terms is lawful and that there are no regulatory or other extraneous restrictions on the trustee's ability to perform the transaction in accordance with the applicable law of the trust or the trust instrument;
- the trust instrument contains no restrictions on the investment or other powers of the trustee and that the trustee does not require the consent of a protector;
- the existing and probable charges to tax do not adversely affect the lending (for example, through application of withholding);
- a viable and cost effective means of enforcement exists; and
- the implications of an insolvency affecting the trustee in each relevant foreign jurisdiction are understood.

In addition to the issues specific to lending to, or taking security from, a trust the lender must have regard to the need, in all cases:

- to complete due diligence in relation to know-your-customer principles (Chapter 3 above);
- to identify and select, by express provision, an appropriate applicable law for all the transaction documents and obtain the express submission to the courts of an appropriate jurisdiction by the trustee (Chapter 2 above); and
- in any case where the trustee is not subject to fixed rules deeming presence within the jurisdiction, to obtain the appointment of an agent for service.

It is important, when considering the issues of trusts, that a lender notes that a trust is a creation of law which may exist in circumstances where the label 'trust' is not expressly used. For example, many of the issues discussed in this chapter may apply where the lender's counterparty is a 'custodian' (frequently encountered in the context of collective or mutual investments funds) or a 'nominee'.

7.1 The validity of the trust

As has been stated in Chapter 4, a trust does not have separate legal personality: it acts through the trustee or trustees who must hold title to the trust fund and contract on behalf of, and in accordance with, the terms of the trust. The lender must determine that the trust has been duly constituted and that the trust property has been validly transferred to and is held by the trustee subject to the terms of the trust. The starting point for determination of validity (and identification of the system of law under which a foreign law opinion should be sought by the lender) is the determination of the applicable law of the trust. Although it is not a completely correct analogy, the applicable law of the trust can be looked upon as an issue which raises, in relation to trusts, those matters for which determination of domicile, residence or place of incorporation, is important in the case of natural persons or companies. The *Hague Convention on the law applicable to trusts and to their recognition [1984]* ('the Convention') (see above, para 4.4.2) provides in Article 8 that the applicable law of a trust determines *the validity of the trust, its construction, its effects and the administration of the trust.* Article 8 further provides an illustrative guide to those matters which are to be determined in accordance with the applicable law of the trust as follows:

- the appointment, resignation and removal of trustees, the capacity to act as a trustee, and the devolution of the office of trustee;
- the rights and duties of trustees among themselves;
- the right of trustees to delegate in whole or in part the discharge of their duties or the exercise of their powers;
- the power of trustees to administer or to dispose of trust assets, to create security interests in the trust assets, or to acquire new assets;
- the powers of investment of trustees;
- restrictions on the duration of the trust, and upon the power to accumulate the income of the trust;
- the relationship between the trustees and the beneficiaries, including the personal liability of the trustees to the beneficiaries;
- the variation or termination of the trust;
- the distribution of the trust assets; and
- the duty of trustees to account for their administration.

7.2 Determining the proper or applicable law of the trust and migration of trusts

A full consideration of this subject is beyond the scope of this book, and, for practical purposes, is unlikely to be a detailed concern of the lender. Nevertheless, as is highlighted by the matters set out at para 2.1 above, the lender must be able to determine the appropriate law under which to seek a foreign law legal opinion or opinions concerning the trust. In this context, the lender should:

- identify, from the instrument constituting the trust, any expressly stated applicable law;

- identify the place in which the administration of the trust is undertaken (and if different, the place of residence or incorporation of the trustee);
- identify the location of trust assets; and
- determine whether the instrument or deed constituting the trust (and the existing applicable law of the trust) allows for a change in the applicable law, or a change in the place of administration of the trust.

In the majority of cases the lender will be concerned with a trust or settlement deliberately constituted under a particular system of law. This is the case not least because a settlor using a trust or settlement will have selected a system of law best lending itself to the fiscal or other purpose of the trust. For example, if the intended purpose is that of asset protection, the settlor may have chosen an offshore centre jurisdiction which has incorporated into its law special protection for transfers of property into trust (for example, Gibraltar). In looking to the express selection of the applicable law of the trust it is relevant that in most of the leading offshore centre jurisdictions where trusts are recognised (particularly those having a predominantly common law system of law), rules exist (or a statute may provide) for a determination of the applicable law of the trust by reference to that expressed in the trust instrument. The Convention, in Article 6, provides that:

> *A trust shall be governed by the law chosen by the settlor. The choice must be express or implied in the terms of the instrument creating or the writing evidencing the trust, interpreted, if necessary, in the light of the circumstances of the case.*

Where, in relation to a trust, there is no express applicable law, Article 7 of the Convention provides:

> *a trust shall be governed by the law with which it is most closely connected. In ascertaining the law with which a trust is most closely connected reference shall be made in particular to (a) the place of administration of the trust designated by the settlor, (b) the situs of the assets of the trust, (c) the place of residence or business of the trustee, and (d) the objects of the trust and the places where they are to be fulfilled.*

The lender should be aware that an express applicable law, or the place of administration of a trust, may be deliberately subject to change. It is not unusual for trusts constituted for inheritance, asset protection, or other fiscal planning reasons to contain provisions which either allow for a change in the applicable law or place of administration of the trust, or, in certain circumstances, deem that it should happen (so-called *'flee provisions'*).

7.3 Determining due constitution of the trust

Having identified the appropriate applicable law, the lender should ensure that the trust is duly constituted and validly existing. Although most jurisdictions recognising a trust as a product of equitable common law provide that there are no formalities required for the creation of a trust, the lender is most likely to be concerned with trusts ordinarily constituted by an instrument or deed in writing. The lender should obtain a copy of the instrument constituting the trust, together with all instruments expressed to be supplemental to it, particularly those relating to the appointment or retirement of trustees. Although the application of the appropriate applicable law to trusts makes generalisation dangerous, the lender should note that the due constitution and valid existence of the trust is likely to involve:

- a valid transfer of property by the settlor to be held by the trustee (risks exist where there are *forced heirship rules* which might make the transfer void under the law of domicile or where the settlor is seeking to put assets beyond the reach of creditors);
- the existence of a trustee in which the trust property is vested;
- other than in the case of a charitable, or non-charitable purpose trust, the existence of one or more persons entitled to benefit from the trust as 'beneficiaries'; and
- enforceable trusts that are not illegal or deemed void or voidable under the relevant applicable law.

The lender should also be concerned to determine that where a trust or settlement has been constituted by an instrument in writing, such instrument is in a proper form (in accordance with its applicable law) and has created the trust, and vested the interests and powers in accordance with its terms.

7.4 The trustee

Having determined the valid constitution of the trust, a lender is most likely to be concerned with issues relating to the administration of the trust by its trustee or trustees. Those issues will include:

- the identification of the jurisdiction in which the trustee undertakes the administration of the trust;
- a determination of the manner in which the trustee holds the trust property (for example, is legal title vested in the trustee, or is the trust property held by some other party to the order of the trustee?);

- identification of the place in which trust assets are held by the trustee (the issues raised as the applicable law for the valid transfer of title or grant of security interests may arise, as discussed in Chapter 9 below);
- the existence and scope of powers which the trustee has to hold, invest and dispose of the trust property;
- whether there is any person appointed as *protector* whose consent is required by the trustee in relation to the transactions contemplated;
- whether there are any relevant investment or other restrictions to which the trustee is subject;
- any limitation on the liability of the trustee (for example, limiting the liability of the trustee to the extent of the trust fund where the trustee contracts in the disclosed capacity as trustee); and
- where there is more than one trustee, the existence of any restriction on delegation, etc.

7.5 Trust powers

This is a fundamental issue for the lender. It will be of the utmost importance to determine that the nature of the transaction proposed is one which lies within the trust powers, determined in accordance with the applicable law of the trust. Where the trustee is to borrow, the lender should ensure that the trust powers:

- include a power to borrow without restriction as to amount;
- where a general power to borrow exists, allow a borrowing for the intended purpose;
- where the transaction contemplated is the grant of security, allow the trustee to create mortgages and charges in respect of the trust property;
- where a guarantee is required, allow the trustee to grant guarantees for the benefit of third parties (who may or may not be existing beneficiaries); and
- that the exercise of the power does not require the consent of a protector.

The lender should, moreover, be concerned not merely with the existence of a relevant power but with its exercise by the trustee in a way which is consistent with the trusts. For example, it is not unusual for a lender to be asked to extend facilities to an onshore borrower (as the beneficiary of a foreign law trust) in circumstances where the trust is to provide security for the borrowing over trust assets. In such circumstances, the lender will be concerned to ensure that the power to create security exists and that it may be exercised for the benefit of the beneficiary. The lender may require, in addition, to determine that the exercise of the power to create the security for the benefit of one beneficiary is not a breach of the trustee's obligations to act impartially between all beneficiaries. The applicable law of the trusts may restrict the trustee's investment powers or impose duties on the trustee which exclude the operation of powers for particular purposes. For example, a trustee may have power to enter into option contracts as a 'hedge' but not for purely speculative investment purposes.

7.6 Vesting of the trust property in the trustee

As has been stated above, the vesting of trust property in the trustee is likely to be a fundamental requirement for the existence of a trust (certainly in relation to the property concerned). The lender should be concerned to establish the manner in which the trustee is holding the property and as to whether there are, in the particular circumstances, any other parties with an interest in, or possession of, the relevant property. It is not unusual for real or other immoveable property held subject to a trust to be held by a limited company, the share capital of which is wholly owned by the trust, or for possession to be held by somebody other than the trustee. In such circumstances, the lender will take the creation of a relevant security from the limited company as the holder of legal title to the charged property. In other cases, the lender may find that intangible moveable property (in the form of cash and securities) may be held by a professional investment manager through a further custodian or nominee. In such circumstances, while the security may be created by the trustee, notice may need to be given to the investment manager, custodian or nominee. In any event the lender should note that the issues of selection of applicable law for creation of valid security rights and interests should follow the rules set out in Chapter 9, below.

7.7 Restrictions on trustee's liability

In some offshore centre jurisdictions the liability of the trustee may, where the trustee contracts in disclosed capacity as trustee, be limited to the value of the trust fund. While, in the ordinary course, if the lender is lending to a trust (or taking security over assets of the trust) it will not ordinarily seek to look to the assets of the trustee, the lender should not lose sight of the fact that quite independently of the liability or obligation incurred to the lender, the trustee may incur liabilities and obligations elsewhere diminishing or totally dissipating the trust fund. In such circumstances, the lender should consider obtaining and monitoring appropriate covenants not to incur further borrowing or liabilities without the lender's prior consent, and take negative pledge covenants.

7.8 The place of administration

The lender may find, notwithstanding the applicable law of a trust, that the trustee (particularly a professional trust corporation) is domiciled, resident or incorporated in a different jurisdiction to that of the applicable law of the trust and that the trust is actually administered from such jurisdiction. The existence of the administration of a trust within a territory may mean that the courts of that territory have jurisdiction in relation to the trust. In any such case, the lender should ensure that there are no issues arising out of the existence of such jurisdiction, or otherwise out of the conduct of administration in the territory concerned, which impact on the exercise of the trustee's powers, or on the enforceability or otherwise of the transaction documents.

7.9 Due authorisation

The lender should ensure that the exercise of the trust powers by the trustee has been duly authorised and approved in accordance with the applicable law of the trust and relevant terms of the trust instrument. Professional trustees will almost certainly administer the trust, and take major trust decisions, through use of trustee minutes and resolutions. Where the trustee is a professional trust corporation, these may take the form of a resolution of its directors, a committee of directors or professional managers. In any event, the lender is best protected by insisting upon the production of a certified true copy of minutes recording resolutions entered into by the trustee or trustees:

- in which the trustee or trustees properly consider the terms of the proposed transaction and record the benefit to the trust, the discharge of a trust charitable purpose, or non-charitable purpose;
- in which the trustee or trustees record the existence of the relevant trust power and that the transaction is *ultra vires* such powers;

- which reflect the tabling and consideration by the trustee or trustees of relevant transaction documents;
- which disclose any trustee or trustees' interests or conflicts;
- which set out the trustee or trustees' resolution to approve the transaction and execute the transaction documents; and
- in which the trustee or trustees authorise the execution of the transaction documents under hand, or as relevant, under the common seal of the trust corporation.

7.10 Enforcement against trustees

Assuming that liabilities and obligations are entered into by the trustee of a foreign law trust in accordance with the terms of a transaction document the applicable law of which has been determined in accordance with the principles set out in Chapter 2, the issues on enforcement should be those arising under the applicable law of the transaction. As with any other party to transaction documents, the lender should ensure that there is a valid submission to the jurisdiction of the courts of the appropriate and convenient system of law and that, as necessary, the trustee has appointed an agent for service of process within that jurisdiction. Otherwise, in the context of enforcement and the availability of reliefs and remedies, observations made in Chapter 5 in relation to individuals (where the trustee is an individual) and in Chapter 6 (where the trustee is a corporation) apply.

7.11 Bankruptcy and insolvency

The lender should ensure that, in accordance with the applicable law of the trust, the assets of the trust fund are not treated as assets to which the creditors of the trustee have access. On this basis, it will follow that the bankruptcy, winding-up or dissolution of the trustee ought not to give rise to a claim (other than for unpaid trustee's fees or indemnity) against the trust assets.

8

Double taxation

Introduction

The possibility of double taxation arises where a person (i.e. a natural person, company or other legal personality chargeable to tax under the fiscal law of a particular territory) is assessable and chargeable to tax under the fiscal law of more than one territory in respect of the same income or gain. The incidence of double taxation is seen as a material impediment to free international trade. To meet this problem it is open to sovereign nation states (or territories having responsibility for their own fiscal laws and collection of taxes) (i) to enter into bilateral treaties determining which of the taxing jurisdictions has the right to tax an income or gain in the hands of the taxpayer (a *double taxation treaty*), or (ii) to unilaterally concede relief (usually allowing foreign tax paid as a credit against domestic tax payable and taxing on the net amount), which is referred to as *unilateral relief*. Reference has been made in Chapter 2 to the operation of withholding and to the requirement that a lender seek to avoid its application through 'grossing up' provisions (see above, paras 2.10.8–2.10.9). Double taxation treaties and the availability of treaty relief are intended to reduce the incidence of a source country withholding tax between Contracting States.

8.1 Double taxation treaties: the OECD Model

Where double taxation treaties must, by definition, be the product of negotiation and agreement between two nation states (the 'Contracting States'), their usefulness would be materially undermined in the absence of an internationally agreed and applied approach. Such an approach exists in the form of the precedents provided by the *Organisation for Economic*

Cooperation and Development (OECD). In the case of the United Kingdom, it has, in virtually all cases, entered into double taxation treaties following the *OECD Draft Convention of 1963*, the *OECD Model Convention of 1977* and that of 1992 (the *OECD Model*). The United Kingdom gives effect to its double taxation treaties through Order in Council and, in general, provides that the treaty provisions shall prevail in the case of conflict with domestic law (*Income and Corporation Taxes Act 1988* ss. 788(1) and 788(3)). The OECD Model proceeds on the basis that a treaty will apply to the 'residence' of one or both Contracting States and in respect of all taxes imposed on income or capital.

8.1.1 Residence

The OECD Model provides (in Article 4) that a Contracting State may, through application of the tests of domicile, residence, central control and management test or otherwise, determine that a person is resident. If on the application of the domestic law of a Contracting State a person is domiciled in both Contracting States, charge to tax is determined by the following factors.

8.1.1.1 Permanent home
The question is asked: where does the person (being a natural person) have his permanent home and if he has a permanent home, in both Contracting States, with which centre are his personal and economic relations closer?

8.1.1.2 Habitual abode
Where it is not possible to determine the existence of a permanent home in one or other of the Contracting States, the question is asked: does the person have an habitual abode in either Contracting State?

8.1.1.3 Nationality
Where habitual abode is not determinative, the question is asked: is the person a national of either Contracting State?

8.1.1.4 Mutual agreement
If none of the factors in paras 8.1.1.1–8.1.1.3 above determines the issue, the question is to be determined by mutual agreement.

In the case of a taxpayer who is not a natural person, the OECD Model determines residence by reference to the place in which the entity has its *place of effective management*. Importantly, the OECD Model is intended to exclude from its application a person who is non-resident for tax purposes but who might, under the domestic law of a Contracting State, be chargeable to tax in relation to income or gains sourced in the relevant

Contracting State: see below in relation to anti-avoidance provisions. The OECD Model provides, in the context of determination of residence for other than a natural person, a definition of *permanent establishment* as a 'fixed place of business through which the business of an enterprise is wholly or partly carried on'. The tests used to determine charge to tax in relation to the double taxation are used exclusively in relation to the determination required under the double taxation treaty and will not change the determination of the existence of residence or non-residence under the relevant domestic law.

8.1.2 Taxation of income

The OECD Model differentiates between different types and sources of income as follows.

8.1.2.1 Income and gains from real property
Income derived directly or indirectly from immoveable property (which excludes ships, boats and aircraft) and property ancillary thereto is taxable where the property is situated (the *lex situs*).

8.1.2.2 Business profits
The profits of an *enterprise* are taxable in the Contracting State in which the enterprise carries on its business through a 'permanent establishment' (para 8.1.1 above). In the case of *associated enterprises* incorporated in one Contracting State which are the subject of control in the other Contracting State (or if both associated enterprises are in the same beneficial ownership and the beneficial owner is resident in the other Contracting State) an adjustment may be made so as to exclude the effect of transfer pricing or thin capitalisation (para 6.4.5 above) and provide for a charge to tax as if the adjusted profits had been made.

8.1.2.3 Royalties, interest and dividends
Royalties, interest and dividends payable by a person in one Contracting State to a person in the other Contracting State are, as a general rule, taxable in the hands of the payee, save that the Contracting State of source may charge a limited withholding tax of 5–15%.

8.1.2.4 Self-employed persons
A self-employed person with a permanent home in one Contracting State which is also the source is charged to tax in that Contracting State.

8.1.2.5 Employee income and pensions
Remuneration from employment is taxable in the Contracting State in which it arises if, but only if, the employee has been resident in the other Contracting State for less than an aggregate of 183 days in the relevant year,

the remuneration is paid by an employer not resident in the other Contracting State, and the remuneration is not borne by a permanent establishment or fixed base which the employer has in the other Contracting State. Pensions deriving from an employment in one Contracting State are only taxable in that Contracting State.

8.1.3 Taxation on assets

Any tax on capital values relating to immoveable property is that of the *situs*; tax based on the capital value of ships, boats and aircraft is chargeable in the place where the effective management is situated.

8.2 Exemption and credit relief

The OECD Model allows a Contracting State to prevent double taxation through the provision of *reliefs* or *exemptions*. The United Kingdom (both under double taxation treaties and unilaterally) allows credit relief, while many other jurisdictions allow exemptions.

8.3 Anti-avoidance provisions

The OECD Model proceeds on a premise that double taxation treaties should not be available as a tax avoidance measure to those who are not properly 'resident' and a taxpayer in one or other Contracting State and therefore truly within the scope of the relevant double taxation treaty. The OECD Model is intended only to facilitate international trade and not to facilitate exploitation which may lead to little or no tax being paid. With this in mind, the OECD Model seeks to exclude from the benefits of double taxation, individuals or entities who are not taxable in one or other of the Contracting States by excluding them either as resident or as a qualifying person.

8.4 General provisions

The OECD Model makes provision for (i) specific rules for the determination by a treaty of 'residence', (ii) the prohibition on one

Contracting State subjecting the nationals of the other Contracting State to a charge to tax higher than that imposed on its own nationals, and (iii) allows for the exchange of information between the revenue authorities of the Contracting States.

8.5 Double taxation, implications for lenders

The effect of double taxation treaties (and particularly those following the OECD Model) may be fundamental to the inclusion of a foreign company borrower, or other foreign law connection, in a lending transaction. The existence, or otherwise, of a double taxation treaty may be of particular importance in the context of the imposition of withholding taxes and/or the opportunity to take a credit relief or exemption in respect of interest paid. Reference should also be made to the unilateral relief extended by the United Kingdom Inland Revenue in the case of individuals and of companies. Of particular relevance to lenders are the anti-avoidance provisions relating to *tax sparing* provided for by section 798 of the *Income and Corporation Taxes Act 1988* which provide that where a resident bank or other financial institution makes a loan to a non-resident, spared tax (that is tax reduced or forgone under the law of one Contracting State) is deemed to be interest that the resident bank has received (up to 15%).

9 Considerations when taking security

Introduction

Chapters 6 to 7 have looked at the issues for the lender making available facilities to a borrower resident or incorporated abroad or otherwise having a connection with foreign law (for example, through domicile or source of income or repayment). The focus of concern has been those issues arising from the system of personal law to which the borrower is connected. In this chapter the focus of concern is the creation of security over property which has a connection with a foreign law. In relation to the execution and performance of the agreement under which the security is created, the lender should remain concerned to ensure that in accordance with all relevant systems of law:

- the borrower (which for the purpose of this chapter will include a reference to a third-party provider of security for the obligations of the principal – a *surety* or *guarantor*) exists (in the case of a company, having been duly constituted and not dissolved) and has capacity to grant the security interests and rights and otherwise perform the obligations under the security arrangements;
- the borrower has duly authorised the grant of the security interests and rights in accordance with its constitution;
- the borrower executes the security arrangements in an appropriate form; and
- should it be necessary, the courts of a relevant foreign territory will recognise the choice of applicable law and, in accordance with that law (but subject to proof of it) enforce the lender's security rights against the borrower and/or the secured property.

In the case of the creation of security interests, issues arise not only from qualities attributable to the borrower by the borrower's personal system of law but also from the system or systems of law under which an interest by way of security is acquired. Without the identification of the system of law relevant to the creation of the security, the lender does not know (i) how to perfect the security, (ii) what if any priority it gives, (iii) how it can be enforced, or (iv) which lawyers to take an opinion or assistance from. In this regard it is important that the lender should:

- identify the system or systems of law which will govern the creation of a security interest in the relevant property and regulate competing priorities (the *proper* or *applicable* law of the security);
- identify and comply with all necessary formalities for the perfection (in accordance with the applicable law) of security interests in the relevant property;
- identify and consider any onerous obligation or liabilities that may arise under the applicable law or otherwise out of the holding of security interests in the property concerned;
- identify the method of enforcement and, in particular, any stay on enforcement, formality or cost which may materially impede the ability to realise the value in the security; and
- identify the consequences of a foreign law insolvency or rehabilitation process.

The most fundamental of mistakes in taking security with a foreign law connection is that of failing to recognise that such a connection exists and, thereafter, to properly ascertain the applicable law. The questions and issues which follow are designed to highlight the existence of a potential foreign law connection and the consequences of such a connection.

9.1 What is the nature or classification of the property provided as security?

The proper or applicable law is a product of the type of property concerned. Where the property to be taken as security may have a connection with a foreign law, the lender should put to one side as potentially misleading domestic descriptions of property such as 'land', 'realty', 'leasehold property', 'equitable interests' or 'chattels' and should be prepared to look for classification applied pursuant to the rules of private international law, as follows.

9.1.1 Immoveable property

Although it may be possible, in the absence of a determined proper or applicable law, to identify types of property which may be within the 'class' of property likely to constitute immoveable property, the ultimate status of a particular type of property will, as set out in para 9.2 below, be determined in the place in which the property is located (the *lex situs*). Although not exhaustive, the class of such property may include (i) estates in land such as freehold fees, (ii) interests in land including mortgages and charges, (iii) buildings or structures on, fixed to or otherwise forming part of a corporeal estate in land, and (iv) minerals under or other rights arising above or below the surface of the land. Although there may be no material uncertainty in classifying proprietary interests in land, other forms of interests or rights in relation to land may be differently classified under different systems of law. A lease may be classified as 'moveable' property and may, in consequence, be incapable of mortgage or charge. Similarly, a foreign system of law may exclude from the definition of immoveable property structures on the land and other resources and materials under it. Variations in classification may mean that a lender's security by way of mortgage, charge or their equivalent may be immoveable property in accordance with the law of the *situs*, with consequent implications for its transferability.

9.1.2 Moveable property

Moveable property can take the form of *tangible moveable property* or *intangible moveable property*. Tangible moveable property may be that which English law classifies as 'chattels' and may include such items as valuable paintings or motor cars. Under some systems of law, however, a distinction may be drawn between property represented by a certificate of title to 'securities' (for example, a share certificate) classified as tangible moveable property and the rights which a shareholder may have as against the company as issuer which may be classified as intangible moveable property. By contrast, while a debt may represent intangible moveable property, certain forms of debt instrument evidencing such debt (which may be in negotiable form) may be treated by some systems of law as tangible moveable property.

9.1.3 Present or future property

Not all systems of law allow security interests to be created by a person over property to which such person has not yet acquired title, that is future property. Although this issue is not one strictly of classification under private international law principles, it is convenient to highlight the issue at this point, and return to it in the context of perfection and floating charges at paras 9.5 and 9.6 below.

9.2 What is the governing or applicable law for the creation of the security?

It has been suggested, in connection with transaction documents relating to the loan or facility generally, that the lender should be concerned to determine by express choice the proper or applicable law (para 2.3 above). When dealing with the creation of rights to immoveable or moveable property the role of party autonomy in the selection of the proper or applicable law is displaced by a concern to select the system of law of a territory which will provide a valid and enforceable interest in favour of the lender. The lender should note that a law selected to govern the principal loan and other transaction documents may be wholly inappropriate to govern the rights in or to immoveable or moveable property. The rules of private international law relating to the determination of the proper or applicable law to govern the grant of rights in or to, or the transfer of, property are complex. As a general proposition, and therefore as an over-simplification, the following may be used as a guide only.

9.2.1 Security over immoveable property

Rights relating to the grant of security to those forms of property which may be within the class of immoveable property are governed by the law of the place where such property is situated or rights in or to it enjoyed (the *situs*). As a consequence, the lender should note that the English courts will not assume jurisdiction in relation to matters concerning interests or title in land, or the right to possession of land, situated in a foreign territory. In relation to a Contracting State to the *Brussels Convention* the position is governed by the *Civil Jurisdiction and Judgments Acts 1982 and 1991* and, as a matter of common law, the case of *British South Africa Co v Companhia de Mozambique* [1893] A.C. 602. The domestic law of the *situs* will determine both the *formalities for alienation* of land or interests in land, and the *essential validity* of such alienation or transfers. In the former case, the lender must comply with the formalities required by the domestic law of the *situs* relating to the manner in which the security is created (in some jurisdictions that may, for example, mean documentation in particular form, or involve court proceedings). In the case of essential validity the creation of certain types of interests may be totally unrecognised by the law of the *situs*: for example, an assignment of lease although valid by the law of the domicile of the parties entering into the transaction may not be valid in accordance with the *situs* of the immoveable property to which the lease relates.

9.2.2 Security over moveable property

As a starting point, the lender should note the distinction between *tangible* moveable property and *intangible* moveable property.

9.2.2.1 Tangible moveable property

Tangible moveables, by their nature, constitute property in a form the location or *situs* of which may change by transport and delivery. Where the location and *situs* are changed, so that the property is transferred from one territory to another, at least two possible systems of law could govern the creation of a contemporaneous grant of security. In such a case, available modern English authority suggests that the proper law determining the transfer of title to all rights in the tangible moveable property will be that of the *situs*, so that if a foreign resident and/or domiciled borrower deposits tangible moveable property with the lender in England, the lender should take the chattel mortgage or pledge (as appropriate) in accordance with English law. In the case of tangible moveable property this rule is most frequently underlined by the almost universal application of a requirement for delivery up of possession (either actual or constructive) as an element in a valid creation of title to tangible moveables, whether absolutely or by way of security. The lender should therefore note that in the creation of security over tangible moveables, any change in the location of the place of deposit or custody of the tangible moveables may materially impact on enforceability of any previously obtained legal or equitable title by way of security. In particular, the movement of tangible moveables from one territory to another may expose the tangible moveables to the claims of creditors capable of overriding the title validly given by way of security under the law of the original territory; see *Inglis v Robertson* [1898] A.C. 616.

9.2.2.2 Intangible moveable property

In the case of intangible moveable property (for example, a debt) the fundamental difficulty is that of determining location or *situs* at all. In seeking to deal with the issue from a practical standpoint the lender should identify factors which may connect the property with a foreign territory and/or system of law, for example:

- the system of law of a foreign territory in which a cash deposit maintained with a bank or financial institution is held;

- the system of law of a foreign territory in which a corporate issuer of shares or other securities is incorporated;
- the system of law of a foreign territory in which a share or other register in relation to securities is maintained (noting that the register may be maintained in a territory different to that in which the issuer is incorporated);
- the system of law of the territory in which the security is created (described in the case of *MacMillan and Bishopsgate Investment Trust plc and others (No 3) 1996   1 ALL ER 585* as the *lex loci actus*);
- the system of law of a foreign territory in which securities (or a dematerialised form of the securities) is maintained with a settlement system or depository (for example, Euroclear or CEDEL); and
- the system of law of a foreign territory in which amounts due in respect of a debt or other receivables are payable.

It is increasingly the case that sophisticated high net worth individuals maintain a substantial part of their assets in portfolios of cash, securities and other investments held by portfolio or investment managers offshore. Where security is offered in such a portfolio, or in the assets comprising such a portfolio, difficult issues may arise as to the choice of proper or applicable law to govern the security. The location in which the investment management is undertaken may misleadingly suggest that that is the location in which the assets are also held. That may or may not be the case. One possible solution in such cases (or, indeed, in any situation in which the appropriate *situs* for intangible moveable property is difficult to determine) is to take a security by way of assignment (i) of the benefit of the portfolio or investment management arrangements, (ii) of the nominee agreement under which title to such assets can be held, or (iii) of other contractual rights of redelivery or restitution. There may be circumstances in which such an assignment should be supplemented by express security taken over underlying assets (although this is not always possible if they are tangible) and any such express security may need to take account of the actual location in which certificates of title representing the assets etc. are deposited or held. An example of the type of problem which can be encountered when dealing with intangible moveable property is that of the difficulties which, until relatively recently, made it difficult to perfect a security over bonds held in the Euroclear settlement system and obtain a clean foreign law legal opinion under Belgian law as the proper law. The problems have now been largely solved through provision under *Belgian Royal Decree No 62*, being the system of law under which the Euroclear settlement system operates, allowing for the creation of security interests in the *Caisse interprofessionelle de depots et de vivrements de titres* maintained by bondholders with Euroclear.

9.3 Issues relating to title to property having a foreign law connection

Assuming that the lender has established whether the relevant property is immoveable property, tangible moveable property, or intangible moveable property, and the identity of each system of foreign law with which the relevant type of property is connected, the lender should next determine the capacity in which the proposed grantor of security holds an interest in or right to the property concerned (that is, the borrower or grantor's *title*). There is no way in which it is possible to catalogue the varied manner in which immoveable property in particular may be held or enjoyed, but the lender should note the importance of identifying the nature of the title which a borrower or grantor of security may have under a relevant foreign law. In particular, the lender should be concerned to identify any defects in, or limitations of, the borrower or grantor's title. Accordingly, the lender should have regard to the following potential issues.

9.3.1 True or beneficial ownership, the problem of nominees, custodians and trustees

In lending with an offshore centre connection, or other foreign law connection, it is likely that title to assets is held through a nominee, custodian or other trustee (whether merely a bare trustee or otherwise, see Chapter 7 above). Care should also be taken where, in the case of holding through nominees/custodians, there may exist sub-custodians (who may be located in yet a further foreign law jurisdiction). In the absence of the titleholder being both the legal and true or beneficial owner, questions may arise under a foreign law as to the capacity of such titleholder to grant a relevant form of security interest in favour of the lender. In any case where a nominee holder of title is identified, consideration must be given to joining the true or beneficial owner in the grant of security, unless it is clear under the relevant proper or applicable law that the holder of legal title or possession is entitled to grant a security which will be valid and enforceable against the true owner (particularly in the case of bankruptcy or insolvency affecting the true owner). In the case of layers of custodial ownership or possession, the lender should ensure that the custodian at the head of the chain is able to redeliver or perform in accordance with the obligations undertaken by the grantor of security and can call for redelivery or performance by a sub-custodian free of equities or other rights affecting the sub-custodian.

9.3.2 Two or more owners

Where property (and in particular immoveable property) is or may be subject to a foreign law, and where ownership of the relevant property is held through two or more persons, the lender should ensure that the capacity in which the property is held is fully understood and that there is nothing arising from the capacity in which such property is held that may be detrimental to the security rights. An English lender may be familiar with the types of joint ownership existing under English law (for example, joint tenancies and tenancies in common). Under a foreign law the nature of joint ownership may be fundamentally different. Care is required in relation to this issue because the characteristics of forms of joint ownership may only become relevant in the context, for example, of an insolvency in respect of one joint owner, or on death or other incapacity. These are problems which may not necessarily be highlighted by the terms of a foreign law opinion dealing with capacity, due authority and due execution, and may need to be dealt with by appropriate certificates or reports on title.

9.3.3 Execution on behalf of a titleholder by power of attorney, mandate holder or other agent

In transactions involving a foreign law connection, additional care is required where transactions are completed on behalf of the party with relevant title by a person operating under power of attorney, or some other mandate or agency. In addition to the question of capacity to grant the relevant power of attorney, or the authority in favour of the mandate holder or agent (an issue which has been examined in the context of the issues when lending to individuals) the lender may be concerned with yet a further and quite distinct foreign law connection relating to the form and validity of the power of attorney, mandate or agency contract. The lender should seek to ensure (i) capacity to grant the power, (ii) grant in due form (for example, is there a requirement for witnessing or registration of notarisation?), and (iii) whether the power actually provides necessary authority for the act concerned. Where transaction and/or security documentation is to be executed pursuant to a power of attorney or other third-party mandate or agency arrangement, it may be necessary to obtain a separate foreign law opinion on the form, validity and extent of the powers granted.

9.3.4 Obligations on the lender imposed through holding the foreign law security

The lender should take steps to ensure that the acquisition of a security interest, particularly any such acquisition involving acquisition by assignment or otherwise of 'title' to, for example securities, does not bring with it any onerous obligations. So, for example, it may be necessary to ensure that the registration of registrable securities in the name of the lender or its nominee does not give rise to any obligation (under the relevant proper or applicable law) on the part of the lender (or the nominee) to act in relation to notices received, exercise voting rights and/or otherwise incur responsibility for any action taken or any omission to act in relation to the securities (possibly subject to any such loss arising through the negligence or wilful default of the lender or its nominee). Similarly, the lender should ensure that the acquisition of security does not expose the lender to any liability for payments (whether in respect of unpaid capital contributions or otherwise) to the issuer or its creditors. Where the security interests are over immoveable property, the lender should take particular care to ensure that the existence of the security interest does not, under the relevant foreign law, give rise to any liability for property taxes, maintenance obligations or third-party liability (for example, arising out of any environmental hazards on the land).

9.4 General terms and conditions of security documentation with a foreign law connection

What follows is a summary of provisions which are likely to be significant in the context of security with a foreign law connection, and which, therefore, may be the subject of an express choice of such foreign law and submission to the jurisdiction of the courts of the territory of that system of law. The issues that are raised, and the observations that are made, can do no more than highlight for the lender the significance of certain types of provisions and those areas in which significant variation in the forms of documentation may exist from that ordinarily applicable, say, under English law.

9.4.1 The choice of proper or applicable law clause

In Chapter 2 (paras 2.1–2.3 above) and in the preceding part of this chapter, extensive consideration has been given to the selection of the applicable law for transaction documents, and, in particular, the taking of security. Notwithstanding the application of a rule of private international law which may determine the identity of an appropriate system of law to govern the transfer of, or grant of rights in, relevant property, security documentation should (consistent with that appropriate law) expressly select the law to govern the grant of the security rights. As will be seen in Chapter 10, the recognition of the choice of law can be confirmed as a valid choice of law by an appropriate foreign law opinion.

9.4.2 Submission to jurisdiction

General consideration of the issues arising from jurisdiction, and the desirability of an express submission to the courts of a chosen jurisdiction is set out in Chapter 2 (para 2.4 above). In the context of documentation under which security rights are granted, the nature of the property (for example, immoveable property) may dictate that the courts of the jurisdiction in which the property is located have exclusive jurisdiction, irrespective of any other factor, including the domicile of the parties. Where the subject matter of the security documentation is either tangible moveable or intangible moveable property, the lender may wish to elect to have the borrower or grantor submit to a provision granting *non-exclusive jurisdiction*, thereby allowing the lender to bring proceedings in any other court of competent jurisdiction. For a fuller consideration of the choice between exclusive and non-exclusive jurisdiction, reference should be made to para 2.4 above.

9.4.3 The governing language of the security documentation

Where security documentation is required to be taken under a foreign applicable or proper law, such law may require that the documentation be in the language of that territory. In any such case, and although the lender's interests may be appropriately protected through relevant legal advice in the jurisdiction concerned, particular care should be taken if reliance is placed upon any translation of the relevant security documentation and it should be expressly stated both in the original language documents and in any translation that it is the foreign law language document which contains the governing terms and provisions and which is to prevail in the case of inconsistency.

9.4.4 Representations and warranties

Subject to the application of a relevant foreign law to the transaction documents, the lender should ensure that a security agreement contains relevant representations and warranties and that the representations and warranties contained within the security agreement are consistent with those contained within any other transaction document (which may be governed by a different proper or applicable law). As a matter of English contract law, there is a distinction to be drawn between the nature of a *representation, warranty* and *condition*, such that different reliefs and remedies may be available arising from the significance of a breach in each case. Where the security agreement (or a relevant other transaction document) is governed by a law other than English law, the lender should ensure that the drafting of representations and warranties and, as relevant, conditions and covenants, does not give rise to unintended results in terms of the available reliefs and remedies. As a matter of English law, a representation is a statement of fact made by one party to the other before the contract is entered into and on which a party to the contract relies. As such, a representation is not a term or condition of the contract. By contrast, a warranty is, as matter of English law, a contractual term, breach of which may amount to a breach of the contract. There is then (again as a matter of English law) a distinction to be made between a warranty and condition such that (and at the risk of over-simplification) a breach of warranty may give rise to a right in damages, whereas a breach of condition may give rise to both a claim for damages and a right to terminate the contract. These problems may be overcome by the inclusion of an appropriate event of default making it clear that the rights and remedies flowing from such an event of default arise as a consequence of the occurrence of any breach of a term of the contract and/or in the event that any representation and/or warranty proves to have been incorrect, incomplete or misleading. For the purposes of a security agreement (perhaps as distinct from the loan or other transaction agreement), the following may be the principal representations and warranties required.

9.4.4.1 Due incorporation, valid existence, capacity, due authorisation and execution by the grantor

The following should form the subject of appropriate representations and warranties as, not least, a checklist relating to the borrower/grantor:

- that in the case of a body corporate or other entity which is not a natural person, it is duly constituted and validly existing, and that there is no event causing, or any event which with the passage of time causes, the winding-up, dissolution or striking-off of the grantor/borrower;
- that the borrower has power to borrow or grant the security and to be bound by and perform the obligations set out in the security agreement;
- that the grant of the security, or the performance of any of the other obligations contained within the security agreement do not contravene or cause a breach of any law, regulation or other provision to which the borrower/grantor is subject; and
- that the security agreement constitutes the valid and binding obligation of the borrower/grantor.

9.4.4.2 Title to the secured property, absence of default and financial condition

The lender should also be concerned to establish by representation and warranty (although it will almost certainly also be covered by a direct covenant) that the grantor has unencumbered title to the secured property and that:

- in the case of a grantor/borrower which is not a natural person, that the grant of the security interest has been duly authorised in accordance with its constitutive documents and all other provisions of corporate control or governance;
- the borrower or grantor holds all governmental and other consents, permissions and licences which may be required to give effect to the valid grant of the security interest;
- there is no litigation, arbitration or other proceedings outstanding or threatened against the borrower which might adversely affect the grantor/borrower's ability to perform; and
- where the grantor/borrower is a sovereign state or entity controlled by or linked with a sovereign state, the grantor/borrower is subject to the relevant commercial law.

9.4.4.3 Cross-default

Where representations and warranties are contained within security documentation which is separate from and additional to other transaction documents, for example a loan or facility agreement, and where, in particular, the security documentation may be taken from a third party other than the borrower, the lender should ensure that there is appropriate consistency between representations and warranties contained within all of the documentation. Moreover, care should be taken to ensure that appropriate cross-default provisions are contained within relevant 'events of default' (as to which, in the context of security, see para 9.4.5 below) relating to breaches of representations and warranties.

9.4.5 Events of default

In addition to standard boiler-plate type events of default (for example, non-payment, breach of representation and warranty, etc) security documentation under a foreign law may require specific events of default relevant to, for example, events indicative of insolvency or bankruptcy. In this context, it may be important that the lender's rights under the security documentation are available, or crystallised, at a point in time prior to the commencement of a bankruptcy or other insolvency (for example, pursuant to the making of an order) and that this can be achieved through the casting of appropriate events of default.

Where foreign law opinion is sought in relation to the capacity of a borrower or grantor, but where otherwise the security documentation is drawn pursuant to a law different to that under which the opinion is granted, the lender should, nevertheless, require that the foreign lawyers confirm the sufficiency of events of default in security documentation (this notwithstanding that the foreign law opinion may confirm, in terms, that the document is valid and enforceable in accordance with its terms).

9.4.6 Waivers

General consideration of the issue of waiver of sovereign immunity in transaction documents has been considered in relation to individuals at para 5.7.2 above. In the case of security documentation (particularly that taken under a foreign law in connection with property located in a foreign territory), it may be singularly important to determine that no sovereign or other immunity from suit arises in connection with the property. In the previous consideration of sovereign immunity, attention has been drawn to the requirement of securing jurisdiction and of securing a waiver of immunity. In the case of security documentation, it may be particularly important to ensure that the documentation includes a provision which does not allow the borrower or grantor of security to preclude recourse by the lender to remedies of enforcement. In addition to waivers relevant to sovereign immunity, the lender should consider (taking foreign law advice as appropriate) whether any other waivers of rights and immunities should be taken in accordance with the applicable or proper law. It may, for example, be that a party to the security (for example, a spouse, tenant, or usufructuary) has rights in relation to the property which is the subject matter of the security interests. There may, in addition, be rights to certain reliefs in proceedings, for example that proceedings be commenced or undertaken against particular parties or in a particular way (for example, when enforcing security against a guarantor or surety, a requirement that proceedings be brought and exhausted against the principal debtor). Any such issue should be identified and an appropriate waiver obtained.

9.4.7 Exchange controls

The lender must be concerned to ensure that the realisation of value in the secured property will not be impeded by the application of currency control under any system of law to which the property (or the proceeds of its realisation) are subject. For practical purposes, the lender should ensure that the security agreement (or as relevant, the loan or other transaction agreement) contains appropriate conditions precedent in relation to the obtaining of prior exchange control consents if necessary, or representations or warranties as to the existence of relevant exchange controls or other restrictions on repatriation of currency. If a judgment or realisation of the property subject to the security could occur in a currency different from that of the loan, the security agreement should provide for authority to convert the judgment or realisation currency into the currency of the debt at a rate of exchange determined or determinable by the lender (and so as to be agreed as binding between the parties), and the grantor or borrower should as a separate stipulation agree to indemnify the lender in respect of any loss arising out of the conversion.

9.5 Perfection: requirements for creation in particular form, execution, attestation and registrations and filings

Wherever security documentation is taken with a foreign law connection, whether because the security documentation is, itself, subject to a foreign applicable or proper law or because the borrower or other grantor of such security is domiciled, resident or constituted under a foreign law, the lender should be concerned to ascertain whether perfection of the relevant security, or the determination of the lender's priority in relation to such security, requires any registration, filing or other recording to be undertaken in the foreign law jurisdiction or elsewhere. The lender should similarly identify and comply with any time periods relating to registration, recording or filing. For practical purposes, and for the fullest possible protection of the lender's position, it may be appropriate (not least where a foreign law opinion is also being sought) to instruct the relevant foreign lawyers to complete any such registration, filing or recording (or at least to confirm that it has been appropriately completed) on behalf of the lender.

9.5.1 Form of execution

In any case where the applicable or proper law of the security documentation is a foreign law, the form of the security documentation and its execution should be the subject of confirmation by lawyers competent in the foreign law concerned. In any case where the security documentation is governed by the domestic law of the lender, but where the borrower or other grantor of the security is domiciled, resident or incorporated in a foreign law jurisdiction, the lender should ensure that execution of the documentation by such party is in proper form. For example:

- Is there a requirement for witnessing or notarial certificates?
- Must the document be attested in a particular way (e.g. signed and delivered as a deed)?
- In the case of a company, must it (notwithstanding anything to the contrary in the company's constitution) be executed under common seal?

9.6 Floating or universal business charges and non-possessory security

Many jurisdictions having a system of law based on civil law do not recognise those forms of charge which either (i) purport to create a security interest in present and future acquired property which crystallises on the happening of certain specified events and which allow the lender, in the result, to obtain a security interest over the entirety of a business undertaking, or (ii) allow a lender to acquire a fixed charge over after-acquired property. In the context of such charges, two issues arise, the first being the capacity of the grantor to enter into such a security and the second being the recognition of such a security by a relevant system of foreign law. Most frequently, the problems arising in relation to floating or universal business charges arise not out of an absence of capacity to validly create such security under a relevant foreign law, but rather out of the difficulty of obtaining recognition for the validity of such security in respect of assets outside of the lender's home territory. In many cases, the only manner in which a foreign court can consider a foreign law floating or universal business charge is if the relevant courts can identify such security as being closely compatible with available local security interests. Wherever the lender's security documentation contains either a floating charge or other form of universal charge, or a fixed charge over future assets, if it is intended that such charge should apply to assets outside of the lender's home territory, a foreign law legal opinion should be sought concerning the validity, priority and enforcement of such charges. There may, in some jurisdictions, be difficulties in obtaining recognition of the right of possessory management through a receiver acting either as agent of the relevant borrower and/or as the party in whom assets are deemed to vest.

9.7 Enforcement

Issues relating to enforcement which may arise out of the nature of the borrower have been addressed in Chapters 5, 6 and 7. In the case of security, the lender should ensure that:

- there is no material delay likely to the enforcement of security under foreign law, pursuant to any formality such as a stay on enforcement if the borrower has commenced a formal rehabilitation procedure (for example, such as that existing under the United States Chapter 11);
- there is no requirement for the lender to deposit security with the courts of the foreign law territory;
- there is no restriction requiring sale only in a local currency;
- there are no exchange control restrictions on the repatriation of sale proceeds to the lender;
- in the case of floating or universal business charges, the powers or title of a receiver will be recognised;

- the realisation of the security can proceed other than exclusively through an insolvency; and
- there are no untoward costs of enforcement in the form of court, custodial, legal or auctioneer's fees, or that there is a requirement for the creditor to deposit security or a bond as a prerequisite for enforcement.

Chapter

10 Foreign law legal opinions

Introduction

References in this chapter to a *foreign law legal opinion* mean a form of opinion which, in its subject matter and, to a lesser extent, in its presentation, has become a recognised and recognisable tool in reducing the lender's exposure to risk. The private international banker is usually concerned to address one or other or both of two potential foreign law connections, these being:

- issues arising from the domicile, residence or place of incorporation of a borrower and/or grantor of security or the place in which a payment or other obligation is to be performed; and
- the validity and enforceability of transaction or security documents expressed to be governed by a foreign proper or applicable law.

The requirement for an opinion has found its way into the conditions precedent of facilities extended in private international banking in a way similar to the requirement of more complex international syndicated or project finance facilities. In particular, (i) the extension of facilities to trust or privately held investment holding companies incorporated within offshore financial centres, and/or (ii) the taking of security from or over the assets of such companies (most frequently for facilities extended to a third-party borrower or to leverage the investments of the company) gives rise to the need for a foreign law opinion. A foreign law opinion should be viewed as an essential part of the lender's due diligence (in particular, in the case of an opinion sought on the basis of a borrower/grantor of security having a foreign domicile, residence or place of incorporation or constitution) and as part of the *know-your-customer* compliance regime. Foreign law legal opinions should not, however, be viewed as passing to lawyers (or their indemnity insurers) risks that are properly the lender's credit risks based on factual circumstances beyond the scope of a statement of relevant law or mixed fact and law.

The appendix to this chapter sets out a specimen foreign law legal opinion, to which reference is made, as appropriate, in the course of this chapter. The specimen contains more assumptions and qualifications than may ordinarily be encountered in a single opinion so as to provide an illustration of possible assumptions and qualifications.

10.1 When should an opinion be sought?

In preceding chapters, reference has been made to the prospect that a *foreign law connection* may arise as a result of:

- the application of the *personal system of law* to which the borrower/grantor of security is connected by domicile, incorporation (or other constitution), residence or nationality; and
- the connection to a system of law which a transaction document has through the express or implied application of such system of law as the proper or applicable law of the transaction document.

In the context of the practice of private international banking, a requirement for a foreign law legal opinion will most frequently arise where the borrower and/or a grantor of security is a company (most likely an investment holding company), trust (or nominee), or, possibly, a limited partnership which is incorporated, registered or otherwise constituted in an offshore centre. In such circumstances, the opinion should be sought notwithstanding that transaction documents may themselves be subject to a proper or applicable law which is the domestic law with which the lender is familiar. A foreign law legal opinion should, similarly, be sought whenever a material transaction document (which may include a grant of security) has an express or implied proper or applicable law which is that of a foreign jurisdiction. Of course, it may be that both features are present in a single facility or lending arrangement.

10.2 Who should give the legal opinion?

A legal opinion should be sought only from reputable lawyers practising and competent in the relevant foreign law. Lawyers giving opinions should not be asked to consider the application of a system of law which they do not hold themselves out as competent to advise upon. In fact, most legal opinions will expressly state that the opinions rendered are restricted to issues arising as matters of the stated system of law: see para 6 of the specimen opinion. In identifying appropriate firms of lawyers to provide opinions, where the lender has no such existing knowledge, assistance may be gained through:

- panel lawyers and/or knowledge of foreign lawyers held by the lender's in-house legal function, if any; and
- the correspondent or foreign lawyers known to, and recommended by, external law firms used by the lender within their domestic jurisdiction.

10.3 What is the function of a foreign law opinion?

The function of a foreign law opinion is, as stated above, to inform the lender. The foreign law legal opinion should be restricted in scope to those matters on which the opinion of the relevant lawyers is of value. Ideally, and not least with a view to reducing the potential cost of a foreign law legal opinion, the opinion should be restricted to issues exclusively of law. In practice, however, a foreign law legal opinion is in large part a mixed statement of law and fact; so that, for example, due incorporation may require the lawyers concerned to undertake searches showing whether, as a fact, certain filings and registrations have been properly undertaken. In seeking a foreign law legal opinion, the lender should resist the temptation to require lawyers to confirm matters which are exclusively matters of fact and which are properly the subject matter of the contractual representations and warranties given by the borrower and/or grantor of security. For example, the question of whether or not execution of the transaction documents gives rise to a breach of negative or other covenants contained within contractual obligations by which the borrower is bound, is primarily one of fact which ought to be within the knowledge of the borrower or its officers. The lawyers rendering an opinion could only add to the value of the relevant contractual representation and warranty by undertaking comprehensive and expensive due diligence and, even then, any opinion or statement contained within the legal opinion is likely to be subject to material assumptions (for example, as to completeness of disclosure) which is likely to qualify the usefulness of such an exercise. Where, as a matter of convenience, the lender wishes to see statements concerning issues of fact within the knowledge of the borrower and/or grantor of security or its officers (and although the practice of lawyers on this issue varies), the best approach is that of requiring the lawyers to receive from the borrower and/or grantor of security a 'certificate' or 'declaration' given by its directors and/or secretary confirming those issues of fact which the foreign lawyers are unable to establish or verify through an external enquiry or source (a *secretary's certificate* or *director's certificate*). For example, in some offshore centre jurisdictions it may be possible to verify the identity of directors and/or registered shareholders from a public entry in the Companies Register. In other jurisdictions, such details may not be available. It should be noted (see the relevant references under paras 10.6.3 and 10.6.5 below) that entries in public registers may not be complete or up to date. It is not unusual to find that shareholder resolutions are effective when made, notwithstanding breach of a requirement to file such resolutions within a stated period (in most cases, 15 to 21 days). In these cases, the foreign law legal opinion may append a secretary's or director's certificate:

- confirming the status and capacity of the party providing the certificate (for example, a duly appointed secretary or director);
- appending to the certificate a certified true copy of the certificate of incorporation, memorandum of association and other constitutional documents of the company, confirming that they have not been amended (these documents will be reviewed by the lawyers giving the opinion);
- appending a certified true copy extract of the relevant board minute or other resolution pursuant to which the transaction is considered and approved and the execution of transaction documents confirmed through nominated signatories or the affixing of the company's seal and that such resolution remains duly made and not varied as at the date of the certificate;
- confirming, as relevant, the adoption of an official seal, or any other sealing regulations;
- confirming the identity of the company's directors or other relevant officers as at the date of the certificate;
- confirming the absence of any resolution to wind up or dissolve the company as at the date of the certificate;
- confirming the absence of receipt of notice of any claim made against, or proceeding affecting the company as at the date of the certificate; and
- confirming, where appropriate, that the company has recorded the grant of charges/mortgages etc in any relevant charges and mortgages register maintained by the company.

The lender should note that where such statements of fact are incapable of independent verification by the foreign lawyers, they will invariably be the subject matter of an assumption as to their completeness and correctness (as to which, see para 10.6.3 below and para 3(c) of the specimen opinion). Of course, where the statements of fact can properly be the subject of independent verification, the lawyers concerned should be required to make such enquiries and undertake such searches as may be appropriate or necessary. In some offshore centres it may be possible to conclusively determine that there are no proceedings commenced against the borrower and/or grantor of securities and that, in particular, there are no insolvency proceedings commenced. In other jurisdictions, it may not be possible to determine conclusively (or indeed in any useful way) the absence of such proceedings where, for example, there is not a publicly available register of information.

10.4 What is the liability of the foreign lawyers for their opinion?

Although it has been stated above that the purpose of the foreign law opinion is to inform and not to insure the lender against credit risk, it is important to understand the extent and scope of the foreign lawyers' liability in respect of the legal opinion. In this regard there are two relevant aspects:

- the scope and extent, in law, of the lawyers' liability in respect of the completeness and accuracy of the statements contained within the legal opinion; and
- the identity of those persons who have a right to recover as against the lawyers in respect of any such liability arising.

It is relevant to both issues to determine the proper or applicable law under which the lawyers' liability may arise. It is likely that the opinion will, itself, state that it is to be governed by an expressly stated system of law: see para 6 of the specimen legal opinion. In the absence of such an express statement, some uncertainty may exist as to the extent of liability (for example, as a matter of the tort of negligence) of the lawyers providing the opinion, the application of such issues as time limitation on the bringing of actions in contract or the tort of negligence and the application of those principles which determine the identity of persons entitled to recover against the lawyers. The lender should, therefore, take care in the selection of the law to govern the opinion, although it should be noted that the foreign lawyers may themselves insist that the opinion is governed by the system of law under which the opinion is given. In any such case, it may be relevant that the lender understands any limitation that may apply to the lawyers' liability. It is equally relevant for the lender to appreciate the significance of any limitation on liability that may arise out of the status of the lawyers providing the opinion, or from any express limitation of liability contained within the terms of the opinion. For this purpose, and at a practical level, where it remains the case that law is almost universally practised by sole practitioners and/or partnerships, it may be relevant to determine the worth, or, more particularly, the value of third-party indemnity cover carried by the relevant lawyers. It may also be the case that the lawyers concerned are formed as a *limited liability partnership*, pursuant to which recourse other than to the assets proper of the partnership may be limited. Finally, it is possible (but it is not a widespread practice) that lawyers seek to limit the extent of their financial liability for opinions through the terms of an express statement contained within an opinion. So, for example, the opinion may expressly state that the liability of the lawyers for loss and damage arising out of the opinion shall not exceed a stated sum. Those lawyers who seek to incorporate such a limitation of liability of course run the risk that lenders will simply seek out lawyers prepared to give an opinion not so qualified and it is probably the case that the practice is, at present, limited by competition between law firms for work. Nevertheless, it is appropriate to reflect that the real value in a foreign law legal opinion is, as stated above, that of informing the lender and of identifying any particular issue which may increase materially the lender's credit risk. Insofar as it is valid to suggest that a legal opinion should not be looked upon by the lender or any other person as an insurer of such credit risks, it may, arguably, be valid to see a limitation on lawyers' liability as both legitimate and not necessarily material to the efficacy and purpose of the opinion. More generally, and in the absence of a relevant limitation of liability in, or otherwise affecting the opinion, the liability of lawyers for a foreign law opinion is likely to arise under principles of law applicable to contract or to the tort of negligence. Liability in contract is usually based on an identifiable breach (for example, of a term that the opinion will be a correct statement of the law) causing loss or damage to a person who was a party to the contract concerned (that is where there is *privity of contract*). Negligence may be an additional or alternative remedy and, as a matter of English law, the rules governing the opportunity to obtain relief (and in particular the scope of those persons potentially able to recover against the lawyers for reliance on the opinion) are set out in the line of authorities deriving from the English case *Hedley Byrne & Co Ltd v Heller & Partners Ltd* [1964] A.C. 465, extending the tort of negligence to misstatements where the maker of the statement owes a duty of care. In this context it is important to determine the identity of those persons who may, as a matter of the relevant law, rely upon the opinion as an addressee or otherwise.

10.5 Providing for the scope of reliance in a foreign law opinion

As a starting point, it should be noted that as a matter of practice lawyers rendering a foreign law legal opinion will seek to qualify the scope of reliance to the addressee or addressees of the opinion and, further, prohibit disclosure of the opinion by the addressee to any other person without the consent of the lawyers concerned: see para 6 of the specimen legal opinion. All those not identified as being a party to the contract (by providing instructions to the lawyers) or otherwise entitled to rely upon the opinion as an addressee may be excluded from any remedy against the lawyers. The lender should ensure, therefore, that all of those intended to have the benefit of the legal opinion are expressly included within the stated scope of any addressees and of those to whom the opinion can be disclosed. Particular care should be taken where the opinion is received by an addressee as agent or security trustee and best practice is to have the opinion expressly addressed to the agent or trustee and each participating lender. It may also be necessary to consider expressly providing, as appropriate, for disclosure to any assignees or transferees (or other participants) anticipated in the lending structure.

10.6 The contents of the legal opinion

Reference has been made above to the broad substantive issues which a lender will wish the legal opinion to address. Although presentation and form may vary between both jurisdictions and lawyers, a foreign law legal opinion will almost always contain the following principal elements:

* details of the addressees;
* a statement concerning the retention of the firm of lawyers by the addressees;
* a recital of relevant aspects of the transaction;
* a recital of those transaction documents reviewed for the purposes of the opinion;
* details of searches and enquiries undertaken for the purposes of the opinion;
* assumptions made for the purposes of the opinion;
* the substantive opinion terms; and
* a statement as to the governing law of the opinion, limitation on liability of the lawyers rendering the opinion, and restrictions on scope of dissemination of the opinion.

The paragraphs which follow will consider those issues which most frequently arise under each of the identified headings.

10.6.1 Addressees

The identity of those persons to whom the opinion is to be addressed (as the parties able to rely on the opinion through privity of contract and/or liability in negligence) should be carefully established and included as specific addressees of the opinion.

10.6.2 Description of transaction, identification of documents examined and statement of searches and other enquiry made

The opening part of a foreign law legal opinion should, in favour of the lender (here taken to mean all appropriate addressees as those entitled to rely upon it both in contract and in the tort of negligence), (i) provide a statement of the capacity in which the lawyers act, (ii) provide a statement of any matter likely to be material to the state of knowledge of the lawyers acting, (iii) clearly identify the documents reviewed for the purpose of the opinion, and (iv) identify the nature and extent of searches and other enquiries made by the lawyers for the purpose of the opinion.

10.6.2.1 Capacity and knowledge of the foreign lawyers

At its most simple, this statement may merely record that the lawyers have been retained to provide an opinion in accordance with the laws of the relevant jurisdiction, but may, in some cases (largely as a matter of style), go on to state that the lawyers are competent to practise in the law of the jurisdiction concerned. More significantly, the lender should consider whether this statement needs to include language reflecting any special knowledge on the part of the lawyers concerned. In particular, where the borrower is a company incorporated in an offshore centre, it is not unusual for the opinion to be provided by lawyers who through the relevant partnership (or possibly through partnership-owned trust and corporate administrators) provide corporate administration services which may include partners or employees of the law firm acting as directors, nominee shareholders and/or secretary and include custody and control of statutory and other corporate records relating to the borrower. If the lender is prepared to accept an opinion from lawyers acting for the borrower in this way, it is appropriate that the lender insists on the recital to the opinion reflecting this fact. As will be discussed below, where partners of the law firm providing the opinion may also act as directors of the company, it will be right for the lender to question any attempt to qualify the extent of knowledge of the company's affairs contained within the assumptions to the opinion.

10.6.2.2 Description of the transaction and identification of transaction documents

The opinion should next state a brief summary of the transaction and, in particular, identify those transaction documents examined by the lawyers providing the opinion. The description of the transaction will further serve to describe the state of knowledge and completeness or otherwise of the instructions provided to the lawyers concerned. The lender should ensure that any description of the transaction documents reviewed by the lawyers includes:

- all of the documents on which issues relevant to the foreign law connection arise (this will generally include all of those to which the foreign law connected entity is a party, together with those in respect of which the foreign law is the proper or applicable law);
- a statement of whether the transaction documents as reviewed are executed and dated; and
- if reviewed in draft, a statement that such is the case together with, where appropriate, a statement identifying the version of the draft reviewed.

10.6.2.3 Statement of searches and enquiries made

The lender should, when providing instructions to lawyers for a foreign law opinion, expressly require that the lawyers concerned conduct all such searches and make all such enquiries and investigation as the lawyers deem appropriate in order to protect the lender's interests. Instructions given in these terms (which can be reflected in the form of precedent/draft opinion, if any, provided by the lender to the lawyer) will require that the lawyers providing the opinion identify for the lender any limitation or other deficiency restricting the scope of the lawyers' ability to confirm relevant issues. It may be that the lawyers concerned will address this issue by setting out in their opinion details of all of those enquiries and searches made and any limitation on the correctness or completeness of the results.

10.6.3 Assumptions*

The lawyers providing a foreign law legal opinion will wish to state that certain issues of fact are assumed for the purpose of their opinion as given. It is entirely proper for assumptions to be made in a foreign law legal opinion in relation to facts (and issues of law) which are not within the knowledge or competence of the lawyers providing the opinion. By way of

*See para 3 of the specimen legal opinion at the end of this chapter.

example, at para 3(e) of the specimen opinion an assumption is made in relation to transaction documents expressed to be governed by a law other than that in respect of which the opinion is given. It is, therefore, assumed, for the purpose of the opinion given, that the transaction documents concerned are a 'legal, valid and binding obligation' of the company in respect of which the opinion is given, and that they are 'enforceable in accordance with … their terms', under their relevant proper or applicable law. This assumption may be particularly important where the foreign law legal opinion is directed at the validity and enforceability of a collateral security interest, the right to enforce which, amongst other things, may depend upon the enforceability of the principal debt or, for example, a guarantee. Other material assumptions may, in effect, point to limitations in the scope of the opinion, or the extent to which it may be relied upon. So, for example, at para 3(c) and (h) of the specimen legal opinion, assumptions are made as to the accuracy of statements of fact made in the secretary's certificate (as to which see para 10.3 above) and as to the accuracy and completeness of information obtained arising from a search at a relevant public registry. The inclusion of an assumption of this type should be seen as identifying a risk which will be the lender's risk and which is not the subject of a confirmation provided in the terms of the opinion. At para 3(i) of the specimen opinion, an assumption is set out which is intended to reflect a limitation in the scope of the opinion in determining the absence or otherwise of a risk to the transaction based on transactions at an undervalue, preferences and/or on any challenge to the capacity of the directors to enter into the transaction that might be brought by members. This is an example of a form of assumption that should not be accepted where the opinion is to be delivered by lawyers who also provide corporate administration services and, in particular, directors of the company in respect of which the opinion is provided.

10.6.4 Statements of opinion

The statements of opinion are, subject to the assumptions on which they are made (para 10.6.3 above) and subject also to the matters which qualify them (para 10.6.5 below), the purpose and substance of a foreign law opinion. The scope and nature of such statements will vary depending on whether:

● no opinion is given on transaction or security documents governed by the relevant foreign law and where the opinion is, therefore, restricted exclusively to matters arising out of the connection of a borrower/grantor of security to the relevant system of law (sometimes referred to as a *capacity and due authority opinion*); or

- the relevant lawyers are called upon to provide confirmation as to the effect and enforceability of a transaction or security document expressed to be governed by the relevant foreign law.

Because the terms of the opinion in relation to a transaction document are very particular to the nature and law of such document, the consideration of the opinion terms which follows (and those contained in the specimen legal opinion) is restricted to those usually found in a capacity and due authority opinion.

10.6.4.1 Due constitution, existence and capacity

The purpose of the opinion under this heading is to provide the lender with confirmation that under the relevant system of foreign law the borrower and/or grantor of security has appropriate *legal personality* (that is, the borrower or grantor is a natural person with full and appropriate capacity or is otherwise duly incorporated or constituted and continues in existence with the appropriate capacity). For the purpose of confirming due incorporation or other constitution, the opinion will require the lawyers concerned to have examined relevant (and usually determinative) evidence of proper incorporation in accordance with the relevant law (including certificates of incorporation of a company) and to undertake searches at any relevant public registry. It is preferable that the opinion should identify by appropriate description the manner in which an entity other than a natural person is incorporated or constituted so as to distinguish, for example, a corporation incorporated pursuant to a statutory framework, or some other body (for example, a corporation constituted by some other authority such as a charter or, in the case of some Middle Eastern states, sovereign edict or promulgation). Having stated that the relevant entity has (as a passed event) been duly incorporated or constituted (para 4(a) of the specimen legal opinion), the opinion should state (i) any relevant characteristic of the company, for example that it is a company limited by guarantee or by shares and guarantee, (ii) that the entity continues to exist with full appropriate capacity as at the date of the opinion, and (iii) that it will continue to exist (either as an entity with perpetual succession or until some specified date or happening of some specified event). The lender should be aware of the implications of references within a foreign law legal opinion to the status of a corporate entity as a *limited life* or *limited duration* company, where the memorandum of association or other constitutional document is likely to specify a date and/or an event on the earlier of which the company is to be wound up. In many cases the relevant law will deem the commencement of a winding-up from such date or event, notwithstanding that the company, its shareholders and directors omit to take any relevant step. The lender should also note that a corporate borrower and/or grantor of security may continue to validly exist as being duly constituted but have no capacity to act through its directors or shareholders after the commencement of a winding-up, receivership, administration or other rehabilitation procedure. The lender should look carefully for any indication on the face of the opinion (particularly arising from the terms of an assumption or qualification) which suggests that enquiries and searches made by the lawyers are incapable of determining conclusively the commencement of such a procedure under the law of the jurisdiction concerned. Ultimately, in such circumstances, the lender may simply be forced to rely upon the factual representations and warranties contained within a secretary's or director's certificate. Finally, in connection with the statement of opinion contained under this heading, a frequently encountered risk is that a failure on the part of the company to make certain annual filings, for example of shareholders, mortgages and charges and to pay certain annual fees can lead to the company registrar or other similar official seeking the striking-off or dissolution of the company. In most cases, it is to be expected that appropriate searches and enquiries made by the foreign lawyers would determine the absence of compliance with any such formality and, therefore, the risk of such a step being taken. This issue, in some jurisdictions, is dealt with by the issue by the registrar of companies of a *certificate of good standing*. As a matter of style, a statement as to the full capacity of the borrower and/or grantor of security to enter into and be bound by the relevant transaction documents may form part of the statement dealing with the due constitution and valid existence of the borrower and/or grantor of security. The issue addressed under this heading is that of identifying any restriction on the capacity of the borrower and/or grantor to validly enter into the transaction documents and to be bound by their terms, and, in particular, the application of any doctrine of *ultra vires.*

10.6.4.2 Due authorisation

The opinion must contain a statement that the borrower and/or grantor of the security has, fully in accordance with the relevant foreign law, and in particular, in accordance with any requirements set out in its memorandum and articles of association, authorised and approved the entry into the transactions contemplated by the transaction documents and their execution (see para 4(b) of the specimen legal opinion). To give the necessary opinion, the foreign lawyers will require to have considered the articles of association, statutes or by-laws of the relevant company, together with the relevant evidence of directors and/or shareholder resolutions. Although, in that context, there will be a requirement that a meeting be duly convened (by notice or otherwise) and properly held (for example subject to quorum requirements or the place in which such meetings should be held), it will be usual for the foreign lawyers to rely upon the correctness of statements contained within the resolutions as to compliance with all such formalities as an assumption, although if the lawyers are aware of any apparent defect they should not rely on the assumption and should draw the matter to the attention of the lender.

10.6.4.3 *Valid and binding*

The statement in the legal opinion confirming that the transaction documents constitute the valid and binding obligation should not be misunderstood. In those cases where the transaction documents are governed by a proper or applicable law which is a system of law different to that covered by the legal opinion, it has already been noted that it will be assumed by the foreign lawyers that the transaction documents are valid and enforceable in accordance with such proper or applicable law. The issue for the foreign law legal opinion is, therefore, a very narrow one, being that of confirming that the obligations and agreements contained within the transaction documents are of a type which will be enforced by the courts of the foreign law jurisdiction (on proof of issues arising as a matter of the proper or applicable law) so that there is no supervening issue of law or public interest under the relevant foreign law that would give rise to the courts of the foreign law jurisdiction refusing to enforce, as against the borrower and/or grantor, the terms of the agreement. This confirmation, when taken together with the confirmation of capacity on the part of the borrower and/or grantor to enter into the transaction documents, means that the lender can look to the courts of the foreign law jurisdiction to enforce, as against the borrower and/or grantor, the transaction documents as they would be enforced by the courts of the jurisdiction of the proper or applicable law, subject only to proof of such law. The confirmation does not mean that all the rights and remedies that would be available to the lender in proceedings before the courts of the jurisdiction of the proper or applicable law will be available.

10.6.4.4 *No requirement for filing, registration, consents, licences etc and no requirement for payment of material fees or taxes*

This statement is intended to identify any requirement (i) that the transaction documents should be filed, registered, recorded or enrolled in order to be valid and enforceable (and obtain the stated priority if a security), (ii) that no material registration fees, stamp or similar duty is required, or (iii) that any consents, authorisations or approvals are required in connection with the validity or enforceability of the transaction documents. In some jurisdictions (for example, the Isle of Man) it is necessary to register the grant of security at a central registry; others may require entry in a register maintained at the company's registered office. Failure to register may have differing consequences, in some cases making the security ineffective as against a liquidator, in others merely constituting an offence committed by the company.

10.6.4.5 Conformity with laws and no contravention of constitution

This statement confirms that the execution and delivery of the transaction documents does not contravene any law of the relevant jurisdiction and that there is no contravention of the provisions of the memorandum or articles of association or other constitutional documents of the borrower.

10.6.4.6 Immunity

This statement should confirm that the borrower and/or grantor of security does not have the benefit of any immunity from suit under the relevant foreign law and, as appropriate, that its assets may be the subject of rights and remedies by way of relief.

10.6.4.7 Absence of withholding tax

The lender should look for a clear statement that all payment obligations imposed on the borrower and/or grantor of security may be met without the application of any withholding tax. Where the borrower and/or grantor of security is incorporated in an offshore centre jurisdiction, it is likely that the ability to give such confirmation will depend upon the tax status of the borrower and/or grantor of security, for example, pursuant to it being exempt or otherwise non-resident for the purposes of the foreign tax law. Where this is the case, it is the better practice for the lawyers to state that such is the case in order that it can be confirmed that the company has the appropriate status and so that the lender is aware of the significance of the borrower and/or grantor of security failing to maintain such status (usually by the payment of annual fees).

10.6.4.8 Choice of law and submission to jurisdiction

Where the transaction documents contain an express choice of a proper or applicable law being other than that covered by the terms of the foreign law opinion, the opinion should contain a statement that such express choice of law will be recognised as valid and binding on the parties by the courts of the foreign law jurisdiction. It is usual for such statement to be subject to an assumption that the selection is valid in accordance with the proper or applicable law and, moreover, subject to a qualification that the selection has been made in the absence of a bad faith intention to evade the application of a system of law to which the transaction has a closer or more real connection. The opinion should, in similar vein, confirm that the submission to jurisdiction by the borrower and/or grantor is a valid submission. In most cases, the effect of this confirmation is that it ought to be arguable as against the borrower and/or grantor seeking to contest the jurisdiction selected (or on an application to stay proceedings brought in any other jurisdiction) that the courts selected are the appropriate forum and that any other proceedings should be stayed.

10.6.5 Qualifications

In almost all cases, a foreign law legal opinion will, in addition to the assumptions on which the opinion statements are made, contain express qualifications to the terms of the opinion. In most cases, the qualifications will be extracted and set out separately to the opinion statements which, otherwise, will read as if unqualified. In some cases the opinion statements may themselves contain language intended to qualify the scope and nature of the conclusion reached. The specimen foreign law legal opinion contains the most frequently encountered qualifications at paras 5 (a) to (k). In relation to such qualifications the following should be noted.

10.6.5.1 Insolvency, winding-up and creditors' rights
In the form of the specimen opinion, this qualification is given in the very general terms in which it will generally be encountered. The difficulty is that the qualification is intended to draw attention to all of those issues that may arise for the lender where the borrower and/or grantor of security is subject to an insolvency pursuant to the foreign law jurisdiction. The legal opinion cannot summarise all of the relevant implications and the lender should, therefore, assume (unless further enquiries are made) that the qualification is intended to draw attention to the following:

- the existence of claims treated as preferential;
- that proofs of debt may require prior operation of mandatory or other agreed set-off arrangements in respect of amounts due as between the lender and borrower;
- that interest and other costs and expenses may not be recoverable for any period after the commencement of the winding-up;
- that there may be administration or other rehabilitation processes giving time to the debtor and staying proceedings for enforcement; and
- that the insolvency process may allow for the setting aside of transactions which are deemed to have been prejudicial to the creditors (for example, *transactions at an undervalue*, or *preferences*).

10.6.5.2 Limitation on availability of discretionary remedies and relief
This qualification draws attention, again usually in general terms, to limitations on the availability of certain types of relief (and in particular discretionary remedies).

10.6.5.3 Limitation on ability to recover or enforce through the operation of time-bar, prescription or estoppel
Statements under this heading identify the existence of limitations operating as a matter of the general law of the jurisdiction concerned.

10.6.5.4 Limitations on the enforcement of certifications, default interest rates, pre-estimate of damage provisions and provisions relating to severability of contract terms

Qualifications of this type are intended to cover all of those qualifications which may address the limitations of enforcement of particular contract terms, so that the lender should be aware that the opinion may and should contain a qualification in relation to any particular provision of the transaction documents which may not be enforceable or which may only be enforceable at the discretion of the courts of the foreign law jurisdiction.

10.6.5.5 Restriction of the scope of the opinion to matters stated as at its date and exclusively to matters arising under the stated foreign law

The lender should note that, invariably, the opinion will state that the opinion applies only as at its date. Where, therefore, the lender is concerned that it should have the protection of relevant opinion statements as at a date important in the context of the transaction (for example draw-down) it will be important to ensure that the opinion is delivered as at such date.

The opinion will normally close with a statement containing the following:

- a statement of the governing law;
- a statement of limitation on disclosure to parties other than the addressee (see above, para 10.5); and
- the signature of the provider of the opinion.

Appendix: Specimen foreign law legal opinion

Re: [   ] ('the Borrower')

1. We have been requested to provide you with a legal opinion on matters of the law of [specify foreign territory] in connection with the following document, [final drafts/certified copies] of which we have examined ('the Documents'):

[specify the relevant transaction documents]

2. In addition, we have examined:

   (a) the public records of the Borrower on file and available for inspection at the [specify the identity of any relevant registry] ('the Public Records');

   (b) a [certified true] copy of the Memorandum and Articles of Association of the Borrower; and

   (c) a certificate of the Secretary of the Borrower ('the Secretary's Certificate') relating to certain questions of fact, together with the Minutes of a meeting of the board of directors of the Borrower referred to therein, a copy of which is attached.

3. **Assumptions**

   In our examination of the Documents and as relevant the Documents set out in paragraphs 2(a) to (c) above, we have assumed:

   (a) that all parties other than the Borrower have the capacity, power and authority to enter into the Documents and that such parties have duly authorised, executed and delivered those documents to which they are a party;

   (b) the genuineness and authenticity of all signatures on all documents, the authenticity of all original documents and the conformity to original documents of all documents produced to us as copies;

   (c) the accuracy and completeness of the Secretary's Certificate;

   (d) that the Documents as executed do not differ in any material respect from the drafts which we have examined; (This statement would be included where the documents have been examined in draft.)

   (e) that each of the Documents when executed and delivered by the Borrower and the other parties thereto will constitute the legal, valid and binding obligation of the Borrower, enforceable in accordance with its terms under [specify proper or applicable law] law, by which law the Documents are expressed to be governed;

   (f) that there is no provision of the law of any jurisdiction other than [specify foreign law] which would have any adverse implication in relation to the opinions expressed hereunder;

(g) that the choice of [proper or applicable] law to govern each of the Documents is bona fide and not made with any intention to evade the laws of the jurisdiction with which the transaction under each of the Documents has the closest and most real connection;

(h) that the information and documents disclosed by our searches of the Public Records are accurate and there is no information or document which had been delivered for registration, or which is required by the law of [specify foreign law territory] to be delivered for registration, which was not included in the Public Records; and

(i) that in resolving that the Borrower enter into the Documents the directors of the Borrower were acting in the interests of and for the purposes of the Borrower.

4. **Opinion**

On the basis of and subject to the foregoing we are of the opinion that:

(a) the Borrower is a company duly incorporated under the laws of [specify foreign territory] with power to enter into the Documents and to exercise its rights and perform its obligations thereunder and all corporate or other acts required to authorise the execution by the Borrower of the Documents and the performance by it of its obligations thereunder have been duly taken;

(b) each of the Documents when executed and delivered by the Borrower and the other parties thereto will constitute the legal, valid and binding obligation of the Borrower, enforceable in accordance with its terms;

(c) it is not necessary in order to ensure the legality, validity, enforceability or admissibility in evidence of any of the Documents in [specify foreign law]:

   (i) that they be filed, recorded or enrolled with any court or governmental authority in [specify foreign law]; or

   (ii) that any registration fees, stamp or similar duty (other than the payment of court fees in the event of litigation before the [specify] Courts) be paid on or in relation to any of the Documents; or

   (iii) that any consents, authorisations or approvals of any court or governmental authority in [specify foreign law] be obtained by the Borrower in relation to any of the Documents;

(d) the execution and delivery of the Documents and the performance of the Borrower's obligations thereunder will not contravene:

   (i) any applicable provision of [specify foreign law] law to which the Borrower is subject; or

   (ii) any provision of the Borrower's Memorandum and Articles of Association;

(e)   the Borrower is not entitled to claim immunity from suit, execution, attachment of other legal process in [specify foreign territory];

(f)   the Borrower is not required to make any withholding or other deduction from any payment due by the Borrower pursuant to the Documents;

(g)   the choice of [proper or applicable law] law to govern each of the Documents will be upheld as a valid choice of law and [proper or applicable law] law will, accordingly, be applied by the courts of [foreign law] if the said Documents or any claims thereunder come under their jurisdiction upon proof of the relevant provisions of [proper or applicable law] law. The submission by the Borrower to the jurisdiction of the [proper or applicable law] courts in the Documents is valid and binding on the Borrower;

(h)   a final and conclusive judgment under which a sum of money is payable (not being a sum payable in respect of taxes or other charges of a like nature or in respect of a fine or penalty) obtained in the [specify the courts of the foreign territory] against the Borrower in respect of the Documents would be recognised as a valid judgment by the Courts of [specify foreign law] and be enforceable without reconsideration of the merits;

(i)   it is not necessary under the laws of [foreign law]:

(i)   in order to enable the Lender to enforce its rights under the Documents; or

(ii)   by reason of the execution of the Documents or the performance by the Lender of its obligations thereunder;

that the Lender should be licensed, qualified or otherwise entitled to carry on business in [specify foreign territory]; and

(j)   the Lender is not nor will it be deemed to be resident domiciled or carrying on business in [foreign territory] by reason only of the execution, performance and/or enforcement of the Documents.

5. **Qualifications**

This opinion is subject to the following qualifications:

(a)   enforcement of the Documents may be limited by dissolution, bankruptcy, liquidation, reorganisation, insolvency or similar laws affecting creditors' rights generally;

(b)   enforcement of the Documents may be limited by general principles of equity; in particular equitable remedies are discretionary and are not available where damages are considered to be an adequate remedy;

(c)   the Courts of [the foreign territory] may decline to accept jurisdiction in an action where it determines that a court of competent jurisdiction has already made a determination of the relevant matter or where there is litigation pending in respect thereof in another jurisdiction or it may stay proceedings if concurrent proceedings are instituted elsewhere;

(d) claims may be barred under the laws relating to the prescription and limitation of actions or may become subject to the general doctrine of estoppel in relation to representations, acts or omissions of any relevant party or may become subject to defence of set-off or counterclaim;

(e) the Courts of [specify the foreign territory] will not enforce provisions of the Documents to the extent that the same may be illegal or contrary to public policy in [specify the foreign territory] or if obligations are to be performed in a jurisdiction outside [specify the foreign territory] to the extent that such performance would be illegal or contrary to public policy under the laws of that jurisdiction;

(f) information available in public registries in [specify the foreign territory] is limited and in particular there is no publicly available record of charges or security interests over the shares or assets of [specify the foreign territory] companies;

(g) the enforcement of the obligations of the parties to the Documents may be limited by the provisions of [specify the foreign territory] law applicable to Documents held to have been frustrated by events happening after their execution;

(h) the question of whether or not any provision of the Documents which may be invalid on account of illegality may be severed from the other provisions thereof would be determined by a Court in [specify the foreign territory] in its discretion;

(i) any provision of the Documents which purports to give conclusive effect to any calculation, determination or certification may be held by the Courts of [specify the foreign territory] not to be conclusive as such Courts may review the grounds on which such calculation, determination or certification is made or given;

(j) any provision in any of the Documents purporting to provide for a certain payment to be made in the event of breach of any term of the Documents would not be enforceable to the extent that a Court in [specify the foreign territory] was to construe it to be a penalty which was excessive (i.e. it unreasonably exceeds the maximum damages which an obligee could have suffered as a result of the breach of an obligation); and

(k) the effectiveness of terms exculpating any party from a liability or duty otherwise owed may be limited by law.

6. This opinion shall be governed by and construed in accordance with the laws of [specify the foreign territory] and is limited to the matters expressly stated herein. This opinion is confined to and given on the basis of the laws and practice in [specify the foreign territory] at the date

hereof. We have made no investigation and express no opinion in relation to the laws of any jurisdiction other than [specify the foreign territory]. This opinion is given for your benefit in connection with the Documents and with the exception of your professional advisers it may not be disclosed to or relied upon by any person or used for any other purpose or referred to or made public in any way without our prior written consent.

Yours faithfully

Part **II**

Introduction

The island of Jersey is the larger of two Bailiwicks which make up the Channel Islands (the Bailiwick of Jersey comprising the main island and two rocky islets, the Ecréhous and Minquiers). The island, which measures some 45 square miles, is located approximately 15 miles from the west coast of Normandy and approximately 90 miles south of the south-west coast of England. The principal population centre (and the location of most of the financial institutions and professional support services) is St Helier, situated on the south coast of the island. The island has a population of approximately 80 000, predominantly English-speaking.

11.1 Currency and exchange control

The currency of Jersey is sterling, although it prints its own notes and mints its own coins which are legal tender within the island. At the present time there is no exchange control.

11.2 Constitution

Jersey is regarded as being politically stable. It is part of the British Isles (as a Crown dependency) but is not a part of the United Kingdom. Jersey's relationship with the English Crown is central to its constitution, in that prior to the invasion of England by William the Conqueror, Jersey was part of his lands as the Duchy of Normandy. When, in 1204, the English Crown lost its lands in mainland Normandy, Jersey remained loyal to the English Crown, which has over the centuries accorded to Jersey the right to internal self-governance and, in particular, the right to control its own fiscal affairs. Primary permanent legislation passed, in the first instance, by the States of Jersey (comprising 53 elected representatives who hold office in a non-party system) requires ratification by the Crown in Council. The United Kingdom retains responsibility for Jersey's external affairs. The island's Lieutenant-Governor is a representative of the English Crown and the Bailiff and law officers are appointees of the Crown subject to consultation with the insular authorities. At the present time, any treaty obligation entered into by the United Kingdom which is either silent as to its territorial extent or makes reference to territories for whose international affairs Her Majesty's government is responsible, is taken to extend to Jersey, but the Home Office consults with the island's authorities prior to accession to such treaties.

11.3 Legal system

Jersey's legal system reflects its original ties to the Duchy of Normandy. The island's laws relating to immoveable property, its contract law and the law relating to testate and intestate succession reflect its Norman French roots and require reference to Norman French jurisprudence together with the customary law of the island. Otherwise the modern legislation of the States of Jersey passes into law in the English language and, both in the framework for such legislation and in its interpretation, draws on the experience of the legislature and courts of the United Kingdom. Jersey has its own separate judiciary, the principal court of which is the Royal Court. The Royal Court administers civil and criminal justice through the office of the Bailiff, Deputy Bailiff, the Jurats and Judicial Greffier. The Jurats (who sit as arbiters of fact) represent the independence of the island's judiciary as an ancient office capable of being traced back in time beyond the consolidation of the English Crown and Duchy of Normandy. In civil matters, appeals from the Royal Court are to the Jersey Court of Appeal, comprising the Bailiff, the Bailiff of Guernsey and senior English barristers and Scottish advocates. From the Jersey Court of Appeal, appeal lies to the Judicial Committee of the Privy Council. Proceedings in the Royal Court are conducted in English, although the principal language of conveyancing remains French.

11.4 Constitutional relationship with the European Union

In common with Guernsey and the Isle of Man, Jersey's relationship with the European Union is determined pursuant to *Protocol No 3 to the Treaty of Accession (1972)*, in accordance with which the island has preserved its constitutional position relative to the English Crown, together with its fiscal independence. Jersey is within the provisions of the *Treaty of Rome* for the purposes of the *Common External Tariff* and *Agricultural Levy System*, and is therefore able to enjoy free trade in goods. The island is not required to apply European Union directives relating to, for example, movement of capital, company law, and the provision of financial services in insurance and banking.

11.5 Banking and professional confidentiality

Jersey does not have any statutory framework for bank or professional secrecy. Banking and other professional confidentiality arises as a matter of an express or implied contractual obligation. Decisions of the Royal Court in Jersey confirm the existence of a duty on the part of a banker or other professional not to disclose to a third party information which is in its nature confidential to the customer or client. Insofar as the Royal Court has regard to English authority on commercial matters, it is likely that the principles set out in the English decision *Tournier v National Provincial and Union Bank of England* [1924] 1 K.B. 461 as to the scope of such duty will be applied. As a contractual term, the duty of confidentiality can, in appropriate circumstances, be modified and limited (for example, to allow compliance with regulatory disclosure which may not amount to 'compulsion of law'). A recent example of where modification by contract has been necessary has arisen where US dollar accounts are made available with cheque books requiring a US dollar 'payment through' clearing facility, and so that account-holder details may be disclosed to the US clearing agent at its request.

11.5.1 Jersey companies: disclosure of beneficial ownership

It is a requirement on incorporation of a Jersey company that its ultimate beneficial ownership be disclosed to the Financial Services Department. This information is not thereafter available on the Public Companies Registry file and is maintained as strictly confidential.

11.5.2 Disclosure to bankers by financial intermediaries

Know-your-customer standards reflected in the Guidance Notes issued jointly by the Financial Services Department and the Jersey Bankers Association/Jersey Fund Managers Association require the account-holding bank to obtain and retain in its records details of ultimate beneficial ownership of accounts and the source of funds. If, however (as is very often the case), an account is maintained by the deposit-holding bank for a Jersey trust corporation as the trustee of a settlement and/or for a private investment-holding company, corporate administration of which is provided by a Jersey trust or company administrators, then, provided the bank regards them as *reputable*, there is no requirement that the account-holding bank must establish ultimate beneficial ownership, it being the obligation of the trustee or company administrator to do so.

11.5.3 Disclosure under compulsion of law

Bankers and other professionals may be subject to an order to disclose made pursuant to the *Fraud Investigation (Jersey) Law 1991*, the *Drug Trafficking Offences (Jersey) Law 1988*, the *Prevention of Terrorism (Jersey) Law 1996*, the *Income Tax (Jersey) Law 1961* and the *Bankers Book Evidence (Jersey) Law 1986* and, otherwise, in accordance with an order of the Royal Court made pursuant to its jurisdiction in proceedings before it.

11.6 Regulation in the financial sector

The Finance and Economics Committee of the States of Jersey ('the Committee') is responsible for the supervision, development and promotion of Jersey's finance industry. The executive functions of the Committee are undertaken by the Financial Services Department ('the Department'). It is proposed that, with the coming into force of a law (during the course of 1997) intended to regulate the conduct of investment business, there will be established a commission to replace the functions presently undertaken by the Department. At the present time, however, the Department operates as the primary regulator in accordance with the terms of the following key legislation:

- The *Banking Business (Jersey) Law 1991*, pursuant to which the Department acts as a relevant supervisory authority in relation to licensed institutions engaged in deposit-taking (whether locally incorporated subsidiaries of foreign banks, or their branches).

- The *Insurance Business (Jersey) Law 1996*, pursuant to which the Department acts as a supervisory authority in respect of licensed insurers and insurance managers.
- The *Companies (Jersey) Law 1991* and the *Limited Partnerships (Jersey) Law 1994*, pursuant to which the Department acts through the office of Registrar in the regulation of companies and limited partnerships.
- The *Collective Investment Funds (Jersey) Law 1988*, pursuant to which the Department supervises the constitution and provision of functionary services to collective investment funds.
- The *Borrowing (Control) (Jersey) Law 1947* and the *Control of Borrowing (Jersey) Order 1958*, pursuant to which the Department regulates the issue of shares or securities by Jersey companies and the raising of moneys in the island by the issue of securities and/or the circulation of a prospectus by companies incorporated elsewhere.

In addition to the above primary legislation relating directly to financial regulation, business activity is also regulated pursuant to the *Regulation of Undertakings and Development (Jersey) Laws 1973 and 1975*, pursuant to which a licence is required for the commencement of any new undertaking in the nature of a trade, business or profession. Jersey is, through its connection with the United Kingdom, a party to the Organisation for Economic Co-operation and Development. Jersey participates as a member of the Offshore Group of Banking Supervisors and has designated territory status under the United Kingdom *Financial Services Act 1986*, s. 87.

11.7 Anti-money laundering legislation and best practice

Although Jersey is not a member of the Financial Action Task Force (FATF), in the Guidance Notes for Mainstream Banking, Lending and Deposit Taking Activities issued by the Joint Money Laundering Steering Group pursuant to the United Kingdom Money Laundering Regulations, the island is referred to as having enacted legislation which is equivalent to the EU directive and therefore is required to be judged by United Kingdom banks and building societies as meeting an FATF required standard so as to be assumed to pass the *equivalence test* referred to at paragraph 49 of the Guidance Notes. The legislative regime in place in relation to the combating of money laundering is as follows.

11.7.1 The Drug Trafficking Offences (Jersey) Law 1988

The *Drug Trafficking Offences (Jersey) Law 1988* makes provision for:

- the making and enforcement of confiscation orders against persons convicted of drug trafficking offences;
- the offence of assisting drug traffickers to retain the proceeds or benefits of trafficking;
- the offence of making any disclosure likely to prejudice an investigation; and
- the making of production and enforcement orders in relation to production of and access to materials required in connection with a police investigation.

The offence of assisting a drug trafficker to retain the proceeds or benefits of drug trafficking is committed by a person:

- who knows or suspects that another is a drug trafficker or has benefited from trafficking; and
- who is concerned in an arrangement which facilitates the retention or control of such proceeds by the drugs trafficker, or which facilitates the acquisition of property by way of investment.

It is a defence to the offence to show:

- that he has disclosed to a police officer his relevant suspicion or belief, either before the doing of the act concerned (being an act done with the consent of the police officer), or after the act but voluntarily and as soon as is reasonable; or
- that he did not know or suspect that the arrangement related to another's proceeds of drug trafficking; or
- that he did not know that he was facilitating such control; or
- that, although he intended to make disclosure to a police officer, there is reasonable excuse for his not doing so.

Where disclosure is made to a police officer there is deemed to be no breach of any duty of confidentiality. The law has now been amended by the provisions of the *Drug Trafficking (Miscellaneous Provisions) (Jersey) Law 1996* which has, amongst other things, added a new Article 18A which in relation to a person acquiring knowledge or suspicion in the course of an employment in a trade, business or profession creates an offence of failing to disclose knowledge or suspicion of drug money laundering.

11.7.2 The Prevention of Terrorism (Jersey) Law 1996

The *Prevention of Terrorism (Jersey) Law 1996* provides for:

- the making and enforcement of exclusion orders against persons concerned in the commission, preparation or instigation of acts of terrorism or similar matters connected with Northern Ireland;
- the offence of provision of financial assistance for terrorism; and

- the offence of assisting another in the retention or control of terrorist funds.

The offence of assisting another in the retention or control of terrorist funds is committed by a person who enters into or is concerned in an arrangement whereby the retention or control of terrorist funds by or on behalf of another is facilitated. It is a defence to show:

- that the assistance is given with the consent of a police officer, or followed by timely voluntary disclosure;
- that the person did not know or believe that the arrangement related to terrorist funds;
- that, although the person intended to make disclosure to a police officer, there is reasonable excuse for his not doing so.

Where disclosure is made to a police officer there is deemed to be no breach of any duty of confidentiality.

11.7.3 Drug Offences (International Co-operation) (Jersey) Law 1996

This law enables the island to co-operate with other countries in investigations of proceedings relating to drug offences and to the connected purposes.

11.8 Lending with a Jersey foreign law connection

The sections which follow will highlight those issues which may arise in connection with a lending which has a Jersey foreign law connection in that, either the borrower is domiciled, resident and/or incorporated or constituted in the island, or because a transaction or security document has a proper or applicable law which is Jersey law. Building on the issues set out in Chapters 4, 5, 6 and 7, the paragraphs which next follow highlight, by reference to borrower type, issues which arise for a lender where the borrower is domiciled, resident or incorporated in Jersey. For each borrower type the issues considered are those which will, in the normal course, form the subject matter of a Jersey foreign law opinion, being:

- legal personality (i.e. does the borrower have a separate legal existence and if not, who may contract on behalf of the borrower?);
- capacity;
- due authorisation of the transaction;
- due execution; and
- taxation including withholding.

The remaining paragraphs deal collectively with:

- the creation of security;
- enforcement and insolvency; and
- recent or anticipated developments.

11.8.1 Capacity to grant a foreign law security

The *Security Interests (Jersey) Law 1983* as amended provides in Article 12 that after the commencement of the law a person incorporated, resident or domiciled in Jersey who gives security over *property* situated outside of the island governed by *a foreign law* shall be deemed to have had capacity to give it under the law of the island. For this purpose references in the Article to *property* are references to all property, whether tangible or intangible, vested, contingent, or future, whether or not regarded by the law of Jersey as *immeuble* and including choses in action. References to a foreign law are references to a law other than that of the island.

11.8.2 Lending to natural persons

The following issues are relevant when lending to, or taking a grant of security from, an individual domiciled and/or resident in Jersey.

11.8.2.1 Capacity
An individual is a *mineur* and without legal capacity to contract (other than possibly for necessities) until attaining the age of 20 years. If, however, the mineur is subject to a *tutelle* (a form of court-administered protectorship allowing interests in property to be held for the account of the mineur) full age will not be reached until 21 years. In the case of mental incapacity, an individual may be subject to the appointment of a *curateur* pursuant to the *Mental Health (Jersey) Law 1969* as amended. There is no distinction drawn between the capacity of men and women, and no limitation on the capacity of a married woman. See also para 11.8.1 above.

11.8.2.2 Tax and withholding
An individual resident or ordinarily resident within the island is liable to assessment to tax on profits or gains wherever arising. A non-resident person is liable to assessment on profits or gains having a Jersey source (excluding, by concession, bank deposit interest). Profits or gains are taxed at a single rate of 20% after allowances. There is no separate tax on capital gains, capital transfers or death, although a probate duty is payable on proving a Jersey estate.

11.8.3 Lending to companies

The legislative framework relating to a company incorporated under the law of the island is to be found in the *Companies (Jersey) Law 1991* as amended ('the Companies Law'). In relation to a company incorporated under the Companies Law, the lender should note the following.

11.8.3.1 Legal personality, due incorporation and good standing

A company incorporated under the Companies Law has separate legal personality and may hold assets, incur liabilities, and sue and be sued in its own name. Such existence becomes effective on the registration of a memorandum of association at the Companies Registry (a division of the Financial Services Department) and upon the issue of a certificate of incorporation by the Registrar of Companies, so that, from the date of incorporation mentioned in the certificate, the members of the company are deemed to be a 'body corporate' capable forthwith of exercising all functions of an incorporated company. The Companies Law allows only for the incorporation of limited liability companies, liability being limited by registrable shares (a Jersey company may not issue bearer shares). Requirements for incorporation are dictated by the provisions of Article 7 of the Companies Law and the terms of the *Companies (General Provisions) (Jersey) Order 1992* requiring that the following information must be disclosed to the Registrar of Companies:

- the name of the company;
- the names and addresses of the subscribers to the memorandum;
- the amount and denomination of the company's authorised share capital;
- the period (if any) fixed for the duration of the company;
- whether the whole or any part of the standard table of articles of association is to be adopted by the company; and
- in the case of a public company, the name, address, nationality, occupation and date of birth of each proposed director.

The Companies Law draws a distinction between *public companies* and *private companies*. A company is a public company if (i) it has more than 30 members; or (ii) it states in its memorandum that it is a public company. Importantly, only a public company may circulate a *prospectus* (which means, for this purpose, an invitation to the public to acquire or apply for any securities) (see also 11.8.3.5 below relating to shares, securities and prospectuses). Otherwise, in relation to incorporation, the lender should note the following:

- a minimum of two subscriber shareholders is required (they may be nominees) who may not be minors or interdicts (but the Companies Law does provide for a single member company where shares are held by a holding company in its wholly owned subsidiary);

- the information required on incorporation is set out within a combined application for the prior consent of the Finance and Economics Committee in accordance with the provisions of the *Control of Borrowing (Jersey) Order 1958* as amended (known as *COBO consent*), all such information being contained within Form C2;
- Form C2 requires the disclosure of the identity of the ultimate beneficial owners of the company, together with a description of the nature of the company's intended activities;
- Form C2 must be signed by an Advocate or Solicitor of the Royal Court of Jersey, or by a Chartered or Certified Accountant who is practising in Jersey as a principal or a partner of such a firm;
- the memorandum of association may be in a 'short form' but must contain (i) the name of the company, (ii) the amount of the share capital and the number, value and currency of the shares into which it is divided, (iii) a statement that the liability of the members of the company is to be limited, (iv) the period (if any) fixed for the duration of the company, and (v) a statement that the company is a public company (if that is to be the case); and
- the full name and addresses of the subscribers of the company.

The Companies Law makes express provision for the status of pre-incorporation contracts, providing that they may be adopted by the company after it is incorporated, but otherwise providing that a contract entered into by a person purporting to act for the company or as agent for it is personally bound by the transaction (and entitled to its benefits) unless otherwise stated in the agreement concerned. The term 'good standing' is not, generally, used as a term of art in the context of the Companies Law. The standing of the company pursuant to the Companies Law, if taken by the lender to require that the company borrower is not at risk of dissolution and has not committed offences under the Companies Law, requires that the lender determine, among other things, the following (this is not an exhaustive list of offences):

- that the company has complied with an obligation to submit an annual return to the Registrar made up as at the first day of January of each year and to be submitted not later than the last day of February together with the appropriate fee (in default of such filing the Registrar of Companies has power to seek the striking-off and dissolution of the company);
- that the company is maintaining and has notified the Registrar of Companies of a registered office within the island;
- that the company has (unless its members have in the case of a private limited company waived such requirement) held an annual general meeting in accordance with the provisions of the Companies Law and its articles of association;
- that, if the company is a public company for the purposes of the

Companies Law, it has appointed an auditor, and has produced and filed with the Registrar of Companies audited accounts for each completed financial period; and

- that the company has at least one director (if private) and at least two directors (if public) and has a secretary qualified to act.

11.8.3.2 Capacity

Pursuant to the terms of Article 18 of the Companies Law, the capacity of a Jersey company (whether incorporated before or after coming into effect of that law) is not subject to any limitation contained within its memorandum of association, but the capacity of its directors to enter into a transaction on behalf of a company incorporated prior to 2 March 1992 (when the law came into force) will be subject to any limitation contained within the company's memorandum prior to that date, unless amended by special resolution. Companies incorporated after the coming into effect of the Companies Law will usually be found to have a short form memorandum stating, for example, that the company shall have 'unrestricted corporate capacity'. It is still the practice for a memorandum of a Jersey company to incorporate an objects clause where, for example, the company is regulated as a bank or insurance company, or provides trust or corporate administration services. Article 19 of the Companies Law provides that there is no concept of constructive notice of those records which are available at the Companies Registry, or are made available pursuant to the Companies Law for inspection by a company. For capacity to grant a foreign law security, reference should be had to the provisions of Article 12 of the *Security Interests (Jersey) Law 1983* (para 11.8.1 above).

11.8.3.3 Due authorisation

There are no general limitations on the borrowing powers of a Jersey company, although the lender should note that such restrictions may be contained within the articles of association and, in particular, of those relating to a collective investment fund (see para 11.8.6 below). A company incorporated under the Companies Law acts through its directors, who are bound by the terms of the articles of association and any objects set out in the company's memorandum of association. The Companies Law provides that a private company must have at least one director and a public company must have at least two directors. Corporate directors are not permitted. Notwithstanding the protection afforded by the Companies Law to a third party transacting with a Jersey company, and in particular the absence of an obligation to enquire as to any limitation on directors' powers or otherwise as to due authorisation by the directors or the company of a relevant transaction, it is suggested that the lender should, in all cases, require sight of a minute or extract of minute of the directors dealing with the following:

- confirming that the meeting was duly convened and quorate;
- consideration of the relevant aspects of the proposed transaction and in particular the commercial benefit to the company;
- consideration of the terms of relevant transaction documents;
- approving the execution of transaction documents substantially in the considered form (and, as appropriate, allowing for the negotiation or agreement of amendments to such documents);
- stating the manner in which such documents are to be executed, designating one or more persons to attest the common seal of the company or designating individuals as signatories to the documents; and
- disclosing the extent and nature of a director's material conflicts of interest as necessary.

It is the general practice to settle articles of association for Jersey companies which allow directors to convene and conduct meetings by telephone and to allow for written resolutions, if signed by all of the directors entitled to receive a notice of the meeting. Although the Companies Law does not prevent the holding of meetings outside of the island, the lender should ensure that there is no prohibition on the holding of meetings in particular jurisdictions (for example, the United Kingdom or United States) expressed in such a way as to make invalid any resolution passed at a meeting purportedly convened in any such place. Where shareholder resolutions are required as an aspect of due authorisation for the transaction (for example, in relation to confirmation of benefit, or where it is necessary to deal with a financial assistance point), the lender should note the following:

- although it is possible to have a single member holding company, it is arguable that the Companies Law does not provide for a 'meeting' of shareholders to be convened in such circumstances, such that shareholder resolutions may only safely be made in writing, or through a meeting convened at which two or more persons are present as representatives of the single member;
- notice of an annual general meeting (other than an adjourned meeting) must be called by notice in writing given not less than 21 days in advance, provided that time may be abridged by the consent of all members entitled to attend and vote at such meeting;
- notice of any other meeting of shareholders (including a class meeting) must be convened by notice in writing of not less than 14 days, provided that such time may be abridged by the consent of a majority together holding not less than 95% in nominal value of the shares giving a right to attend and vote at such meeting; and
- anything that may be done by a resolution (including a special resolution but excluding a resolution removing an auditor) to be dealt with at a meeting of the company (or at a class meeting) may be done by

resolution in writing signed by or on behalf of each member who, at the date when the resolution is deemed to be passed, would be entitled to vote on the resolution if it were proposed at a meeting.

The Companies Law defines a *special resolution* as a resolution passed by a majority of not less than two-thirds of members who (being entitled to do so) vote in person, or by proxy, at a meeting of the company (or at a class meeting) in respect of which the notice provisions have been complied with. A special resolution is required to be filed with the Registrar of Companies within 21 days. Failure to comply will not invalidate the resolution but it will constitute an offence by the company.

11.8.3.4 Due execution

The Companies Law provides that a person acting under due authority of a Jersey company may make, vary or discharge a contract or sign an instrument on behalf of the company in the same manner as would a natural person. Accordingly, and subject to the provisions of the company's articles of association, there is nothing in the terms of the Companies Law which imposes upon a company an obligation to enter into a contract in any way other than that prescribed for a natural person. Nevertheless, the Companies Law further provides that every Jersey company shall have a common seal and allows, where the company engages in business outside of the island that it may, if authorised by its articles, have for use in such country or territory an *official seal*. Pursuant to authority in writing under the common seal of the company, the company may authorise an agent to make use of the official seal and in respect of a third party dealing with the agent, the agent's authority is deemed to continue until that person has actual notice of the termination of the authority. Where a Jersey company has granted a power of attorney (in respect of which Jersey law is the proper law) the provisions of the *Powers of Attorney (Jersey) Law 1995* apply, requiring a body corporate to execute a power of attorney 'in the manner permitted by its articles of association or other internal regulations without any further attestation'. In this context, it should be noted that articles of association will generally provide that powers of attorney be granted under the common seal of the company.

11.8.3.5 Issue of shares and circulation of a prospectus

On the incorporation of a Jersey company, capital duty in respect of authorised share capital of £10 000.00 (or its currency equivalent) at the rate of 0.5% is prepaid, with further capital duty at the same rate being payable on any authorised share capital in excess of £10 000.00 (or its equivalent). Bearer shares are not permitted. There must be a minimum of two initial subscribers, otherwise there is no minimum capital for a private company and no requirement that shares be paid-up on subscription. Shares may be issued at a premium, in which case the value of the premium must be shown in a *share premium account* which is then treated (with certain limited exceptions) as part of the paid-up capital of the company. Shares may be issued as redeemable shares, provided that there are also in issue non-redeemable shares. The Companies Law provides for the redemption or repurchase by a company of its own shares, subject to conditions which include prescribed sources of funds (the proceeds of a new issue of shares made for that purpose, distributable profits and the balance on a share premium account), sanctioned by special resolution and subject to the directors being satisfied as to the solvency of the company. Redeemable shares are a particular feature of collective investment fund scheme companies, to which special provisions apply allowing for flexibility in relation to the source of funds from which to effect redemption. The Companies Law provides for the variation by a Jersey company of its share capital by alteration to its memorandum (pursuant to special resolution), although a capital reduction may only be undertaken in accordance with the Companies Law and pursuant to court sanction. Only a public company may circulate a prospectus and the company must (unless the offer contained in it is not an offer to the public, in that it is made to a restricted circle of persons) have the prior consent of the Financial Services Department.

11.8.3.6 Licences and consents

If the activity of the company as borrower is undertaken from or within the island of Jersey and is banking business, insurance business or that of a collective investment fund, the lender should note the requirement for the appropriate registrations and licences as set out at para 11.6 above. At the present time there is no requirement for registration or licensing applicable to the operation of a trust corporation (other than for the purposes of the *Probate (Jersey) Law 1949*, or for the provision of services as a financial intermediary). The lender should confirm that:

- the raising of money by the proposed borrowing does not constitute, in the hands of the borrowing company, the taking of a deposit for the purposes of the *Banking Business (Jersey) Law 1991*;
- to the extent that the proposed borrowing contemplates the issue of shares or securities by the company, the prior consent of the Finance and Economics Committee (through the Financial Services Department) has been obtained in accordance with the *Control of Borrowing (Jersey) Order 1958*, provided that no such consent is required where (i) the issue is of securities made for the sole purpose of securing money borrowed by the company, (ii) the borrowing is in the ordinary course of the company's business and is from a person carrying on a banking undertaking, or (iii) such securities are not bearer securities and the number of persons in whose names the securities are to be registered

does not exceed ten, or if the securities are bearer securities, they are not capable of being held by more than ten persons; and
- no consent is required in connection with the raising of money (as a subscription or investment) in a collective investment fund as defined by the *Collective Investment Funds (Jersey) Law 1988* as amended (see para 11.8.6 below).

11.8.3.7 Financial assistance

The Companies Law as amended contains provisions in Article 58 which prohibit the giving of financial assistance in connection with the purchase by a Jersey company of its own shares, but allows, subject to certain limitations and safeguards, financial assistance to be given, (i) in the ordinary course of the company's business, (ii) by means of a lawful distribution of the company's assets to its shareholders, for the purpose of an employees share scheme, (iii) by way of loans to employees (other than directors) to finance the purchase of shares, or (iv) subject to such financial assistance being authorised by a special resolution (both of the company giving assistance and of a holding company which is not itself a wholly owned subsidiary) provided that immediately after the assistance has been given the company is able to comply with minimum solvency requirements. Occasionally, the requirement that the holding company of the company giving the financial assistance provide a members' special resolution as part of the 'white wash' gives rise to difficulties.

11.8.3.8 Disclosure of directors' interests

There is an obligation upon directors to disclose, whether generally, or in a particular case, the existence and extent of an interest in a transaction in respect of which the director has a material conflict.

11.8.3.9 Commercial benefit

The directors of a Jersey company are under a duty to act honestly and in good faith with a view to the best interest of the company and, although a breach of such duty (arising if the directors resolve that the company should enter into a transaction for which there is no commercial benefit to the company) may give rise to an action by the shareholders against the directors. Knowledge or deemed knowledge of the breach of duty may also give rise to a lender being unable to enforce the obligations against the company, or their being set aside on insolvency. The lender should seek to establish that the appropriate consideration has been given by the directors to the existence of commercial benefit to the company, or, in any marginal case (most frequently those involving the grant of upstream guarantees), ensure (i) that the shareholders authorise and require the directors to enter into the transaction, (ii) that the directors note and act on the shareholders' authority and request, and (iii) that the directors note on relevant evidence the solvency of the company.

11.8.3.10 Transactions at an undervalue/preferences

The Companies Law as amended contains provisions, in relation to an insolvent winding-up, which allow a liquidator or the Viscount (an officer of the States of Jersey) to set aside *transactions at an undervalue* or *preferences*. In relation to transactions at an undervalue there is an unqualified risk period of two years, and a risk period of up to five years if the company was insolvent at the time of the transaction or becomes insolvent in consequence of the transaction.

11.8.3.11 Tax and withholding

The *Income Tax (Jersey) Law 1961* as amended ('the Taxes Law') allows that a company (whether or not incorporated in Jersey) may, for tax purposes, be:

- *resident*, being a company incorporated in Jersey (or incorporated elsewhere but having management and control located in Jersey) which is not an exempt company. A resident company pays tax at the rate of 20% on its profits or gains wherever arising, assessed by reference to financial statements and a tax return for each financial period;
- *exempt*, being a company which, for a relevant financial period, applies for exempt status in accordance with Article 123A of the Taxes Law, on the basis that it is beneficially owned by persons not resident in Jersey for tax purposes (notwithstanding that it may be subject to management and control in Jersey). An exempt company is deemed non-resident and is not assessable to Jersey tax on profits or gains arising from a non-Jersey source or (by concession) on Jersey source bank deposit interest. Exempt status requires a payment of an annual fee of £500.00; or
- an *International Business Company* (IBC), being a company (whether or not incorporated in Jersey) in respect of which prior application has been made to the Comptroller of Income Tax, no later than 31 October of the year of assessment, stating that no Jersey resident has a beneficial interest in the company. An application for status as an IBC must disclose the company's proposed activities and estimate the tax yield. An IBC is deemed resident in Jersey, but is subject to tax on its non-Jersey source income at an effective rate of tax which may vary between 0.5% and 30% and which moves incrementally in bands. A fee of £1200.00 is payable as an advance of tax.

Where the company is an exempt company, and is therefore deemed non-resident, no withholding applies in relation to payments of interest or on distributions. In the case of a company which is resident or an IBC, by concession, there is no withholding in respect of interest payments made to a bona fide bank or building society outside of the island and, otherwise, withholding may only apply where payments are made out of Jersey source income to a person resident in Jersey for tax purposes.

11.8.4 Lending to Jersey trusts

The law of the island of Jersey has consolidated its recognition of trusts into the *Trusts (Jersey) Law 1984* ('the Trusts Law'). For the purpose of this paragraph, references to a 'trust' are references to a Jersey trust, meaning a trust which, in accordance with the Trusts Law, has a proper law being Jersey law (this distinguishes the provisions of the Trusts Law relating to *foreign trusts*). The Trusts Law allows for the proper law of the trust to be changed subject to the terms of the trust instrument. The lender should note the following broad classification by use of trusts under Jersey law.

- *Private trusts*, which may be discretionary (and usually are) and/or vested interest trusts. The Trusts Law as amended makes express provision for the validity (as a matter of Jersey law) of transfers to a Jersey trust of property by a non-resident settlor (of full age and mental capacity) made during the settlor's lifetime notwithstanding any rule applicable under the law of the settlor's domicile restricting the right to dispose of property (*forced heirship*).
- *Unit trusts* (which must be created in writing), used as collective investment fund vehicles.
- *Pension or employee benefit trusts*, which may be used as an efficient vehicle through which to provide employee pension or incentive schemes.
- *Charitable trusts*, which may be used as part of defeasance, asset securitisation, note issues or other financing structure.
- *Non-charitable purpose trusts*, which allow for the creation of a trust without beneficiaries but with a stated non-charitable purpose.

In dealing with a trust as borrower and/or provider of security over property comprising the trust fund, the lender should note the following.

11.8.4.1 Legal personality
The trust does not, itself, have separate legal personality. The trust acts through its trustee or trustees who hold (or have held to their order) title to the trust fund.

11.8.4.2 Due constitution and validity of the trust
The Trusts Law allows for the creation of a trust without requirement for specific form but subject to requirement for certainty of intention to create a trust. There is no requirement for registration of a trust. In most cases the trust will be created by instrument in writing. The exception as to a requirement for form is a unit trust which must be created in writing. The following are primary characteristics of a validly constituted trust:

- there must be property comprising the initial trust fund transferred to the trustee;

- the trust must have two or more trustees, unless originally constituted with only one trustee;
- the trust property may comprise any form of property other than immoveable property under Jersey law;
- the trustee or settlor may also be a beneficiary of the trust;
- other than in the case of a charitable trust, a trust has a maximum duration of 100 years;
- subject to the trust powers, there is the opportunity to accumulate during the entire perpetuity period;
- the trust must, unless it is a charitable or non-charitable purpose trust, in accordance with the Trusts Law and the *Trusts (Amendment No 3) (Jersey) Law 1996*, have one or more beneficiaries;
- in the case of a trust which is a charitable trust it must have an exclusively charitable purpose, and in the case of a non-charitable purpose trust, it must have a person who is an *enforcer*; and
- a trustee must, in the execution of his duties and in the exercise of his powers and discretions, act with due diligence, as would a prudent person, and to the best of his ability and skill observing the utmost good faith.

A trust is invalid to the extent (but only to the extent) that:

- it purports to do anything the doing of which, or purports to confer any right or power or impose any obligation the exercise or carrying out of which, is contrary to the law of Jersey;
- it purports to apply directly to immoveable property situated in Jersey; or
- it is created for a purpose in relation to which there is no beneficiary, not being a charitable purpose or in respect of which purpose there has been no enforcer appointed in respect of a non-charitable purpose trust.

A trust will become invalid to the extent that the court declares that:

- it was established by duress, fraud, mistake, undue influence or misrepresentation;
- the trust is immoral or contrary to public policy;
- the terms of the trust are so uncertain that its performance is rendered impossible.

11.8.4.3 Capacity

The capacity of the trustee and the extent of the trustee's powers are of crucial importance to a lender contracting with the trustee and must be confirmed in accordance with the Trusts Law and the terms of the instrument constituting the trust. The Trusts Law provides that the trustee shall have all of the powers of a beneficial owner, but the lender should obtain and review the trust instrument (or ensure that the lawyers providing a relevant Jersey law opinion have sight of it) to ensure that there are no restrictions on the trustee's powers and that exercise of the relevant trustee powers does not require the consent of a protector, if any.

11.8.4.4 Trustee's liability

Where, pursuant to the Trusts Law, the trustee of a public trust contracts in that disclosed capacity, the trustee's liability to a third party is limited to the value of the trust fund. The lender should note that if transaction documents are expressed to be governed by a law other than the law of Jersey, the trustee is likely to require an express limitation of liability to the value of the trust fund within the transaction documents.

11.8.4.5 Due authorisation

The lender should seek production of a trustee's minute pursuant to which:

- the trustee or trustees properly consider the terms of the proposed transaction and record the benefit to the trust, the discharge of the trust's charitable purpose, or non-charitable purpose;
- there are tabled and considered by the trustee or trustees the transaction documents;
- there are disclosed any trustee's or trustees' interests or conflicts;
- the trustee or trustees resolve to approve the transaction and execute the transaction documents; and
- the trustee or trustees authorise the execution of the transaction documents by their signature.

In the case of a corporate trustee, the lender will, in addition, be concerned with its internal corporate governance and should, therefore, require to be considered, in the context of a relevant foreign law legal opinion, the articles of association and the internal authorised signatory arrangements of the corporate trustee.

11.8.4.6 Tax and withholding

Where the trustee of a Jersey trust is resident in Jersey (and would, therefore, be assessable to tax) by concession no assessment is raised in respect of a trust or settlement the beneficiaries of which are non-resident and in respect of non-Jersey source income. By concession, bank deposit interest accruing to the trust is not assessable to tax. There is no withholding on payments made to beneficiaries who are non-resident, or otherwise in relation to payments made to a non-resident individual.

11.8.5 Lending to partnerships and limited partnerships

For the purpose of this paragraph a limited partnership is taken to be one that is registered in accordance with the *Limited Partnerships (Jersey) Law 1994* ('the Limited Partnerships Law'). Where the lender is dealing with a limited partnership as a prospective borrower and/or grantor of security, the following is relevant as a matter of Jersey law.

11.8.5.1 Legal personality, constitution and valid existence

A limited partnership does not have separate legal personality. The Limited Partnerships Law provides that a limited partnership is established when the Registrar of Limited Partnerships has issued a certificate following the delivery to him of a *declaration* signed by each person who is, on the formation of the limited partnership, to be a general partner, stating:

- the name under which the limited partnership is to be conducted;
- the intended address of the registered office of the limited partnership (which must be in Jersey);
- the full name and address of each general partner or, in the case of a body corporate, the place where it is incorporated and has its registered or principal office;
- the term, if any, for which the limited partnership is to exist or, if for an unlimited duration, a statement to that effect; and
- such other particulars as may be prescribed (at the present time, none has been prescribed).

A certificate issued by the Registrar of Limited Partnerships is conclusive as to the delivery of the declaration and the establishment of the limited partnership. Otherwise, the following are relevant features of a duly constituted and validly existing limited partnership:

- a limited partnership is constituted by an association of one or more general partners and one or more limited partners;
- the limited partnership must have a registered office in the island;
- the limited partnership must have a partnership agreement (meaning any agreement in writing of the partners as to the affairs of the limited partnership and the rights and obligations of the partners amongst themselves) and such agreement, together with each amendment made to it, must be kept at the registered office together with (i) details of the name and address of each limited partner and the percentage or unitised extent of their interest in the limited partnership, (ii) a copy of the declaration of limited partnership and each amendment made to it, (iii) a statement of the amount of any contributions agreed to be made by the limited partners and the time at which, or the events on the happening of which, the contributions are to be made, (iv) a statement of the amount of money and nature and value of any other property contributed by each limited partner and the dates of such contribution, (v) a statement and amount of the contributions returned to the limited partners and the dates of the returns of such contributions and (vi) such

other particulars as may be prescribed (there are no such particulars prescribed to date);

- a limited partner is not liable for the debts or obligations of the limited partnership unless such partner participates in the management of the limited partnership (the Limited Partnership Law expressly excludes certain activities from constituting participation in management, generally allowing limited partners to participate, for example, on investment advisory committees);
- the death, insanity, retirement, bankruptcy, commencement of liquidation proceedings, resignation, insolvency or dissolution of the sole or last remaining general partner will cause the immediate dissolution of the exempted limited partnership which is required forthwith to be wound up in accordance with the provisions of the partnership agreement or orders of the court, unless within 90 days of the date of such dissolution the limited partners unanimously elect one or more new general partners, in which case the exempted limited partnership is deemed to have continued as provided for in the partnership agreement;
- there is no limitation on the number of limited partners; and
- both a general partner and limited partner may be a body corporate.

11.8.5.2 Capacity

The Limited Partnership Law provides that a general partner in a limited partnership has all the rights and powers and is subject to all the restrictions and liabilities of a partner in a partnership without limited partners. Otherwise, in relation to the capacity of a general partner to hold assets for, and incur liabilities on behalf of, the limited partnership, the lender should note the following:

- the general partner does not, without the written consent or ratification of all the limited partners, have any authority to (i) do any act which makes it impossible to carry on the activities of the limited partnership, (ii) possess limited partnership property, or dispose of any rights in limited partnership property, for other than the limited partnership purpose, or (iii) admit a person as a general partner or admit a person as a limited partner unless the right to do so is given in the partnership agreement;
- the general partner is deemed to hold limited partnership property as an asset of the limited partnership in accordance with the terms of the partnership agreement and if there are two or more general partners, they are deemed to hold such property jointly;
- a debt or obligation incurred by a general partner in the conduct of the activities of the limited partnership is a debt or obligation of the limited partnership;
- a limited partnership is insolvent only when the general partner is unable

to discharge the debts and obligations of the limited partnership (excluding liabilities to partners in respect of their partnership interests) as they fall due out of the assets of the limited partnership without recourse to the separate assets of the general partner not contributed to the limited partnership.

The lender should have regard to any restriction or other issue affecting a general partner (where a general partner may be an individual or body corporate domiciled, resident or incorporated outside of the island) and should, as necessary, obtain a further foreign law legal opinion.

11.8.5.3 Due authorisation and execution

Due authorisation of a transaction on behalf of the limited partnership should be resolved upon by the general partners and the lender should obtain and have reviewed in the context of a Jersey foreign law opinion a minute of resolution of the general partners. It may be necessary to consider further foreign law connections if one or more corporate general partners is incorporated outside of the island. For the purpose of determining due execution, it is relevant that the Limited Partnerships Law provides that, where a general partner executes a document on behalf of the limited partnership, it shall be conclusively presumed in favour of any person who is not a partner that the general partner has the authority under which he purports to act and that the executed document has been validly executed.

11.8.5.4 Tax and withholding

The *Income Tax (Jersey) Law 1961* as amended provides specifically for limited partnerships, stating that the limited partnership will not itself be subject to assessment for income tax and that a non-resident partner will not be liable to Jersey income tax except on Jersey source income (but excluding, by longstanding concession, bank deposit interest). The preferred status for a general partner of a limited partnership is that of an exempt company or IBC; either of these enable a general partner to pay interest on loans to the partnership, made by either the limited partners or third parties, without being liable to make a deduction in respect of withholding tax. A tax resident general partner will be required to make an appropriate withholding.

11.8.6 Lending to collective investment funds

A *collective investment fund* is a regulated investment activity undertaken by a body corporate, unit trust (through its trustee) or limited partnership (through its general partner), falling within the scope of the *Collective Investment Funds (Jersey) Law 1988*. The lender should be concerned with the issues of legal personality, capacity, due authorisation and due execution arising from the constitution of the body corporate, trustee of the unit trust or general partner of the limited partnership and should ascertain that all regulatory licences and permissions have been obtained. As a particular issue arising in relation to capacity and due authority, the lender should ensure that there are no *investment restrictions* which prevent either the borrowing or the application of the borrowed moneys in the manner anticipated. It is likely, in addition, in the case of an *open-ended investment scheme* that the assets will be held by a separate *custodian*, who may be required to grant, or join in, any disposition of property by way of security. Similarly, the collective investment fund may operate through a *manager* who would be required to join in the approval and due execution of lending arrangements and transaction documents.

11.8.7 Taking security

Jersey law proceeds on a distinction between immoveable property (*immeuble*) and moveable property (*meuble*) (as to which distinction generally, see Chapter 9 above).

11.8.7.1 Immoveable property
As a matter of Jersey law, immoveable property includes those interests in land and buildings held *à fin d'heritage* (that is, in perpetuity), *rentes* (a form of annuity secured on land), and an *hypothèque conventionnelle simple* (one of two forms of security over land, popularly referred to as an HCS). At the present time, a lease (in respect of which Jersey law draws a distinction between a lease for a period in excess of nine years, a *contract lease* and one for less than nine years, a *paper lease*) is immeuble but not 'biens-fonds' and is incapable of hypothecation or mortgage. An HCS is created through the passing of a contract before the Royal Court. Registration of the resultant Act of the Court in the public registry provides to the lender a preferred security over the subject property but, importantly, does not provide to the lender a 'power of sale'. The lender's rights are to receive the proceeds of sale out of the *désastre* (bankruptcy) of the debtor in priority to other creditors, or to foreclose and buy-in the property free from subsequent encumbrances and creditors of the debtor, in a process known as *dégrèvement*. A second form of security over immoveable property exists by way of *hypothèque judiciaire* (popularly referred to as an HJ) which is a form of consent judgment registered through a summary judicial process against all of the immoveable property of the borrower as at the date of the HJ, or against designated immoveable property of the debtor. Again, it accords the lender no power of sale and only the same remedies are available as in the case of an HCS. The primary distinction between the two forms of security lies in the fact that, historically, the HJ

has been taken in a form which allowed for registration at a subsequent time, thereby saving the stamp duty costs arising on registration, and the fact that the HJ only protects the lender's secured priority against a third-party purchaser for a period of ten years. Although it is not possible to obtain either an HCS or HJ over leasehold interests, it is not uncommon for leasehold interests to be held through a limited liability company with exclusive rights of occupation of the relevant property, so that the shares of such company can be made the subject matter of a security (popularly referred to as a 'share transfer').

11.8.7.2 Tangible moveable property
Jersey law allows for a pledge (*gage*) of tangible moveable property or chattels, provided that possession is granted to the secured party or somebody on the secured party's behalf.

11.8.7.3 Intangible moveable property
The taking of security over intangible moveable property is subject to a statutory framework provided by the *Security Interests (Jersey) Law 1983* ('the Security Interests Law'). Article 14 of the Security Interests Law provides that, as a matter of the law of the island of Jersey, a security interest may only be created in accordance with the Security Interests Law. The Security Interests Law defines a 'security interest' as an interest in intangible 'moveable property' that secures payment or performance of an obligation and defines moveable property as all property, wherever situated, whether tangible or intangible, vested, contingent, or future, which is not regarded by the law of Jersey as 'immeuble', and includes choses in action. For practical purposes, therefore, the lender may take by way of security cash and securities (including cash and securities in a portfolio subject to change) in accordance with the modes of creation provided for by Article 2 of the Security Interests Law. Article 2 provides for the creation of a security interest pursuant to a security agreement in respect of the following specified property and in the following specified way:

- in the case of a cash deposit maintained with the lender pursuant to control vested in the lender;
- in the case of certificates of title representing securities pursuant to possession of such certificates of title by the lender or somebody on the lender's behalf;
- in the case of a policy of life assurance pursuant to possession of the policy; and
- in the case of other intangible moveable property provided that the lender has title to the intangible moveable property and notice of the creation of a security interest has been given to the party from whom the debtor held such title.

The reference in the fourth point above to a security interest being held by way of title is a reference to the obtaining of security, for example over a bank account maintained with a third-party bank or securities, by way of 'assignment'. Whether a security interest is created pursuant to control, possession or assignment, it must be granted pursuant to a 'security agreement' complying with the provisions of Article 3 of the Security Interests Law, which requires that a security agreement must:

- be in writing;
- be signed by the debtor;
- contain specified events of default;
- contain sufficient particulars of the collateral, and of the secured obligation to enable them to be identified; and
- be dated.

A security interest granted in accordance with the law allows the lender a secured priority in the bankruptcy of the borrower (and, if the lender has taken security by way of title, precludes the property from vesting in the Viscount or a liquidator) and grants to the lender a power of sale exercisable after an event of default. Exercise of the rights of the power of sale requires:

- an order of the Royal Court, unless such a requirement is waived in the security agreement;
- notice to the borrower of the event of default breached; and
- if the event of default breached is capable of remedy, the expiry of a period of 14 days.

11.8.8 The use of powers of attorney in connection with the grant of a security interest

The *Powers of Attorney (Jersey) Law 1995* provides, in Article 5, for the creation in connection with the grant of a security interest of a form of power of attorney in favour of the lender which survives the bankruptcy of the borrower. It is, therefore, possible to obtain a security interest over intangible moveable property such as certificates of title to securities by way of possession, provided that such security may be perfected by the obtaining of title through the exercise of the power of attorney both before and after an insolvency or bankruptcy event of default.

11.8.9 Floating charges

The law of the island of Jersey does not recognise the concept of a floating charge. As has been noted, Article 12 of the Security Interests Law does, however, provide that a person having capacity to grant a security right under a foreign law is deemed to have such capacity under the law of the island. Accordingly, a Jersey company may grant a floating charge security and, indeed, fixed charges under a foreign law, albeit that such floating charge and/or fixed charge might not be valid and enforceable against property with a Jersey *situs* (or property to which, otherwise, Jersey law may apply). The lender will, generally, find that debentures and fixed and floating charges granted by Jersey companies under English law (including fixed charges which incorporate floating charges) will lead to a qualification in a Jersey foreign law opinion indicating that the borrower or grantor has capacity to enter into the charge but that the Royal Court may not uphold its validity insofar as it purports to extend, or it is sought to be enforced, against property with a Jersey *situs*.

11.8.10 Guarantees

The law of the island of Jersey recognises the concept of an obligation entered into by a party (the guarantor) for the liabilities of another (the principal), as guarantor, surety and/or indemnifier. If the guarantee is taken subject to Jersey law, it should contain waivers of Jersey customary law rights which would otherwise require the principal and/or any other guarantor or surety to be joined in any proceedings taken for enforcement against the guarantor and/or require that the guarantor contributes rateably in respect of the principal's indebtedness. A guarantee taken under the law of Jersey should also contain provisions preserving the rights of the lender to the guarantee obligations and any underlying security where a liability of the principal may be subject to a claim by a liquidator or the Viscount of voidable preference. It is arguable that the *Security Interests (Jersey) Law 1983* does not allow for the creation of a third-party or surety-type security interest, and the better view may be that the lender should require the grantor to secure a guarantee obligation.

11.8.11 Requirements for registration, filing and recording

Although there is a Companies Registry (maintained by the Financial Services Department), and a Registry of Limited Partnerships, there is no requirement that security given over moveables (that is, by pledge or security interest) be registered or recorded. Likewise, there is no requirement for registration or recording of the grant of security in any formal record maintained at the company's or limited partnership's Jersey registered office (although the relevant minute should record the approval of the grant of such security). A grant of security over immoveable property with a Jersey *situs* requires the passing of a contract before the Royal Court and registration in the Public Registry (a register maintained in relation to ownership of and rights in immoveable property in Jersey). Mortgages given over ships registered in Jersey must be registered with the Registrar of Ships in Jersey.

11.9 Enforcement

The Royal Court in Jersey will register and enforce a foreign judgment if it complies with the provisions of the *Judgments (Reciprocal Enforcement) (Jersey) Law 1960* in that it is a judgment of a superior court of a country in respect of which reciprocity exists (at the present time, the United Kingdom, Guernsey and the Isle of Man). In addition to being a judgment of a reciprocating territory, the judgment must be made by a superior court and must be final and conclusive. Any judgment registered may be set aside if the Royal Court is satisfied that the court making the original order did not have jurisdiction (for this purpose the lender should ensure that relevant transaction documents contain a contractual submission to jurisdiction of the original court) or that, otherwise, the judgment is in respect of tax or contrary to the public policy of the island.

11.9.1 Interim relief

Where the lender is concerned to restrain the borrower from dissipating property pre or post a prospective judgment or other enforcement, the Royal Court will provide relief by way of *Mareva-type injunctions* and *tracing orders.* For such relief to be available, however, the lender must demonstrate either a proprietary claim to the property or assets concerned and not merely a debt claim, or that, otherwise, the Royal Court has jurisdiction (either on the basis of reciprocal enforcement or on the basis of presence or the ability to serve the borrower) before it will grant such relief.

11.9.2 Investigation and obtaining of evidence

At para 11.5 above, a general description has been given of the duty of confidence owed by bankers and professions under the law of Jersey. The Royal Court in Jersey will act in aid of a foreign court in non-Jersey civil proceedings for the purpose of taking evidence pursuant to the *Taking of Evidence (Jersey) Law 1960* where the relevant evidence could be taken in the form requested as a matter of the law of Jersey. A deposit-taker registered under the *Banking Business (Jersey) Law 1991* may be required to comply with an order under the *Bankers Books Evidence (Jersey) Law*

1986 if such institution is a party to proceedings or an order is made by the court for special cause. Pursuant to the *Investigation of Fraud (Jersey) Law 1991* as amended the Attorney-General may, at the request of a foreign investigating authority and on being satisfied that such foreign investigation authority is conducting an investigation relating to serious fraud, issue a notice to a person, requiring the delivery up of information and materials to the Attorney-General. Although the Royal Court will not make an order for the provision of information and delivery up of materials in proceedings brought in respect of a foreign tax liability, where serious tax fraud is in issue, the Attorney-General may provide a notice under the *Investigation of Fraud (Jersey) Law 1991.*

11.9.3 Winding-up and bankruptcy

A company incorporated under the *Companies (Jersey) Law 1991* (that is, a Jersey company) may be wound up in accordance with the provisions of that law either on the coming to an end of a period stated in its memorandum for its existence, or pursuant to a special resolution of its shareholders, in each case as a summary winding-up, provided that the directors are able to make a declaration of solvency. Otherwise, the Jersey company can, pursuant to a special resolution of its shareholders (but not pursuant to any form of proceeding by creditors) be wound up in a creditors' winding-up on the basis that it is insolvent. In a creditors' winding-up, a liquidator (who must be a member of one of the English accountancy bodies) must be appointed. In addition to an insolvent creditors' winding-up of a Jersey company, a person (which expression includes a Jersey or foreign company) may be subject to a *désastre* pursuant to the *Bankruptcy (Désastre) (Jersey) Law 1990.* A désastre, which is commenced by notice to the Viscount, commences by the making of an order by the Royal Court otherwise on the *ex parte* application of the debtor, creditor, or in the case of a company, its directors or shareholders. The making of the declaration *en désastre* vests all of the property of the debtor or borrower in the Viscount who, alone, may exercise interests and powers of the bankrupt. The Viscount, generally, retains external professionals to assist in complex désastres and/or to realise assets. Holders of security by way of HCS, HJ or of a security interest will be secured creditors in the désastre. In the case of immoveable property (or in the case of moveable property where the lender does not have title) the title nevertheless vests in the Viscount who will have conduct of the realisation process and whose costs will be recovered from the sale proceeds prior to distribution to the secured lender. A further insolvency or recovery process is that of *dégrèvement.* This process, which is a form of foreclosure, applies only to immoveable property situated in the island, whether owned by an individual or company. The procedure is carried out by an officer of the Royal Court (the *Judicial Greffier*) who, pursuant to an Act of the Royal Court, convenes creditors of the debtor who are, in reverse order of their priority, required to either take the relevant immoveable property of the debtor subject to all prior encumbrances, or renounce their own interest therein. Accordingly, where the lender has a first priority HCS or HJ it will, in general, have the opportunity to have title to such property vested in it free and clear of subsequent encumbrances. Once having title, the lender may sell the property and retain the entire sale proceeds. Where there is likely to be a surplus arising on the sale of immoveable property subject to a lender's security, the debtor may apply for relief from the *dégrèvement* proceedings in the form either of a *remise*, or apply himself for a *désastre* so that such surplus is available to meet creditors generally.

11.10 Double taxation treaties

At the present time, Jersey has double taxation treaties in existence with the United Kingdom and Guernsey.

11.11 Miscellaneous issues in relation to a Jersey foreign law opinion

There are no generally available public registers likely to disclose the identity of a Jersey company which is a private limited company and, therefore, to the extent that this information is required by a lender, it must generally be sought in the form of a certificate or declaration given by the directors or secretary to the company. Similarly, there is no generally available register of pending litigation, so that, again, it is necessary to rely on contractual representations and warranties by the borrower. Where an opinion is required to deal with the existence or otherwise of insolvency or bankruptcy, because a creditors' winding-up may be commenced pursuant to a special resolution of shareholders which may not have been filed at the Companies Registry on the date of a search (the *Companies (Jersey) Law 1991* requires that such registration takes place within 21 days) and, further, because a désastre may be commenced by *ex parte* application, it is not possible to say with absolute certainty for the purposes of an opinion that the borrower is not subject to an insolvency process.

11.12 Recent or anticipated developments

On 24 September 1996 the States of Jersey approved the third reading of the *Limited Liability Partnerships (Jersey) Law*. The law, which was, effectively, promoted by three of the United Kingdom's leading accountancy firms, is perceived as meeting the need for the partners of leading United Kingdom professional firms to be able to protect their personal assets from the increasing risks of litigation, while enabling partners to continue their business within a traditional partnership structure. Under the law, a limited liability partnership will remain totally liable for its debts and any losses caused by it. The limited liability partnership will have a legal personality distinct from that of its partners. A partnership wishing to become a limited liability partnership will need to register a *declaration* with the Registrar of Limited Liability Partnerships in Jersey. The limited liability partnership will require to include within its name the words *Limited Liability Partnership* or *LLP* and the limitation in liability will require to be disclosed in all correspondence and invoices of the partnership. The limited liability partnership will require to have a registered office in Jersey, where its books and records will be maintained (and which must disclose the names and addresses of the partners) together with a copy of the partnership agreement. A Jersey limited liability partnership will be required to provide a security in the sum of not less than £5 million, to be available on the dissolution of the partnership for the benefit of creditors.

12 Guernsey

Introduction

The island of Guernsey comprises a part of the smaller of two Bailiwicks which make up the Channel Islands. The Bailiwick of Guernsey comprises the island of Guernsey, together with the smaller islands of Alderney, Herm, Sark and Jethou. The main island is approximately 25 square miles in area and is located some 30 miles west of the Normandy peninsula and some 80 miles from the coast of south-west England. The principal population centre (and the location of most of the financial institutions and professional support services) is that of St Peter Port, located on the east coast of the island. The island has a population of approximately 60 000, predominantly English-speaking.

12.1 Currency and exchange control

The currency of Guernsey is sterling. The island nevertheless prints its own notes and mints its own coins, which are legal tender within the Bailiwick. There is no exchange control applicable to the island.

12.2 Constitution

Guernsey is regarded as being politically stable. It forms part of the British Isles (as a Crown dependency) but is not part of the United Kingdom. Guernsey's relationship with the English Crown is fundamental to its constitution, in that Guernsey was, prior to the invasion of England by William the Conqueror, part of the Duchy of Normandy. When, in 1204, the English Crown lost its lands in mainland Normandy, Guernsey remained loyal to the English Crown, which has over the centuries accorded to Guernsey the right to internal self-governance and, in particular, the right to a separate judiciary and to control of its own fiscal affairs. The States of Deliberation acts as the originating source of permanent primary legislation which requires sanction by Her Majesty in Council before becoming law in the island. The island's Lieutenant-Governor is a representative of the English Crown in the island, and the Bailiff and law officers are appointees of the Crown subject to consultation with the insular authorities. The United Kingdom retains responsibility for the defence and external affairs of the island. A treaty obligation entered into by the United Kingdom which is either silent as to its territorial extent or makes reference to territories for whose international affairs Her Majesty's government is responsible, is taken to extend to Guernsey, but the Home Office consults with the island's authorities prior to accession to treaties.

12.3 Legal system

As with Jersey, Guernsey's legal system is drawn from Norman customary source. The island's law relating to immoveable property, its contract law and law relating to testate and intestate succession reflect such roots and require reference to Norman French jurisprudence. Otherwise, the modern legislation of the States of Deliberation passes into law in the English language and, both in the framework for such legislation and in its interpretation, draws on the experience of the legislature and courts of the United Kingdom. The island has its own separate judiciary, the principal court of which is the Royal Court of Guernsey. The Royal Court administers civil and criminal justice through the office of the Bailiff, Deputy Bailiff, 12 Jurats and a Greffier. The Jurats (who sit as arbiters of fact) represent the independence of the island's judiciary as an ancient office capable of being traced back in time beyond the consolidation of the English Crown and Duchy of Normandy. In civil matters, appeals from the Royal Court are to the Guernsey Court of Appeal, comprising the Bailiff, the Bailiff of Jersey and senior English barristers and Scottish advocates. From the Guernsey Court of Appeal, appeal lies to the Judicial Committee of the Privy Council. Proceedings in the Royal Court are now conducted in English, although the principal language for the conveyance of land remains French.

12.4 Constitutional relationship with the European Union

In common with Jersey and the Isle of Man, Guernsey's relationship with the European Union is determined in accordance with *Protocol No 3 to the Treaty of Accession (1972)*, so that the island has preserved its constitutional position relative to the English Crown together with its fiscal independence. Guernsey is within the provisions of the Treaty of Rome for the purpose of the *Common External Tariff* and the *Agricultural Levy System* and (save for particular arrangements in relation to certain agricultural produce) enjoys free trade in goods with Member States of the European Union. Otherwise, the island is not required to apply European Union directives relating to, for example, movement of capital, company law, and the provision of financial services in insurance and banking.

12.5 Banking and professional confidentiality

Guernsey has no statutory framework for bank or professional secrecy. Banking and other professional confidentiality arises as a matter of common law, and as an express or implied contractual obligation. Consequently, the Royal Court in Guernsey has regard to the principles set out in the English decision of *Tournier v National Provincial and Union Bank of England* [1924] 1 K.B. 461, the principles of which are likely to be applied as persuasive.

12.5.1 Guernsey companies: disclosure of beneficial ownership

It is a requirement on incorporation of a Guernsey company that its ultimate beneficial ownership be disclosed to the Guernsey Financial Services Commission. This information is not available on public files and is held as confidential by the Guernsey Financial Services Commission.

12.5.2 Disclosure to bankers by financial intermediaries

Know-your-customer standards reflected in the draft Guernsey Guidance Notes (see below, para 12.7.7) require an account-holding bank or financial intermediary to obtain and retain on its records details of underlying beneficial ownership of accounts and the sources of funds.

12.5.3 Disclosure under compulsion of law

Bankers and other professionals may be subject to an order to disclose made pursuant to the *Criminal Justice (Fraud Investigation) (Bailiwick of Guernsey) Law 1991* which applies to investigations involving serious or complex fraud whether within or without the island, the *Drug Trafficking*

Offences (Bailiwick of Guernsey) Law 1988, the *Prevention of Terrorism (Bailiwick of Guernsey) Law 1990*, the *Income Tax (Guernsey) Laws 1975-1990* and the *Bankers' Books Evidence (Guernsey) Law 1954* and, otherwise, in accordance with an order of the Royal Court made pursuant to its jurisdiction in proceedings before it.

12.6 Regulation in the financial sector

Financial regulation in Guernsey is conducted through the Guernsey Financial Services Commission (popularly referred to as either *the Commission* or *the GFSC*). The Commission operates as the primary regulator in accordance with the terms of the following key items of legislation.

- The *Protection of Depositors (Bailiwick of Guernsey) Ordinance 1971* as amended, pursuant to which the Commission acts as supervisory authority.
- The *Insurance Business (Guernsey Law) 1986*, pursuant to which the Commission acts as supervisory authority in respect of insurers and insurance managers.
- The *Protection of Investors (Bailiwick of Guernsey) Law 1987*, pursuant to which the Commission supervises the constitution and management of collective investment schemes or mutual funds.
- The *Control of Borrowing (Bailiwick of Guernsey) Ordinance 1959*.

More generally, the Commission is charged with the effective supervision and development of the finance sector in Guernsey, reporting to the States Advisory and Finance Committee. Guernsey is, through its connection with the United Kingdom, a party to the Organisation for Economic Co-operation and Development and has designated territory status for the purposes of the *United Kingdom Financial Services Act 1986*, s. 87.

12.7 Anti-money laundering legislation and best practice

Guernsey, like Jersey, is not an FATF country. Its position is reflected in the Guidance Notes for Mainstream Banking, Lending and Deposit Taking Activities issued by the Joint Money Laundering Steering Group pursuant to the United Kingdom Money Laundering Regulations which, in a footnote to paragraph 49, suggests that Guernsey is judged to meet the FATF required standard, so as to be assumed to pass the *equivalence tests*. The legislative regime in place in relation to the combating of money laundering is as follows.

12.7.1 The Drug Trafficking Offences (Bailiwick of Guernsey) Law 1988

The *Drug Trafficking Offences (Bailiwick of Guernsey) Law 1988* makes provision for:

- the making and enforcement of confiscation orders against persons convicted of drug trafficking offences;
- the offence of assisting drug traffickers to retain the proceeds or benefits of trafficking;
- the offence of making any disclosure likely to prejudice an investigation; and
- the making of production and enforcement orders in relation to production of and access to materials required in connection with a police investigation.

The offence of assisting a drug trafficker to retain the proceeds or benefits of drug trafficking is committed by a person:

- who knows or suspects that another is a drug trafficker or has benefited from trafficking; and
- who is concerned in an arrangement which facilitates the retention or control of such proceeds by the drugs trafficker, or which facilitates the acquisition of property by way of investment.

It is a defence to the offence to show:

- that he has disclosed to a police officer his relevant suspicion or belief, either before the doing of the act concerned (being an act done with the consent of the police officer), or after the act but voluntarily and as soon as is reasonable; or
- that he did not know or suspect that the arrangement related to another's proceeds of drug trafficking; or
- that he did not know that he was facilitating such control; or
- that, although he intended to make disclosure to a police officer, there is reasonable excuse for his not doing so.

Where disclosure is made to a police officer, there is deemed to be no breach of any duty of confidentiality. Disclosure is made by banks and other institutions in a standard disclosure format to the Financial Investigation Unit of the Guernsey police.

12.7.2 Drug Trafficking (Amendment) (Bailiwick of Guernsey) Law 1992

The *Drug Trafficking (Amendment) (Bailiwick of Guernsey) Law 1992* provides for the offence of concealing or transferring the proceeds of drug trafficking in order to avoid prosecution or the impact of a confiscation order.

12.7.3 The Prevention of Terrorism (Bailiwick of Guernsey) Law 1990

The *Prevention of Terrorism (Bailiwick of Guernsey) Law 1990* provides for:

- the making and enforcement of exclusion orders against persons concerned in the commission, preparation or instigation of acts of terrorism or similar matters connected with Northern Ireland;
- the offence of provision of financial assistance for terrorism; and
- the offence of assisting another in the retention or control of terrorist funds.

The offence of assisting another in the retention or control of terrorist funds is committed by a person who enters into or is concerned in an arrangement whereby the retention or control of terrorist funds by or on behalf of another is facilitated. It is a defence to show:

- that the assistance is given with the consent of a police officer, or followed by timely voluntary disclosure;
- that the person did not know or believe that the arrangement related to terrorist funds;
- that, although the person intended to make disclosure to a police officer, there is reasonable excuse for his not doing so.

Where disclosure is made to a police officer there is deemed to be no breach of any duty of confidentiality.

12.7.4 Money Laundering (Disclosure of Information) (Guernsey) Law 1995

The *Money Laundering (Disclosure of Information) (Guernsey) Law 1995* provides for an immunity from any duty of confidentiality in favour of a person who discloses a reasonable suspicion concerning the proceeds of criminal conduct (*criminal proceeds*), or information or document-ation relating to such proceeds to an 'officer' (being HM Procureur, a police officer, a customs and excise officer, or any servant of the Commission).

12.7.5 The Criminal Justice (Fraud Investigation) (Bailiwick of Guernsey) Law 1991

This law allows application to be made to the Attorney-General by an authority engaged in the investigation of serious fraud, for an order requiring persons to produce documents or for copies of such documents to be taken. Such material obtained may be used for the prosecution of an offence either within the island or elsewhere. Information covered by legal professional privilege is excluded from the ambit of a notice issued under the law and, in relation to documents and materials in the custody and control of those engaged in banking business or the provision of trustee services, disclosure can only be given either with the consent of a relevant person, or on the specific direction in the notice of the Attorney-General.

12.7.6 Company Securities (Insider Dealing) (Bailiwick of Guernsey) Law 1989

This law makes it an offence for a person to deal with securities listed on a recognised stock exchange where such person is connected with the relevant company and where (i) such person holds information by virtue of being connected with the company, (ii) the information arising from the connection is of a type which it would be reasonable to expect such person not to disclose except for the proper performance of the position from which his connection arises, and (iii) such person knows that the relevant information is *unpublished price-sensitive information* in relation to the relevant securities. For the purposes of the law, a person is connected with a company if they are (i) a director of the relevant company, or of an associated company, (ii) an officer or employee of that company, or (iii) engaged in a business transaction or relationship either directly with the company or related company or as an employee of a company so engaged.

12.7.7 Guidance notes

At the present time, the Commission has circulated in draft form a set of Guidance Notes intended to apply to those institutions licensed in relation to banking business and those licensed in relation to collective investment schemes. There is no present indication of when, if at all, regulations in the form of the draft are likely to be introduced.

12.8 Lending with a Guernsey foreign law connection

We will now look at those issues which may arise in connection with a lending which has a Guernsey foreign law connection in that either the borrower is domiciled, resident and/or incorporated or constituted in the island, or because a transaction or security document has a proper or applicable law which is Guernsey law. The paragraphs which next follow highlight, by reference to borrower type (building on the issues set out in Chapters 4, 5, 6 and 7), issues which arise for a lender where the borrower is domiciled, resident or incorporated in Guernsey. For each borrower type the issues considered are those which will, in the usual course, form the subject matter of a Guernsey foreign law opinion, being:

- legal personality (i.e. does the borrower have a separate legal existence, and if not, who may contract on behalf of the borrower?);
- capacity;
- due authorisation of the transaction;
- due execution; and
- taxation, including withholding.

Following examination of the above issues in relation to borrower types, the remaining paragraphs deal collectively with:

- the creation of security;
- enforcement and insolvency; and
- recent or anticipated developments.

12.8.1 Capacity to grant a foreign law security

The *Security Interests (Guernsey) Law 1993* provides in section 10 that a person resident, domiciled, or incorporated in Guernsey is not to be considered as lacking capacity, or as ever having lacked capacity to give security governed by a *foreign law* over *property* situated outside of Guernsey, by reason only that the law of Guernsey does not permit security to be given by the method or in the circumstances permitted by the foreign law. For this purpose *property* means any property, whether tangible or intangible, whether vested, contingent or future, and moveable property which would be regarded by the law of Guernsey as *immeubles*.

12.8.2 Lending to natural persons

An individual is a minor and without legal capacity to contract until the age of 18 years.

12.8.3 Lending to companies

The legislative framework relating to a company incorporated under the law of Guernsey is now consolidated in the *Companies (Guernsey) Law 1994* (consolidating the pre-existing companies laws 1907–90) ('the

Companies Law'). In relation to a company incorporated under the Companies Law, the lender should note the following.

12.8.3.1 Legal personality, due incorporation and good standing

Registration is conducted by Guernsey lawyers by application first to the Commission and then to the Royal Court. The Companies Law provides only for the registration of a company limited by shares. The Companies Law draws no distinction through designation between private and public companies, although it imposes reporting obligations in relation to allotments on those companies circulating a prospectus or otherwise issuing shares to the public – see also provisions relating to control of borrowing set out at para 12.8.3.5 below. Otherwise in relation to due incorporation the lender should note the following:

- a company is duly incorporated when its memorandum of association has been registered pursuant to the authority of an Act of the Royal Court;
- the Register of Companies is maintained by the *Judicial Greffier* (an officer of the Royal Court);
- the Companies Law requires that there be at least two founder members (accordingly, at the present time, the Companies Law does not provide for single member companies) although beneficial ownership may be held by a single person through nominee share ownership;
- a company incorporated by registration has continuous and successive existence and may sue and be sued in its own name, exercising all the functions of an incorporated company, including the power to hold land; and
- a company which issues shares to the public may not commence business until it has filed with the Judicial Greffier prescribed details of the shares allotted.

Continued existence and good standing require that the company comply with an obligation to file, within a prescribed period at the beginning of each year, an annual return (stating the position as at 1 January) in relation to (i) the address of the registered office, (ii) the authorised and issued share capital together with the details of registered shareholders, and (iii) details of directors. A company is required to hold an annual general meeting, the first not more than 18 months after incorporation, and thereafter in each calendar year and no more than 15 months may elapse between one meeting and the next. Although, as has been noted in the context of banking and professional confidentiality, details of beneficial ownership are provided to the Commission on incorporation of a company, those details are not available at the Register of Companies or otherwise publicly available to the lender.

12.8.3.2 Capacity

Although the Companies Law provides that on registration a company shall be incorporated for the purposes of the objects set out in its memorandum, it is nevertheless provided (in Part II of the Companies Law under the heading Corporate Capacity) that no act of a company shall be invalidated on the ground of lack of capacity by reason of anything contained in or omitted from the company's memorandum. This provision can be read together with that relating to the contents of the memorandum of association which provides that where a company's memorandum states that the object or one of the objects of the company is to carry on business *as a general commercial company*, such object shall be to carry on any trade or business whatsoever, and the company shall have power to do anything incidental or conducive to the carrying on by it of any trade or business. Such a provision may be relevant as, otherwise, the Companies Law provides that the directors shall be under a duty to observe any limitation on their powers imposed by or deriving from the company's memorandum. As regards third parties dealing with the company in good faith, the power of the company's directors to bind the company, or authorise others to do so, is deemed to be free of any limitation imposed by or deriving from (i) the company's memorandum or articles of association, (ii) any resolution of the company, or (iii) any agreement between the company's members. For this purpose, a person deals with a company if he is party to a transaction or other act to which the company is a party, is presumed to have acted in good faith unless the contrary is proved, and is not regarded as acting in bad faith solely because he knows that an act is beyond the directors' powers. A party to a transaction with a company is not bound to enquire as to whether the transaction is permitted by the company's memorandum or as to any limitation on the directors' powers to bind the company or to authorise others to do so. Part III of the Companies Law provides for the alteration of the memorandum and articles of association of a company in accordance with the provisions of the Companies Law.

12.8.3.3 Due authorisation

A company incorporated under the Companies Law acts through its directors, who are bound by a duty to act in accordance with the articles of association and any objects set out in the company's memorandum of association. The Companies Law provides that there must be at least one director (although a sole director cannot also act as company secretary). Notwithstanding the provision of the Companies Law relieving a third party of any obligation to enquire as to any limitation on directors' powers, or otherwise as to due authorisation by the directors or the company of a relevant transaction, the lender should require sight of a minute or extract of minute of the directors dealing with the following:

- confirming that the meeting was duly convened and quorate;
- consideration of the relevant aspects of the proposed transaction and in particular the commercial benefit to the company;
- consideration of the terms of relevant transaction documents;
- approving the execution of transaction documents substantially in the considered form (and as appropriate allowing for the negotiation or agreement of amendments to such documents); and
- stating the manner in which such documents are to be executed, designating one or more persons to attest the common seal of the company or designating individuals as signatories to the documents.

It is suggested that the lender should require review of the relevant minutes by the Guernsey lawyers providing a relevant foreign law opinion and that the relevant opinion as to due authorisation should be given in the context of a stated review of such minutes. The lender should require a certificate given by the directors and/or secretary of the company confirming the identity of the directors of the company as at the date of the relevant minute. Where shareholder resolutions are required the lender should note the following as relevant to shareholder meetings:

- shareholder meetings must be convened by notice in writing (a *convening notice*) given not less than ten days in advance of the meeting to every member of the company, provided that all members entitled to attend and vote at a meeting may agree that a meeting has been duly called and notice of any intention to propose a special resolution is duly given;
- a special resolution is a resolution passed by a majority of not less than three-quarters of the votes recorded at a general meeting in respect of which notice specifying the intention to propose the meeting has been duly given;
- every special resolution must be delivered to the Greffier 21 days after it was passed or, if it is a resolution amending the company's objects and no application has been made for its annulment within 21 days of it being passed, 15 days following the expiry of the 21 days; and
- if the special resolution is not delivered to the Greffier it is void *ab initio* and the company is guilty of an offence.

12.8.3.4 Due execution
A document signed by not less than one director or any other person duly authorised to act on behalf of the company is deemed to have been validly executed for and in the name of the company, save where, pursuant to the Companies Law, a document is required to be executed under the common seal of the company (for example, in the case of the grant of a power of attorney by a company). A company is required to have a common seal bearing its name and is, if permitted by its articles of association, permitted

to have an official seal for use abroad. Where an official seal is in use, the Companies Law provides for the appointment of a person authorised to affix the official seal, such authority to be given in writing under the common seal of the company. A person affixing an official seal is required to certify thereon the date upon which and the place at which it is affixed.

12.8.3.5 Issue of shares and circulation of a prospectus

On the incorporation of a Guernsey company, capital duty in respect of authorised share capital is payable at the rate of 0.5%, up to a maximum of £5000.00. Bearer shares are not permitted. There must be a minimum of two initial subscribers, otherwise there is no minimum capital for a private company and no requirement that shares be paid-up on subscription. Shares may be issued at a premium, in which case the value of the premium must be shown in a *share premium account* which is then treated (with certain limited exceptions) as part of the paid-up capital of the company. Shares may be issued as redeemable shares, provided that there are also in issue non-redeemable shares. The Companies Law provides for the redemption or re-purchase by a company of its own shares, subject to conditions which include prescribed sources of funds (the proceeds of a new issue of shares made for that purpose, distributable profits and the balance on a share premium account), sanctioned by special resolution and subject to the directors being satisfied as to the solvency of the company. The Companies Law provides for the variation by a Guernsey company of its share capital by alteration to its memorandum (pursuant to special resolution), although a capital reduction may only be undertaken in accordance with the Companies Law and pursuant to court sanction. The raising of moneys by the issue of shares above a prescribed amount requires approval pursuant to either the *Borrowing (Control) (Bailiwick of Guernsey) Law 1946* or the *Protection of Investors (Bailiwick of Guernsey) Law 1987* (see below, para 12.8.3.6). The circulation of a prospectus requires consent, pursuant to the same legislation, and, where a company has offered its shares to the public by means of a prospectus or other offering circular, no allotment may be made until there has been subscribed and paid for (i) the amount fixed in the memorandum of articles and disclosed in the prospectus as the minimum subscription, or (ii) if no such amount has been fixed and disclosed, the whole of the share capital offered.

12.8.3.6 Licences and consents

If the activity of the company as borrower is undertaken from or within Guernsey and is banking business, insurance business or that of a collective investment scheme the lender should note the requirement for the appropriate registrations and licences pursuant to the key legislation identified at para 12.6 above. At the present time no registration of licensing applies to the operation of a trust corporation or the provision of services as a financial intermediary. The lender should further confirm that:

- the raising of money by the proposed borrowing does not constitute, in the hands of the borrowing company, the taking of a deposit for the purposes of the *Banking Regulation (Bailiwick of Guernsey) Law*, as it amends the *Protection of Depositors, Companies and Prevention of Fraud (Bailiwick of Guernsey) Law 1969* (a situation which might arise in relation to the issue of certain forms of debt security);
- any consent required for the borrowing or raising of money in the Bailiwick of Guernsey has been obtained in accordance with the *Borrowing (Control) (Bailiwick of Guernsey) Law 1946* and its subordinate ordinances (this law applies, in particular, to the raising of money by the issue of shares, debentures or other securities, but does not require consent in relation to the borrowing of money by any person in the ordinary course of his business from a banking undertaking); and
- no consent is required in connection with the raising of money (as a subscription or investment) in a collective investment scheme as defined by the *Protection of Investors (Bailiwick of Guernsey) Law 1987.*

12.8.3.7 Transactions at an undervalue/preferences

Section 108 of the Companies Law provides that on the application of a liquidator of a company, the Royal Court may, in respect of a preference at a relevant time, make such order as it thinks fit for restoring the position to what it would have been if the company had not given the relevant preference. For the purposes of the section, a preference is given if (i) that person is one of the company's creditors or is a surety or guarantor for any of the company's debts or other liabilities, and (ii) the company does anything or permits anything to be done which improves that person's position in the company's liquidation. A date is a relevant date when it is the earlier of (i) the date of any application for the compulsory winding-up of the company, or (ii) the date of the passing by the company of any resolution to voluntarily wind up the company and such date occurs within a period of six months preceding the commencement of such winding-up. The court may, however, only make such an order on its being of the opinion that (i) the company was at the time of giving the preference (or became as a result of giving the preference) unable to pay its debts, and (ii) the company was influenced in deciding to give a preference by a desire to produce the improvement of the creditors' position in the company's insolvency.

12.8.3.8 Tax and withholding

The *Income Tax (Guernsey) Law 1950* as amended allows that a company (whether or not incorporated in Guernsey) may, for tax purposes, be:

- *resident*, being a company incorporated in Guernsey for tax purposes if it does not apply to be an exempt company, or if it carries on a trade or profession in Guernsey. A resident company pays tax at the rate of 20% on its profits or gains wherever arising, assessed by reference to audited accounts and a tax return for each financial period;

- *exempt*, being a company which for a financial period applies for exempt status on the basis that it is beneficially owned by persons not resident in Guernsey for tax purposes (notwithstanding that it may be subject to management and control in Guernsey). An exempt company is not assessable to Guernsey tax on profits or gains arising from a non-Guernsey source or on Guernsey source income which is deposit interest, income arising through investment in another exempt company or in an exempt collective investment scheme. Exempt status requires a payment of an annual fee of £500.00; or

- *an international company*, being a Guernsey company which has applied for and obtained from the Administrator of Income Tax in Guernsey such status as being a company beneficially owned by persons non-resident in Guernsey for tax purposes. An international company is deemed to be resident in Guernsey but will be subject to tax on its non-Guernsey source income at an effective rate of tax negotiated as being a rate between 0% and 30% and agreed in advance with the Administrator of Income Tax.

A Guernsey resident company is required to make a withholding of tax at standard rate in relation to dividends, salaries to employees and directors' fees and an exempt or international company may likewise be required to make a withholding from payments made out of Guernsey source income.

12.8.4 Lending to Guernsey trusts

The law of Guernsey has consolidated its recognition of trusts pursuant to the *Trusts (Guernsey) Laws, 1989 and 1990* ('the Trusts Law'). For the purpose of this section, references to a 'trust' are references to a Guernsey trust, being a trust which, in accordance with the Trusts Law, has a proper law which is Guernsey law (this distinguishes the provisions of the Trusts Law relating to *foreign trusts*). The Trusts Law allows for a trust to change its proper law.

The lender should note the following broad classification by use of trusts under Guernsey law.

- *Private trusts*, which may be fixed or vested interest trusts and/or discretionary (which is usual). In such private trusts, which may have the object of estate planning, the validity of the transfer into trust is not, in the case of a Guernsey proper law trust, brought into question through the absence of a recognition of trusts under a foreign law or through the operation of *forced heirship rules*.

- *Unit trusts* (which must be created in writing), used as collective investment fund vehicles.
- *Pension or employee benefits trusts*, used as an efficient vehicle through which to provide employee pension or incentive schemes.
- *Charitable trusts*, which are most likely to be encountered as part of a defeasance, asset securitisation, note issue or other financing structure.

In dealing with a Guernsey trust as a borrower and/or provider of security over property comprising the trust fund, the lender should note the following.

12.8.4.1 Legal personality

The trust does not, itself, have separate legal personality. The trust acts through its trustee or trustees who hold (or have held to their order) title to the trust fund.

12.8.4.2 Due constitution and validity of the trust

There are no requirements as to due form for the creation of a trust under the Trusts Law, save that a unit trust must be created in writing. There is no requirement for registration of a trust. The following are primary characteristics of a duly constituted valid trust pursuant to the Trusts Law:

- the trust may be constituted orally, in writing, or otherwise howsoever (a unit trust must be constituted in writing) and may be constituted by settlement of trust property or by declaration;
- the trust must have two or more trustees, unless originally constituted with only one trustee, or with a sole trustee which is a corporate trustee incorporated in Guernsey;
- the trust property may comprise any form of property other than immoveable property under Guernsey law;
- the trustee of the trust is under a duty to act in the best interests of the trust (*en bon père de famille*), that is, in good faith in relation to the trust and its assets as would a prudent man in relation to his own family's assets;
- a trustee or settlor may also be a beneficiary of the trust;
- a trust may have a 'protector' as a person required to provide consent to exercise of powers by the trustees;
- a trust may have a maximum duration of 100 years;
- trust income may be accumulated during the perpetuity period; and
- the title of the trustee to property transferred into trust by a non-resident settlor during his lifetime is not (as a matter of Guernsey law) invalidated by the operation of *forced heirship rules*.

A trust is invalid:

- if it purports to do anything contrary to Guernsey law;
- if it confers any right or function on the trustee, the exercise or discharge of which would be contrary to the law of the island;
- if it has no ascertainable beneficiaries (and is not a charitable purpose trust); or
- upon the declaration of the Royal Court of Guernsey.

12.8.4.3 Capacity

The capacity of the trustee and the extent of the trustee's powers are of crucial importance to a lender contracting with the trustee and must be confirmed in accordance with the Trusts Law and the terms of the instrument constituting the trust. The Trusts Law provides that the trustee shall have all of the powers of a beneficial owner, but the lender should obtain and review the trust instrument (or ensure that the lawyers providing a relevant Guernsey law opinion have sight of it) to ensure that there are no restrictions on the trustee's powers and that exercise of the relevant trustee powers does not require the consent of a protector, if any.

12.8.4.4 Trustee's liability to third parties

Where, pursuant to the Trusts Law, the trustee of a Guernsey trust contracts in that disclosed capacity, the trustee's liability to a third party is limited to the value of the trust fund. The lender should note that if transaction documents are expressed to be governed by a law other than the law of Guernsey, the trustee is likely to require an express limitation of liability to the value of the trust fund within the transaction documents.

12.8.4.5 Due authorisation

The lender should seek production of a trustees' minute pursuant to which:

- the trustees properly consider the terms of the proposed transaction and record the benefit to the trust and/or its beneficiaries;
- there are tabled and considered by the trustees the transaction documents;
- there are disclosed any trustee interests or conflicts;
- the trustees resolve to approve the transaction and execute the transaction documents; and
- the trustees authorise the execution of the transaction documents by their signature.

In the case of a corporate trustee, the lender will, in addition, be concerned with the internal corporate governance and is, therefore, likely to require consideration, in the context of the relevant foreign law opinion, of the articles of association and internal authorised signatory arrangements of the corporate trustee.

12.8.4.6 Taxation and withholding

Notwithstanding that the trustee of the trust may be Guernsey resident, provided that the beneficiaries of the trust are non-resident, the trustee is assessed to tax only in respect of Guernsey source income other than bank interest.

12.8.5 Lending to partnerships and limited partnerships

For the purpose of this section, a reference to a limited partnership is a reference to a limited partnership registered in accordance with the *Limited Partnerships (Guernsey) Law 1995* as prospective borrower and/or grantor of security in connection with which the following is relevant as a matter of Guernsey law.

12.8.5.1 Legal personality, constitution and valid existence

Pursuant to the *Limited Partnerships (Guernsey) Law 1995* ('the Limited Partnerships Law'), the lender should note the following:

- the limited partnership does not, itself, have legal personality as a matter of Guernsey law;
- a limited partnership is constituted under the law pursuant to registration of the limited partnership agreement (which must be in writing), together with certain details concerning the general partners;
- the limited partnership must have one or more general partners and one or more limited partners;
- a general partner is liable for the debts and obligations of the partnership without limitation (and in the case of more than one general partner is liable jointly and severally);
- the liability of limited partners is limited to the amount of their paid-up or required capital contribution to the limited partnership, provided that such limited partners do not participate, and are not deemed to participate, in the business of the limited partnership;
- there is no restriction on the number of partners;
- partnership interests may, in accordance with the terms of the partnership agreement be assignable or redeemable (in the case of redemption providing that the partnership is solvent); and
- a general or limited partner may be a body corporate.

12.8.5.2 Capacity

The capacity of the limited partnership is determined through that of the one or more general partners in accordance with the terms of the limited partnership agreement, the law of the island and any restriction on the capacity of the general partner.

12.8.5.3 Due authorisation

Due authorisation of a transaction and execution of transaction documents on behalf of the limited partnership should be resolved upon by the general partners and the lender should obtain and have reviewed in the context of the Guernsey foreign law opinion a minute of resolution of the general partners. It may be necessary to consider further foreign law connections if one or more corporate general partners is incorporated outside of the island.

12.8.5.4 Taxation and withholding

A limited partnership is treated by Guernsey tax law as 'transparent' for tax purposes, so that the income of the limited partnership is treated as the income of the individual partners. The partners will not be assessable to Guernsey tax insofar as the source of partnership income arises outside of the island, or, to the extent that it is Guernsey source income, is bank deposit interest.

12.8.6 Lending to collective investment schemes

A collective investment scheme or fund is a classification of an investment activity under Guernsey law and describes a regulated investment activity undertaken by a body corporate or unit trust falling within the scope of the *Protection of Investors (Bailiwick of Guernsey) Law 1987*. The lender should be concerned with the issues of legal personality, capacity, due authorisation and due execution arising from the constitution of the body corporate trustee of the unit trust and should ascertain that all regulatory licences and permissions have been obtained. As a particular issue arising in relation to capacity and due authority, the lender should ensure that there are no *investment restrictions* which prevent either the borrowing or the application of the borrowed moneys in the manner anticipated. It is likely, in addition, in the case of an *open-ended investment scheme* that the assets of the corporate collective investment scheme will be held by a separate *custodian*, who may be required to grant, or join in, any disposition of property by way of security. Similarly, the collective investment scheme may operate through a *manager*, who may be required to join in the approval and due execution of lending arrangements and transaction documents.

12.8.7 Taking security

Guernsey law proceeds on a distinction existing between immoveable property and moveable property (as to which distinction generally, see Chapter 9 above).

12.8.7.1 Immoveable property

As a matter of Guernsey law, the conveyance or other transfer of title to or an interest in immoveable property requires the passing of a contract before the Royal Court of Guernsey. Security is created over immoveable property (and only immoveable property) by hypothèque.

12.8.7.2 Tangible moveable property

Guernsey law allows for a possessory pledge of tangible moveable property or chattels but does not allow for the hypothèque or non-possessory charge to be created in respect of tangible moveable property.

12.8.7.3 Intangible moveable property

The taking of security over intangible moveable property is subject to a statutory framework provided by the *Security Interests (Guernsey) Law 1993* ('the Security Interests Law'), which applies to any security agreement in respect of intangible moveable property entered into on or after 9 December 1992. The Security Interests Law defines 'security interest' as an interest in intangible moveable property that secures payment or performance of an obligation under the provisions of the law, and defines 'moveable property' as all property, wherever situated, whether tangible or intangible, and whether vested, contingent, or future, which is not regarded by the law of Guernsey as *immeuble*, and includes choses or things in action. For practical purposes, therefore, the lender may take, by way of security, cash and securities (including cash and securities in a portfolio subject to change) in accordance with the modes of creation provided for by section 1 of the *Security Interests Law*. Section 1 provides for the creation of a security interest pursuant to a security agreement in any intangible moveable property other than a lease, in the following specified way:

- in the case of a cash deposit maintained by the borrower with the lender where the lender has control of the account, pursuant to a security agreement and where the customer and the debtor are one and the same person (whether or not the debtor or any other person has rights specified in the security agreement to receive interest or otherwise in respect of the account);
- in the case of certificates of title representing securities, pursuant to the possession of such certificates of title by the lender or some person on behalf of the lender;
- in the case of a policy of life assurance, pursuant to possession by the lender or somebody on the lender's behalf, of the policy; and
- in the case of other intangible moveable property, provided that the lender has title to the intangible moveable property and notice of the creation of a security interest has been given by or on behalf of the

secured party to the person from whom the assignor would have been entitled to claim the collateral.

The reference in the fourth point to a security interest being held by way of 'title' is a reference to the obtaining of security, for example over a bank account maintained with a third-party bank or securities, by way of 'assignment'. Where notice is given to the person from whom the assignor would have been entitled to claim the collateral, the person to whom such notice is given may serve a counter-notice indicating that such person is aware that the assignment is disputed and indicating awareness of conflicting claims to or rights in the assigned property. Whether a security interest is created pursuant to control, possession, or assignment, it must be granted pursuant to a 'security agreement' complying with the provisions of section 3 of the Security Interests Law, which requires that a security agreement must:

- be in writing;
- be dated;
- identify and be signed by the debtor;
- identify the secured party;
- contain provisions regarding the collateral sufficient to enable its precise identification at any time;
- specify the events which are to constitute events of default; and
- contain provisions regarding the obligation, payment or performance of which is to be secured sufficient to enable it to be identified.

Section 3 of the Security Interests Law provides that a security interest may be created either before or after the coming into existence of the obligation secured, provided that the obligation can be sufficiently identified. A security interest granted in accordance with the law allows the lender a secured priority in the bankruptcy of the borrower (and, if the lender has taken security by way of title, precludes the property from vesting in the Sheriff on a désastre). The Security Interests Law further provides that the fact of the debtor becoming insolvent, his affairs being declared in a state of désastre, or he or his property being subject (whether in Guernsey or elsewhere) to any other judicial arrangement or proceeding consequent upon insolvency or a declaration of désastre, shall not affect the power of a secured party to realise or otherwise deal with the collateral in the same manner a secured party would have been entitled to realise or deal with it if the debtor or his property had not been the subject of such insolvency, désastre or other judicial proceedings or arrangement. The power of sale or application of the secured property arises on the happening of an event of default and provided that the lender has served on the debtor a notice specifying the particular event of default complained of.

12.8.8 Floating charges

The law of Guernsey does not recognise the concept of a floating charge. However, *section 10 of the Security Interests Law* provides that a person who is resident, domiciled or incorporated in Guernsey is not to be considered as lacking capacity, or as ever having lacked capacity, to give security governed by a foreign law over property situated outside of Guernsey, by reason only that the law of Guernsey does not permit security to be given by the method or in the circumstances permitted by that foreign law. Accordingly, a Guernsey company may grant a floating charge security and, indeed, fixed charges under a foreign law, albeit that such floating charge and/or fixed charge might not be valid and enforceable against property with a Guernsey *situs* (or property to which, otherwise, Guernsey law may apply). The lender will, generally, find that debentures and fixed and floating charges granted by Guernsey companies under English law (including fixed charges which incorporate floating charges) will lead to a qualification in a Guernsey foreign law opinion indicating that the borrower or grantor has capacity to enter into the charge but that the Royal Court of Guernsey may not uphold its validity insofar as it purports to extend to, or it is sought to be enforced against, property with a Guernsey *situs*.

12.8.9 Guarantees

The law of Guernsey recognises the concept of an obligation entered into by a party (the guarantor) for the liability to another (the principal), as guarantor, surety and/or indemnifier. If the guarantee is taken subject to the law of Guernsey, it should contain waivers of Guernsey customary law rights which would otherwise require the principal and/or any other guarantor or surety to be joined in any proceedings taken for enforcement against the guarantor and/or require that the guarantor contributes rateably in respect of the principal's indebtedness. A guarantee taken under the law of Guernsey should also contain provisions preserving the right of the lender to the guarantee obligations and any underlying security where a liability of the principal may be subject to a claim by a liquidator in respect of a preference.

12.8.10 Requirements for registration, filing and recording

The Register of Companies is maintained by the Judicial Greffier as an officer of the Royal Court of Guernsey. Other than in the case of immoveable property, there is no general obligation that transaction or security documents be filed, registered or recorded in the Register of Companies, in any register maintained by the company itself for such purpose, or in any other public office.

12.9 Enforcement

The Royal Court in Guernsey will register and enforce a foreign judgment if it complies with the provisions of the *Judgments (Reciprocal Enforcement) (Guernsey) Law 1957* if it is a judgment of a superior court of a jurisdiction in which reciprocity exists at the present time (such as the United Kingdom and Jersey).

12.9.1 Interim relief

Where the lender is concerned to restrain the borrower from dissipating property pre or post a prospective judgment or other enforcement, the Royal Court will provide relief by way of *Mareva-type injunctions* and *tracing orders*. It should be noted, however, that in the case of *First National Bank of Chicago (CI) Ltd v Arab Monetary Fund* [1986], the Royal Court in Guernsey held that orders for disclosure of information will not be made in circumstances where a bank or other person to whom they are addressed is not holding assets at the time when the order is sought.

12.9.2 Investigation and obtaining of evidence

At para 12.5 above, a general description has been given of the duty of confidence owed by bankers and professionals under the law of Guernsey. The Royal Court in Guernsey will act in aid of a foreign court in non-Guernsey civil proceedings for the purpose of taking evidence pursuant to the *Evidence (Proceedings in other Jurisdictions) (Guernsey) Order 1980*, which applies the *Evidence (Proceedings in other Jurisdictions) Act 1975*, under which a court or tribunal of another territory may make an application to the Royal Court in connection with civil or criminal proceedings, other than those of a political character. In the case of *Rea Brothers (Guernsey) Ltd v Securities and Exchange Commission* [1986] it was held that the Act would not be applied in relation to mere fishing expeditions. Evidence may be obtained from banks pursuant to the *Bankers' Books Evidence (Guernsey) Law 1954* as amended. Pursuant to the *Criminal Justice (Fraud Investigation) (Bailiwick of Guernsey) Law 1991*, the Attorney-General may, at the request of a foreign investigating authority, and on being satisfied that such foreign investigation authority is conducting an investigation relating to a serious fraud, issue a notice to a person requiring the delivery of information and materials to the Attorney-General.

12.9.3 Winding-up and bankruptcy

A company incorporated under the *Companies (Guernsey) Law 1994* may be wound up in one of the two following ways.

12.9.3.1 Voluntary winding-up

A voluntary winding-up may occur when:

- the period fixed for the life of the company has expired, or an event has occurred on the happening of which the articles provide that the company shall be dissolved and, in either event, the company has passed an ordinary resolution that the company be wound up voluntarily; or
- the company has passed a special resolution that the company be wound up.

The *Companies (Guernsey) Law 1994* makes no distinction between a members' and creditors' voluntary liquidation. In a voluntary winding-up a liquidator must be appointed, the assets of the company realised and its liabilities paid.

12.9.3.2 Compulsory liquidation

An application for compulsory winding-up must be made to the Royal Court by the company, by one or more of the shareholders or by a creditor. The Royal Court may order that a winding-up take place where:

- a special resolution has been passed to that effect;
- the company has not commenced business within a year of its registration or has suspended business for a full year;
- the company has less than the required number of members;
- the company is deemed unable to pay its debts;
- the company has failed to provide notice of its registered office within the specified time;
- the company has failed either to hold an annual general meeting or to provide the required directors' reports;
- the company has failed to comply with a requirement that it change a misleading name within the time specified having been so ordered by the Royal Court; or
- the Royal Court deems it just and equitable.

On the making of an application for the compulsory winding-up of the company, or at any time thereafter, any creditor of the company may apply to the Royal Court for an order (i) restraining, on such terms and conditions as the Court thinks fit, any action or proceeding pending against the company, or (ii) appointing a provisional liquidator to ascertain the company's assets and liabilities, manage its affairs and do all acts authorised by the Royal Court. Upon the appointment of a liquidator in a compulsory winding-up, all powers of the directors cease, except to the extent that the liquidator or the Court sanctions their continuance. The Royal Court may not hear an application for the winding-up of a company under the *Companies (Guernsey) Law 1994* unless satisfied that the company has been notified of the date, time and place of the application.

12.10 Recent and anticipated developments

The Commission is understood to have under consideration amendments to the *Companies (Guernsey) Law 1994* that may allow single member companies and/or companies limited by guarantee. It is also understood that consideration is being given to the availability of pre-formed companies and fixed duration companies.

Under the new banking law, the Financial Services Commission has wider control and powers to intervene by attaching conditions to banking licences and to introduce by Ordinance a deposit protection scheme.

The Limited Partnerships (Guernsey) Law 1995 was introduced in 1995 and came into force on 1 February 1996.

13 | Isle of Man

Introduction

The Isle of Man is an island of approximately 220 square miles located in the Irish Sea between England, Scotland, Wales and Ireland. The Isle of Man has a population of approximately 70 000. It is English-speaking.

13.1 Currency and exchange control

The currency of the Isle of Man is sterling, although it prints its own notes and mints its own coins, which are legal tender within the Isle of Man. At the present time there is no exchange control applicable to the Isle of Man.

13.2 Constitution

The Isle of Man is regarded as being politically stable. It is part of the British Isles (as a Crown dependency) but is not part of the United Kingdom. Originally settled by the Vikings, the Isle of Man became subject to the authority of the English Crown in 1765 and was ruled directly from England until 1866. From the time of its Viking occupation (and for a period of some one thousand years) the Isle of Man has had a legislative assembly known as the Tynwald, consisting of two Houses (the Upper House and the House of Keys). The Upper House (also known as the Legislative Council) is an indirectly elected body consisting of eight members elected from the House of Keys, the Bishop of Sodor and Man, and the Attorney-General. The House of Keys consists of 24 elected members. The executive arm of the legislature is that of the Council of Ministers, comprising a Chief Minister and some nine other Ministers. The Council of Ministers is appointed from Tynwald by the Lieutenant-Governor. The Isle of Man enjoys legislative and fiscal autonomy, but has entered into a customs union with the United Kingdom pursuant to the *(United Kingdom) Isle of Man Act 1979*. The United Kingdom retains responsibility for the external affairs of the Isle of Man, but the insular authorities and the Lieutenant-Governor are consulted prior to accession to treaties which, by reference to those territories for whose international affairs Her Majesty's government is responsible, will be taken to extend to the Isle of Man.

13.3 Legal system

The Isle of Man has its own separate court and judiciary. The senior judges of the High Court are known as 'Deemsters' (of which there are two). In originating its primary legislation (which must be sanctioned by the Lieutenant-Governor) the legislature draws on the experience of the United Kingdom and the court's application of the common law draws both on the customary law of the Isle of Man and on the common law of the United Kingdom. It should, however, be noted that the Isle of Man has an ancient customary law known as 'Breast Law'.

13.4 Constitutional relationship with the European Union

In common with Guernsey and Jersey, the Isle of Man's relationship with the European Union is determined pursuant to *Protocol No 3 to the Treaty of Accession (1972)* so that the Isle of Man has preserved its constitutional position relative to the English Crown, together with its fiscal independence. The Isle of Man is within the provisions of the *Treaty of Rome* for the purposes of the *Common External Tariff* together with certain particular provisions with regard to agricultural produce and is therefore able to enjoy free trading in goods. Otherwise, however, the Isle of Man is not required to apply European Union directives relating to, for example, movement of capital, company law, and the provision of financial services in insurance and banking.

13.5 Banking and professional confidentiality

The Isle of Man does not have a statutory framework for bank or professional secrecy. Banking and other professional confidentiality arises as a matter of common law, and therefore as a matter of an express or implied contractual obligation.

13.5.1 Isle of Man companies: disclosure of beneficial ownership

There is no requirement for disclosure of beneficial ownership on incorporation.

13.5.2 Disclosure to bankers by financial intermediaries

The standard of *know-your-customer* compliance dictated by the Financial Supervision Commission requires that on opening accounts and undertaking transactions it is not sufficient for a bank to rely on the reputation and bona fides of a local corporate administrator, or the fact that the principals of such corporate administrator are acting in an executive capacity and have signing powers on the bank account. The Financial Services Commission suggests that compliance with best *know-your-customer* standards requires disclosure by financial intermediaries of ultimate beneficial ownership in respect of administered companies and trusts to the account-holding bank.

13.5.3 Disclosure under compulsion of law

Orders may be made for the production of information held by banks pursuant to the *Bankers' Books Evidence Act 1935*, and an order of the court made thereunder. A court order may permit a party to inspect and take copies of entries in the bankers' books. Disclosure may further be required pursuant to mandatory orders made under the *Drug Trafficking Offences Act 1987*, the *Prevention of Terrorism Act 1990*, and the *Prevention of Fraud Act 1968*.

13.6 Regulation in the financial sector

The Financial Supervision Commission ('the Commission') (an independent body created in 1984) is charged with the promotion of the Isle of Man as a banking and finance centre, and with the primary supervision of banking and finance activities. The Commission operates as the primary regulator in accordance with the terms of the following key items of legislation:

1 the *Banking Act 1975*, the *Banking Amendment Act 1986* and the *Banking Business (Compensation of Depositors) Regulations 1991*, pursuant to which the Commission (and a Banking Supervisor) act as a relevant supervisory authority in relation to licensed *domestic banking institutions* and *offshore managed banks*;

2 the *Building Societies Act 1986*, pursuant to which building society operations in the Isle of Man are licensed and supervised;

3 the *Investment Business Act 1991*, pursuant to which the Commission regulates the conduct of *investment business*;

4 the *Financial Supervision Act 1988*, pursuant to which the Commission regulates the conduct of *collective investment schemes* as defined in section 30 of the Act requiring such schemes to be authorised;

5 the *Insurance Act 1986* and the subordinate *Insurance Regulations 1986*, pursuant to which the Insurance Authority and the Insurance Supervisor regulate the conduct of insurance business in or from within the Isle of Man; and

6 the *Companies Acts 1931–1993* and the *International Business Act 1994*, pursuant to which the Registrar of Companies regulates the incorporation of Isle of Man companies.

13.7 Anti-money laundering legislation and best practice

Although the Isle of Man is not an FATF country, the Guidance Notes for Mainstream Banking, Lending and Deposit Taking Activities, issued by the Joint Money Laundering Steering Group pursuant to the United Kingdom Money Laundering Regulations, refer to the Isle of Man, in the context of 'one-off transactions' (paragraph 49 of the Guidance Notes) as a territory having enacted legislation which is equivalent to the EU directive and therefore to be judged by United Kingdom banks and building societies as meeting an FATF required standard so as to be assumed to pass the *equivalence test*. The legislative regime in place in relation to the combating of money laundering is as follows.

13.7.1 Drug Trafficking Offences Act 1987 and Drug Trafficking Act 1996

The *Drug Trafficking Offences Act 1987* as amended by the 1996 Act makes provision for:

- the making and enforcement of confiscation orders against persons convicted of drug trafficking offences;
- the making of production and enforcement orders in relation to production of and access to materials required in connection with a police investigation;
- the offence of making any disclosure likely to prejudice an investigation;
- the offence of assisting drug traffickers to retain the proceeds or benefits of drug trafficking; and
- the offence of failing to disclose knowledge or suspicion of drug money laundering gained in the course of trade, profession, business or employment.

The offence of assisting a drug trafficker to retain the proceeds or benefits of drug trafficking is committed by a person:

- who knows or suspects that another is a drug trafficker or has benefited from trafficking; and
- who is concerned in an arrangement which facilitates the retention or control of such proceeds by the drugs trafficker, or which facilitates the acquisition of property by way of investment.

It is a defence to the offence to show:

- that such person has disclosed to a police officer his relevant suspicion or belief either before the doing of the act concerned (being an act done with the consent of the police officer) or after the act but voluntarily and as soon as is reasonable; or
- that he did not know or suspect that the arrangement related to another's proceeds of trafficking; or
- that he did not know that he was facilitating such control; or
- that, although he intended to make a disclosure to a police officer, there is reasonable excuse for his not doing so.

Where disclosure is made to a police officer there is deemed to be no breach of any duty of confidentiality.

In addition to legislation aimed at combatting drug money laundering the Isle of Man has the following existing legislation aimed at combatting money laundering:

- *The Prevention of Terrorism Act 1990*;
- *The Criminal Justice Act 1990*; and
- *The Criminal Justice Act 1991*

13.7.2 Companies Securities (Insider Dealing) Act 1987

This law makes it an offence for a person to deal with securities listed on a recognised stock exchange where such person is, or in the preceding six months has been, knowingly connected with the relevant company and where (i) such person holds information by virtue of being connected with the company, (ii) the information arising from the connection is of a type which it would be reasonable to expect such person not to disclose except for the proper performance of the position from which his connection arises, and (iii) such person knows that the relevant information is *unpublished price-sensitive information* in relation to the relevant securities. For the purposes of the law, a person is connected with the company if they are (i) a director of the relevant company, (ii) an officer or employee of that company, or (iii) engaged in a business transaction or relationship either directly with the company or related company or as an employee of the company so engaged.

13.8 Lending with an Isle of Man foreign law connection

The text which follows will highlight those issues which may arise in connection with a lending which has an Isle of Man foreign law connection in that either the borrower is domiciled, resident and/or incorporated or constituted in the Isle of Man, or because a transaction or security document has a proper or applicable law which is Isle of Man law. The paragraphs which next follow highlight, by reference to borrower type (building on the issues set out in Chapters 4, 5, 6 and 7), issues which arise for a lender where the borrower is domiciled, resident or incorporated in the Isle of Man. For each borrower type the issues considered are those which will, in the usual course, form the subject matter of an Isle of Man foreign law opinion, being:

- legal personality (i.e. does the borrower have separate legal existence, and if not, who may contract on behalf of the borrower?);
- capacity;
- due authorisation of the transaction;
- due execution of transaction and/or security agreements; and
- taxation, including withholding.

The remaining paragraphs will then deal collectively with:

- the creation of security;
- enforcement and insolvency; and
- recent or anticipated developments.

13.8.1 Lending to natural persons

The following issues are relevant when lending to, or taking a grant of security from, an individual domiciled and/or resident in the Isle of Man.

13.8.1.1 Capacity
An individual is a minor and without legal capacity to contract (other than possibly for necessities) until attaining the age of 18 years.

13.8.1.2 Tax and withholding
An individual resident or ordinarily resident within the Isle of Man is liable to assessment to tax on income, wherever arising. A person non-resident is liable to assessment on income, having an Isle of Man source. Banks and buildings societies do not deduct income tax from interest payable to non-resident depositors. The Isle of Man has a double taxation treaty with the United Kingdom (*Isle of Man Taxes Act 1970*), pursuant to which credit relief is granted in relation to income arising in the United Kingdom. Unilateral relief is given to residents where tax is chargeable in a foreign territory at the foreign rate or the Isle of Man tax rate, whichever is the lower.

13.8.2 Lending to companies

The legislative framework relating to a company incorporated under the law of the Isle of Man is to be found in the *Companies Acts 1931–1992* ('the Companies Acts'). In relation to a company incorporated under the Companies Acts, the lender should note the following.

13.8.2.1 Legal personality, due incorporation and good standing
A company incorporated under the Companies Acts has separate legal personality and may hold assets, incur liabilities and sue and be sued in its own name. Such existence becomes effective on the registration of a memorandum of association at the Companies Registry and upon the issue of a certificate of incorporation by the Registrar of Companies. A company incorporated under the Companies Acts may (i) have liability limited by shares, (ii) have liability limited by guarantee, (iii) have liability limited by shares and by guarantee (a *hybrid*), or (iv) have unlimited members' liability. Incorporation does not require disclosure of ultimate beneficial ownership and does not require the retention of professionals such as lawyers or accountants. Pre-incorporated companies are available through professional corporate administrators. Otherwise, the lender should note

that the following are the principal elements required for due form incorporation:

- application to the Registrar of Companies for name approval (the use of names related to regulated activities such as 'Bank', 'Insurance' or 'Trust Company' will be dependent upon the appropriate licence or registration for such regulated activity);
- the memorandum of association (to be submitted for registration) must state (i) the name of the company, (ii) whether the company is a limited liability company, (iii) that the registered office is in the Isle of Man, and (iv) the amount and division of the share capital (or, where the company is limited by guarantee, its terms, or in the case of a hybrid, the amount of division of the shares and the terms of the guarantee, or, in the case of an unlimited company, the value of the share capital), and the memorandum must be signed by the subscriber or subscribers whose names and addresses must be given and whose signatures must be attested by a witness;
- the lodging of the memorandum with the Registrar of Companies must be accompanied by a first appointment of directors and by the subscribers;
- the *Single Members Companies Act 1993* (which came into force on 18 August 1993) allows for single member companies, so that a private limited company may have a single subscriber share;
- articles of association may be those set out in Table A to the Regulations subordinate to the Companies Acts, or may be specifically settled.

The Companies Acts draw a distinction between *public companies* and *private companies*. A company is a private company if (i) it prohibits the issue of its shares to the public, and (ii) its memorandum of association so states. The Companies Acts make express provisions for the status of pre-incorporation contracts, providing that a contract that purports to be made by or on behalf of a company at a time when the company has not been formed has effect, subject to any agreement to the contrary, as one made with the person purporting to act for the company or as agent for it, so that he is personally liable on the contract accordingly. A public limited company may only commence business where, if it is not to issue a prospectus in relation to an offer to the public of its shares, it has delivered a statement by the directors that the directors have paid-up any shares for which they have subscribed, or, in any case where an offer to the public is made, the minimum number of shares specified have been subscribed, paid and allotted. In relation to the continued standing of the company, and its valid existence, the lender will wish to know generally that the company borrower is not at risk of dissolution and has not committed offences under the Companies Acts so that, among other things, the following are relevant enquiries (this is not intended to be an exhaustive list of such events or offences).

- Has the company complied with an obligation to submit an annual return to the Registrar of Companies within 28 days of the company's return date (the anniversary of the date of its incorporation, or, if different, the anniversary of the last return date), such annual return providing details of (i) the registered office of the company, (ii) the company's total indebtedness, (iii) the names of the company's directors, (iv) details of the members at a record date 14 days after the annual general meeting (together with details of those members who have ceased to be members since such date), and (v) the annual return fee (there is a fee for late filing where the annual return is made later than one month after the last date for filing)?
- Has the company held an annual general meeting in every calendar year (such meeting may be convened and held by the circulation of a written resolution) and, in the case of a public company, has it held its first meeting within three months of incorporation?
- Does the company have at least two directors (corporate directors are not permitted) and a secretary? (In the case of a public company, private exempt company or international business company, the secretary must be a professionally qualified person.)
- Has the company produced audited financial statements? (A private limited company may waive the requirement that such accounts be presented to a general meeting, and private limited companies need not file the audited financial statements with the Companies Registry.)

13.8.2.2 Capacity

The *Companies Act 1986*, s. 1 provides that where a company incorporated on or after 1 June 1988 does not have an objects clause within its memorandum of association, such company may follow any lawful object. A company incorporated before that date remains bound by any limitation imposed by its existing objects clauses until amended by special resolution, which may adopt the *Companies Act 1986* to provide corporate capacity consistent with any lawful object. This language means that if the company purports to engage in a regulated business (for example banking, insurance, etc) but is doing so in breach of the laws and regulations applicable to such activity, such activity will be beyond the capacity of the company. Otherwise, no act or thing done by a company is invalid, void or unenforceable arising from the fact that the company was without the capacity or power to do it. Nevertheless, the company (acting through its directors) is required to act in accordance with the terms of its memorandum of association as a duty owed to its members such that a lack of capacity can be asserted against the company by a member (or holder of a debenture security) where the company is intending to dispose of property, or against a director, for want of capacity. *Exempt companies* (as to which, see para 13.8.2.10 below) are not permitted to carry on or transact a trade or business within the Isle of Man in the course of which:

- goods are made or offered for sale;
- exploration or extraction of minerals is undertaken;
- there is undertaken any fishing or agricultural activity;
- there is distribution of goods;
- there is the development of land or construction; or
- there is the holding of land for the purpose of trading.

13.8.2.3 Due authorisation

There are no general limitations on the borrowing powers of an Isle of Man company, although the lender should note that such restrictions may be contained within the articles of association and, in particular, of those relating to a collective investment scheme (see para 13.8.5 below). A company incorporated under the Companies Acts, acts through its directors who are bound by the terms of the articles of association and any objects set out in the company's memorandum of association. The Companies Acts provide that a company must have at least two directors who must not be corporate directors. Notwithstanding the general absence of a doctrine of *ultra vires* (see para 13.8.2.2 above) it is suggested that the lender should, in all cases, require sight of a minute or extract of a minute of the directors dealing with the following:

- confirming that the meeting was duly convened and quorate;
- considering the relevant aspects of the proposed transaction and in particular the commercial benefit to the company;
- considering the terms of the relevant transaction documents;
- approving the execution of the transaction documents substantially in the considered form (and as appropriate allowing for the negotiation or agreement of amendment to such documents);
- stating the manner in which such documents are to be executed, designating one or more persons to attest the common seal of the company or designating individuals as signatories to the documents; and
- disclosing the extent and nature of a director's material conflicts of interest as necessary.

An Isle of Man company is required to keep minutes of all proceedings of directors and shareholders at its registered office and available for inspection by any member. A register of directors and secretaries must also be maintained at the registered office, setting out residential addresses, nationality, business occupation and, in the case of a corporate secretary, its corporate name and registered office address. The register of directors is to be available at the registered office for inspection by any member of the public. Where a company is a non-resident company (and not exempt) it must establish its management and control (and therefore must hold its directors and shareholder meetings) outside of the Isle of Man. It is likely, in any such case, that the articles of association will prohibit the convening and holding of meetings within the Isle of Man and will deem any resolution passed or made at any such meeting as invalid and of no effect. Where shareholder resolutions are required as an aspect of due authorisation for the transaction, the lender should note the following:

- private limited companies may have a single member, so that meetings will be constituted by a minute of resolution;
- notice of any general meeting at which a special resolution is to be considered requires 21 days' notice;
- the Companies Acts provide that anything which may be done by a resolution passed at a general meeting of a private company (including a special resolution) may be adopted by unanimous resolution in writing of all of the shareholders (subject to the rights of an auditor to convene a general meeting in the case of a special resolution concerning the auditor).

The Companies Acts require that a special resolution be passed by a majority of not less than three-quarters of members who (being entitled to do so) vote in person, or by proxy, at a meeting of the company. A special resolution is required to be filed with the Companies Registrar within 15 days.

13.8.2.4 Due execution

The Companies Acts and the Regulations made pursuant thereto provide that a company can enter into a contract by its authorised representatives whether made orally, in writing or under its common seal where, in accordance with the proper or applicable law of the contract, it could be concluded in such form by a natural person. An Isle of Man company need not maintain a common seal, and any document executed by two directors or one director and the secretary is deemed to be effective as executed under seal. The company may maintain a common seal and may, likewise, maintain an official or branch seal for use outside of the Isle of Man which must be a reproduction of the common seal, with the addition of the name of each territory or place in which it is to be used. Any document to which the official seal of the company is affixed by an authorised person is valid as if executed by the company under its common seal. The Companies Acts provide that the company may in writing and under its common seal empower a person either generally or specifically as its attorney to execute deeds and documents on behalf of the company. An

Isle of Man company administered in the Isle of Man (particularly an exempt company which must have at least one Isle of Man resident director and a professionally qualified secretary) will not operate under general power of attorney as the directors are bound to conduct the management and control of the company consistently with their duties under the Companies Acts.

13.8.2.5 The issue of shares and circulation of a prospectus

Private limited companies, limited by shares, must have a minimum paid-up capital of one share and, based on the pre-paid capital duty (forming part of the incorporation fee), are usually incorporated with an authorised share capital of £2000.00. Thereafter authorised capital in excess of £2000.00 attracts capital duty of 1.4%, capped at a maximum of £5000.00. Shares may only be issued in a registrable form, but, in respect of shares issued and fully paid up (and as permitted by the articles of association), an Isle of Man company may issue bearer warrants. Shares may be issued at a premium, in which case the premium paid must be reflected in a balance on a *share premium account* which is then treated as part of the paid-up capital of the company. Shares may be issued (subject to the provisions of the articles of association of the company) as redeemable shares, to be redeemed at the option of the company or of the shareholders. Redeemable shares are a particular feature of collective investment scheme companies, to which special provisions apply. Shares may be issued with class rights, for example preferential and cumulative or voting and non-voting. The Companies Acts provide for the variation by an Isle of Man company of its share capital in accordance with its articles of association and by the alteration to its memorandum (pursuant to special resolution), although a capital reduction may only be undertaken in accordance with the Companies Acts and pursuant to court sanction. Only a public company may make an issue of shares to the public pursuant to a prospectus or other offering document.

13.8.2.6 Licences and consents

If the activity of the company as borrower undertaken from or within the Isle of Man is banking business, insurance business, investment business, or that of a collective investment scheme, the lender should note the requirement for the appropriate registrations and licences as set out at para 13.6 above.

13.8.2.7 Financial assistance

The Companies Acts prohibit the giving of financial assistance for the purpose of or in connection with the acquisition by a company of its own shares but contain limited provisions permissive of financial assistance by companies for the purchase of their own shares provided that:

- the financial assistance is given in good faith in the interests of the company; or
- money-lending is an integral part of the company's business;
- the financial assistance forms part of an employee share scheme; or
- in the case of a private company the assistance is sanctioned by special resolution and the directors are reasonably satisfied that the company is solvent.

13.8.2.8 Disclosure of directors' interests
Directors must state any personal financial interest in contracts with the company.

13.8.2.9 Commercial benefit
The Companies Acts do not provide for specific statutory duties of directors. Directors of an Isle of Man company are, however, subject to a common law fiduciary obligation in relation to the company and its members to act in good faith, in the best interests of the company and with due skill and care. The lender should seek to establish that the appropriate consideration has been given by the directors to the existence of commercial benefit to the company, or, in any marginal case (most frequently those involving the grant of upstream guarantees), ensure (i) that the shareholders authorise and require the directors to enter into the transaction by special resolution, (ii) that the directors note and act on the shareholders' authority and request, and (iii) that the directors note the solvency of the company.

13.8.2.10 Tax and withholding
For Isle of Man tax purposes, Isle of Man companies may have any of the following statuses.

- *Resident:* a company which has neither filed a non-resident declaration nor applied for exempt or international company status is deemed resident in the Isle of Man for tax purposes. A resident company pays tax at the rate of 20% on its net profits wherever arising;
- *Non-resident:* being a company which has filed on incorporation and for each successive financial year a *non-resident declaration* signed by its secretary, manager, or a director confirming such status. Non-resident status requires that the company must have a majority of directors that are non-resident, although the secretary may be resident, and its central control and management must be undertaken outside of the Isle of Man. A non-resident company pays no income tax but must pay a non-resident company duty, currently £600.00 per annum.
- *Exempt company:* being a company which, notwithstanding control and management undertaken within the Isle of Man (and which must, in

any event, have at least one Isle of Man resident director and a professionally qualified Isle of Man resident secretary), pays no Isle of Man income tax on income arising outside of the Isle of Man (or on Isle of Man bank deposit interest). To qualify as an exempt company, the company must have no Isle of Man resident beneficial owners and must make application for exemption by 30 June of the year of assessment or within 30 days of the commencement of business. At the present time the exempt duty is payable at the rate of £300.00 per annum, with penalty fees applicable in respect of late payment or application.

- *International company:* being a variation of an exempt company (and also requiring an Isle of Man resident director and qualified professional secretary) but which pays an agreed rate of tax of between 1% and 35% (capable of variation throughout the financial year), subject to staged minimum levels and a minimum level in any event for the full financial year of £1200.00.

A resident Isle of Man company will be liable to deduct tax at source in respect of dividends, rents, royalties and other annual payments due to non-residents.

13.8.3 Lending to Isle of Man trusts

This paragraph sets out the issues relevant when lending to, or taking a grant of security from, a trust (through its trustee) which has as its proper law the law of the Isle of Man. There is no consolidated trust law and the relevant statutory framework is, therefore, contained collectively within the *Trustee Act 1961* (which follows in its scheme and provisions those of the English *Trustee Act 1925*), together with the *Variation of Trusts Act 1961*, the *Perpetuities and Accumulations Act 1968*, the *Recognition of Trusts Act 1988* and the *Trusts Act 1996* (together, 'the Trusts Acts').

- Isle of Man has adopted the *Hague Convention on the Law of Trusts and their recognition.*

In the text which follows, a 'trust' means an Isle of Man trust – a trust which, in accordance with the Trusts Acts, has a proper law being the Isle of Man. In dealing with the trust as a borrower and/or provider of security over property comprising the trust fund, the lender should note the following.

13.8.3.1 Legal personality
The trust does not, itself, have separate legal personality. The trust acts through its trustee or trustees who hold (or have held to their order) title to the trust fund.

13.8.3.2 Due constitution and validity of the trust

The following are the primary characteristics of a duly constituted valid trust pursuant to the Trusts Acts:

- there are no requirements at general law that a trust be created in any specific form, with the law of the Isle of Man applying equitable principles in requiring that there be certainty of intention to create a trust, certainty of objects and certainty of subject matter, but otherwise allowing for a trust to be constituted orally, in writing, or otherwise howsoever;
- a trust of Isle of Man immoveable property must be in writing and the trust instrument must be registered in the Deeds Registry of the Isle of Man;
- the trustee of the trust is under a duty to act in the best interests of the beneficiaries and impartially and in good faith using the powers of the trust in accordance with the terms of the trust;
- the perpetuity period for a non-charitable trust is that of the lives in being (or in the alternative, 80 years) plus 21 years;
- trust income may accumulate during a minority; and
- pursuant to the Isle of Man *Trusts Act 1996* the title of the trustee to property transferred into trust by a non-resident settlor during his lifetime is not (as a matter of the law of the Isle of Man) invalidated by operation of *forced heirship rules*;
- the trustee of a trust has power to lend money on the security of trust property, powers of maintenance, advancement and creation of protective trusts, to use agents and to arrange the reconstruction of trusts and have their personal liability limited by the Statute of Limitations and may apply to court by petition of summons to seek advice on the management of trust property.

The *Trust Act*:

- requires a copy of a will bequesting real estate to a trust and the assignment of personal estate to a trust to be registered in the Deeds Registry;
- requires a certified copy of the order of the Court to be submitted upon appointment of a new trustee by Chancery Division of the High Court or by the other trustees;
- limits the number of trustees to four in a settlement of land and allows new trustees to be appointed by the Court or by the other trustees to replace unwilling or unfit trustees or those who are not in the British Isles for a period exceeding twelve months;
- allows trustees to hold the income at their discretion for the benefit of the principal beneficiary's family or the person who would be entitled to

the income after the death of the principal beneficiary, if the trust fails or
determines during the subsistence of the trust period; and

- requires consent to be given to the trust instrument before allowing
trustees to exercise their discretion with investments.

Isle of Man trusts:

- are not in the public domain and may confer anonymity for the settlor
and the beneficiaries;
- allows assets to be passed from one generation to another without the
need of transferring title and hence offers anonymity; and
- enables trustees to enjoy an indemnity whereby they are only answerable
for money received unless they have acted negligently.

The Isle of Man Trusts Bill 1995, which received the Royal Assent in January
1996, has amended certain provisions to clause 2. The bill intends to ensure
that if the Manx Law is not chosen as the proper law of a Trust, then, in the
Isle of Man Courts, Isle of Man law would apply.

13.8.3.3 Capacity

The capacity of the trustee and the extent of the trustee's powers are of
crucial importance to a lender contracting with the trustee and must be
confirmed in accordance with the Trusts Acts. The Trusts Acts provide the
trustee with statutory powers of investment, cross-referenced to English
law, and provide for a power to invest in securities issued by the Isle of
Man authorities. The statutory powers can be supplemented by express
powers contained in the trust instrument, in which context it is usual to
provide the trustees with wide administrative, investment and dispositive
powers. These may include the power to acquire and hold interests in
companies.

13.8.3.4 Trustees' liability

The Trusts Acts make provision for circumstances in which a third
party dealing with the trustee in good faith (without knowledge of a
breach of trust) may enforce contractual obligations against the trustee as
follows:

- notwithstanding that the contract for sale causes loss to the trust;
- where the trust provide for the application of trust funds for any purpose
or in any manner and the transaction involves the borrowing of money
mortgage or sale of trust property; and
- notwithstanding the absence of enquiry by a lender to ensure that
the money borrowed is in fact required or applied for the purpose
stated.

13.8.3.5 Due authorisation

Notwithstanding the protections referred to at paragraph 13.8.3.4 the lender should seek production of a trustees' minute pursuant to which:

- the trustees properly consider the terms of the proposed transaction and record the benefit to the trust and/or its beneficiaries;
- there are tabled and considered by the trustees the transaction documents;
- there are disclosed any trustee interests or conflicts;
- the trustees resolve to approve the transaction and execute the transaction documents; and
- the trustees authorise the execution of the transaction documents by their signature.

13.8.3.6 Taxation and withholding

In the case of a trust having a non-resident settlor and non-resident beneficiaries (and notwithstanding that it has a resident Isle of Man trustee) it will not be assessable to Isle of Man income tax on income arising from a source outside of the island (or on bank deposit interest arising within the Isle of Man).

13.8.4 Lending to Isle of Man partnerships and limited partnerships

Here, a reference to a partnership or limited partnership is a reference to a partnership or limited partnership constituted in accordance with the *Partnership Act 1909* and the *International Business Act 1994* Part II as a prospective borrower and/or grantor of security. In connection with a limited partnership, the lender should note the following as a matter of the law of the Isle of Man.

13.8.4.1 Legal personality, constitution and valid existence

Pursuant to the *Partnership Act 1909* and the *International Business Act 1994*:

- a limited partnership does not, itself, have legal personality;
- a limited partnership may have a maximum of 20 partners (although the Isle of Man Treasury is empowered to vary the restriction);
- a limited partnership must have at least one general partner which is a Manx resident company and which has a resident director and resident qualified company secretary;
- the one or more general partners are liable for all of the partnership debts and obligations and the one or more limited partners are liable only for the debts and obligations to the extent of their capital contributions, provided that the limited partner takes no part in the management of the partnership;

- a limited partnership is constituted by registration of a statement delivered to the Registrar, which must be signed by all of the partners, stating the name and place and business of each partner and the amount of capital contributions with any changes to be registered within seven days and published in two Isle of Man newspapers.

13.8.4.2 Capacity

The capacity of the limited partnership is determined through that of the one or more general partners in accordance with the terms of the partnership agreement, the law of the Isle of Man and any restriction on the capacity of the general partner.

13.8.4.3 Due authorisation

Due authorisation of a transaction and execution of transaction documents on behalf of the limited partnership should be resolved upon by the general partners and the lender should obtain and have reviewed, in the context of an Isle of Man foreign law opinion, a minute of resolution of the general partners.

13.8.4.4 Taxation and withholding

The *International Business Act 1994* Part II has made provision for taxation of an International Limited Partnership registered under the *Partnership Act 1909* intended to confer upon it certainty as to tax transparency, so that there will be no assessment of non-resident partners to Isle of Man income tax, and with the International Limited Partnership simply paying a fee of £300.00 per annum.

13.8.5 Lending to collective investment schemes

The description 'collective investment scheme' is a classification of investment activity under Isle of Man law and describes a regulated investment activity undertaken by a body corporate or unit trust falling within the scope of section 30 of the *Financial Supervision Act 1988* and which is not exempted pursuant to the provisions of s. 30 paragraph(s). The lender should be concerned with the issues of legal personality, capacity, due authorisation and due execution arising from the constitution of the body corporate or trustee of the unit trust and should ascertain that all regulatory licences and permissions have been obtained. As a particular issue arising in relation to capacity and due authority, the lender should ensure that there are no *investment restrictions* which prevent either the borrowing or the application of the borrowed moneys in the manner anticipated. Where an open-ended investment company is an authorised scheme pursuant to the *Financial Supervision Act 1988*, s. 3(1) it will have a separate manager and custodian/trustee who may be required to grant, or join in, any disposition of property by way of security.

13.8.6 Taking security

In its treatment of immoveable, tangible moveable and intangible moveable property, the law of the Isle of Man follows, very closely, that of England, with consequent recognition of the obtaining of security interests by way of registered mortgage/charge in respect of immoveable property, possessory assignment and/or mortgage or pledge in respect of tangible moveables and charge/assignment in respect of intangible moveables.

13.8.7 Requirements for registration, filing and recording

The *Companies Acts 1931–1992* require that an Isle of Man company should maintain a register of charges created by or against the company, including floating charges, if they are to provide the creditor with a secured position as against a liquidator and the creditors of the company. In addition, the Isle of Man company must maintain a charges register at its registered office, details of all secured indebtedness being required to be given in its annual return.

13.9 Enforcement

The High Court of the Isle of Man will register and enforce a foreign judgment if it complies with the provisions of the *Judgments (Reciprocal Enforcement) (Isle of Man) Act 1968*, where the judgment is obtained in the superior courts of the prescribed territory and where the judgment is (i) final and conclusive between the parties; (ii) for a liquidated sum; (iii) has been obtained within 6 years of the judgment; and (iv) capable of enforcement by execution in the jurisdiction of the original court.

13.9.1 Interim relief

Where a lender is concerned to restrain the borrower from dissipating property pre or post a prospective judgment or other enforcement, the High Court in the Isle of Man will provide relief by way of *Mareva-type injunctions* and *tracing orders*.

13.9.2 Investigation and obtaining of evidence

At para 13.5 above, a general description has been given of the application of the common law duty of confidence owed by bankers and other professionals under the law of the Isle of Man. The High Court in the Isle of Man has, in the past, shown a clear inclination to recognise and support such existence of duty of confidence so as to restrain the obtaining of information by third parties. Nevertheless, the following provide a statutory framework for the obtaining of information in criminal and civil proceedings.

13.9.3 Winding-up and bankruptcy

The *Companies Acts 1931–1992* provide that a company may be wound up voluntarily where:

- the period fixed for the life of the company has expired, or an event has occurred on the happening of which the articles provide that the company shall be dissolved and, in either event, the company has passed a resolution requiring that the company be wound up voluntarily;
- the company resolves by special resolution that it be wound up voluntarily;
- the company resolves by special resolution, and pursuant to a request by creditors, that it should be wound up.

The company may be wound up by the court:

- if an application is made by the company, its directors or creditors on the basis that it is insolvent;
- following a special resolution by the company that it be wound up by the court;
- where default is made in delivering the annual report, or in holding an annual general meeting;
- where the company does not commence business within a year of incorporation or suspends its business for a complete year; or
- where the court is of the opinion that it is just and equitable that the company should be wound up.

Where a company seeks to conduct a voluntary but solvent winding-up, it is dissolved by certificate of the Registrar of Companies and such winding-up may be conducted without the appointment of a liquidator. In a court sanctioned winding-up (as a creditors' winding-up), the company or a creditor may apply for stay of proceedings before the winding-up order is made. The court has power to appoint an official receiver, liquidator or special manager.

13.10 Recent and anticipated developments

The Financial Supervision Commission has under continuing review the regulation of corporate administrators and, in particular, the regulation of non-resident companies. It is thought that the Financial Supervision Commission is also considering the prospect for legislation allowing for limited liability partnerships.

The Isle of Man Trusts Bill 1995 received the Royal Assent in January 1996. The new legislation deals with the protection of trusts in the Isle Of Man from forced heirship provisions in foreign jurisdictions.

The financial supervision commission has set out its proposals in 1995 to revise the regulation of restricted and collective investment schemes.

The International Business Act 1994 introduced the concept of an International Company and the International Limited Partnership. The Act replaces the concept of the 'Exempt Company' and extends tax exemption to limited partnerships.

Changes to VAT regulations were introduced on 1 January 1993 under which the Isle of Man can offer corporate tax benefits and VAT applications for overseas business.

The Isle of Man company law has been amended and the Isle of Man *Single Member Companies Act 1993* allows private companies to have a single member.

Anticipated changes to Company Law in respect of legislation for Limited Liability Companies, Regulation of Corporate Managers and tightening of control in respect of non-resident companies operations is expected.

14 Gibraltar

Introduction

The territory of Gibraltar comprises a peninsula at the southern most tip of the Spanish mainland, to which it is connected by a narrow isthmus. The very small land area of some two and three-quarter square miles incorporates the principal population centre of Gibraltar Town, the location of most of the financial institutions and professional support services. Gibraltar has a population of approximately 30 000. Its business language is English, although Spanish is also widely spoken.

14.1 Currency and exchange control

The currency is the Gibraltar Pound, which has parity with sterling. There is no presently applicable exchange control.

14.2 Constitution

Gibraltar is regarded as being politically stable although its relatively recent history has included an ongoing dispute over sovereignty between the United Kingdom and Spain, an issue which appears to have assumed less significance since the accession of Spain to the European Union. Gibraltar is a Crown Colony, its territory having been captured and claimed on behalf of the English Crown in 1704. Gibraltar is self-governing (with, in particular, fiscal independence), possessing its own legislature in the form of the House of Assembly. The House of Assembly is an elected body from which the Government as an Executive is formed. The Government of Gibraltar has insular responsibility for domestic matters, although it continues to rely on the United Kingdom for its external relations, as a territory for which the United Kingdom government has foreign policy responsibility. The Government of Gibraltar is conducted through two Councils, the Council of Ministers (the Chief Minister and seven other Ministers) and the Gibraltar Council (comprising the Chief Minister, the Governor, the Attorney-General, together with four Ministers and three other officials). Legislation originated in the House of Assembly (Ordinances) requires sanction of the Governor.

14.3 Legal system

Gibraltar has an autonomous legal system and judiciary. Its system of law is based on English common law, and its legislation, both in its origin and in its interpretation, draws on the legislation and common law of England. The principal commercial court in Gibraltar is the Supreme Court, equivalent to the High Court of England.

14.4 Constitutional relationship with the European Union

Gibraltar is within the European Union pursuant to the application of Article 227(4) of the *Treaty of Rome* and is a territory for whose external relations the United Kingdom as a Member State is responsible. Although within the EU, Gibraltar enjoys such position without the requirement for harmonisation or application of value added tax, the *Common External Tariff*, or the *Common Agricultural Policy*. Otherwise, however, Gibraltar must, generally, give effect to EU directives (an obligation for which the United Kingdom remains responsible) and, in general, enjoys the benefits of marketability of financial services within the EU and freedom of establishment. In particular, Gibraltar has adopted UCITS legislation, allowing for the marketing of its collective investment schemes or funds within the EU.

14.5 Banking and professional confidentiality

Gibraltar has a common law based implied duty of professional confidentiality following the English decision in *Tournier v National Provincial and Union Bank of England* [1924] 1 K.B. 461. The common law duty of confidentiality is supplemented by a limited statutory framework in relation to bank disclosure contained in the *Banking Ordinance 1992* which, in Part XI, provides for an offence of disclosing information obtained under the Ordinance (section 82(9)). A person guilty of the offence is liable, on conviction, to a sentence of imprisonment for two years and to a fine. The offence is not committed where the relevant disclosure is (i) of information permitted or required under the Ordinance, (ii) of information to or by a person concerned in the administration of the Ordinance, (iii) of any information by the Commissioner or Banking Supervisor to a professional for the purpose of obtaining advice, (iv) of information with relevant consent, (v) of information which is within the public domain, (vi) of information concerned with the conduct of criminal proceedings or proceedings arising under the Ordinance, (vii) of information in connection with a winding-up under the *Companies Ordinance 1974*, (viii) of information by the Commissioner or Banking Supervisor relating to the nature or conduct of business of an authorised institution, or (ix) of any information in the form of a summary in such manner as not to enable information relating to any particular person to be ascertained from it.

14.5.1 Gibraltar companies: disclosure of beneficial ownership

There is no requirement on incorporation for disclosure of ultimate beneficial ownership. If, however, an application is made for the company to be an exempt company and to receive an exemption certificate then, on such application, a declaration must be made of beneficial ownership. Such information is itself covered by a statutory secrecy provision pursuant to the *Companies (Taxation and Concessions) Ordinance 1983*, which makes it an offence for any person to disclose information deriving from the application to any other person other than in connection with the Ordinance, or for the purpose of civil and criminal proceedings in which ownership of the shares is in issue.

14.5.2 Disclosure to bankers by financial intermediaries

Current practice for banks where the 'Applicant for Business' is a third-party intermediary is set out in the Money Laundering Guidance Notes produced by the supervisory authorities listed under sub-section 19(2) of the *Criminal Justice Ordinance 1995*.

14.5.3 Disclosure under compulsion of law

Bankers and other professionals may be subject to an order to disclose made by the Gibraltar courts or to disclosure required by statute (for example, pursuant to the *Banking Ordinance 1992*, in which case the bank is released from its duty of confidentiality) or pursuant to a right to disclose, such as that provided by the *Drugs Trafficking Offences Ordinance 1995*.

14.6 Regulation in the financial sector

The Financial Services Commission ('the Commission') is responsible for the supervision, development and promotion of Gibraltar's finance industry. The Commission was originally established pursuant to the provisions of the *Financial Services Ordinance 1990*, as subsequently reenacted and amended. The *Financial Services Ordinance* provides for the regulation of investment business and for the supervision and licensing of collective investment schemes, trust and company management operations, investment brokers and portfolio managers. The Commission also has overall supervisory responsibility for deposit-taking institutions and insurance companies, although there is a separate specialist Banking Supervisor. At the present time, the Commission operates as regulator in accordance with the terms of the following key legislation:

- *The Banking Ordinance 1992*, pursuant to which the Commission, through the Banking Supervisor, regulates deposit-taking activity.
- The *Insurance Companies Ordinance 1987*, *Insurance Companies (Solvency Margins and Guarantee Funds) Regulations 1987* and *Insurance Companies (Prescribed Particulars) Regulations 1987*, pursuant to which the Commission, through an Insurance Supervisor, regulates the conduct of insurance business.
- The *Companies Ordinance 1974*, pursuant to which the Commission provides for the incorporation of companies under Gibraltar law, through the Registrar of Companies.
- The *Financial Services Ordinance 1989* and the *Financial Services (Collective Investment Schemes) Regulations 1991*, pursuant to which the constitution and supervision of open-ended corporate schemes and unit trusts are regulated, together with the provision of management, administrative and custodial services to such collective investment schemes.

14.7 Anti-money laundering legislation and best practice

As a dependent territory to which EU directives apply, Gibraltar has transposed into its law the EU Money Laundering Directive (91/308/EEC), introducing the provisions into its law on an 'all-crimes' basis. The *Criminal Justice Ordinance 1995* has put in place measures to prevent the use of the financial system for the purposes of money laundering. Part III of the Ordinance applies to:

- all banks, building societies and other credit institutions;
- all persons authorised to conduct investment business under the *Financial Services Ordinance 1989;*
- bureaux de change, encashment centres and money transmission services;
- all insurance companies covered by the EU Life Directives; and
- solicitors and accountants when undertaking relevant financial business.

The Ordinance imposes on regulated financial business duties and obligations in relation to the identification/verification of new business, record-keeping procedures and training. The Ordinance also creates new criminal offences in relation to the laundering of the proceeds of criminal conduct and of tipping-off.

14.7.1 Drug Trafficking Offences Ordinance 1995

The *Drug Trafficking Offences Ordinance 1995* (based on the *English Drugs Trafficking Offences Act 1986*) makes provision for:

- the making and enforcement of confiscation orders against persons convicted of drug trafficking offences;
- the making of production and enforcement orders in relation to production of, and access to, materials required in connection with a police investigation;
- the offence of making any disclosure likely to prejudice an investigation; and
- the offence of assisting drug traffickers to retain the proceeds or benefits of drug trafficking.

The offence of assisting a drug trafficker to retain the proceeds or benefits of drug trafficking is committed by a person:

- who knows or suspects that another is a drug trafficker or has benefited from drug trafficking; and
- who is concerned in an arrangement which facilitates the retention or

control of such proceeds by the drug trafficker, or which facilitates the acquisition of property by way of investment.

It is a defence to the offence to show:

- that such person has disclosed to a police officer his relevant suspicion or belief, either before doing the act concerned (being an act done with the consent of the police officer) or after the act but voluntarily and as soon as is reasonable; or
- that he did not know or suspect that the arrangement related to another's proceeds of drug trafficking; or
- that he did not know that he was facilitating such control; or
- that although he intended to make a disclosure to a police officer, there is reasonable excuse for his not doing so.

Where disclosure is made to a police officer there is deemed to be no breach of a duty of confidentiality.

14.8 Lending with a Gibraltar foreign law connection

The text which follows will highlight those issues which may arise in connection with a lending which has a Gibraltar foreign law connection, either in that the borrower is domiciled, resident and/or incorporated or constituted in Gibraltar, or because a transaction or security document has a proper or applicable law which is Gibraltar law. The paragraphs which next follow highlight, by reference to borrower type (building on the issues set out in Chapters 4, 5, 6 and 7), issues which arise for a lender where the borrower is domiciled, resident or incorporated in Gibraltar. For each borrower type, the issues considered are those which will, in the usual course, form the subject matter of a Gibraltar foreign law opinion, being:

- legal personality (i.e. does the borrower have separate legal existence, and if not, who may contract on behalf of the borrower?);
- capacity;
- due authorisation of the transaction;
- due execution of the transaction and/or security agreements; and
- taxation, including withholding.

The remaining paragraphs will deal collectively with:

- the creation of security;
- enforcement and insolvency; and
- recent or anticipated developments.

14.8.1 Lending to natural persons

The following issues are relevant when lending to, or taking a grant of security from, an individual domiciled and/or resident in Gibraltar.

14.8.1.1 Capacity
An individual is a minor and without legal capacity to contract (other than possibly for necessities) until attaining the age of 18 years.

14.8.1.2 Tax and withholding
An individual who is ordinarily resident in Gibraltar is liable to be assessed on their income wherever arising and will be liable to pay tax at rates between 20% and 50% of net taxable income. There are, however, three categories of tax residence for individuals, which are intended to provide favourable tax regimes, being those applicable to high net worth individuals taking up residence in Gibraltar and agreeing to pay tax assessed producing a maximum liability of approximately £20 000.00 and an annual tax liability of approximately £10 000.00, a special tax status for those who are essentially employed in Gibraltar who may be taxed in a round sum amount of £10 000.00 per annum, and a tax status for non-resident individuals with no Gibraltar source income, who may be treated as tax resident on their worldwide income at an agreed rate of not less than 2%, subject to a maximum tax liability of approximately £20 000.00 per annum. Gibraltar is not a party to any double taxation agreements, but unilateral credit relief is given where income is from United Kingdom or Commonwealth income tax. An individual pays a state duty, if resident, on worldwide moveable and Gibraltar immoveable property, and, where the individual is non-resident, on moveable and immoveable property in Gibraltar.

14.8.2 Lending to companies

The legislative framework relating to a company incorporated under the law of Gibraltar is to be found in the *Companies Ordinance 1974* (based on the United Kingdom *Companies Act 1929*) ('the Companies Ordinance'). In relation to a company incorporated under the Companies Ordinance, the lender should note the following.

14.8.2.1 Legal personality, due incorporation and good standing
A company incorporated under the Companies Ordinance is from the date of its incorporation (as stated in its certificate of incorporation) a body corporate having perpetual succession. Provision is made in the Companies Ordinance for pre-incorporation contracts which if made by a person on behalf of a company prior to due incorporation are made, subject to any agreement to the contrary, as the personal contract of such person and for

which they are liable. The certificate issued by the Registrar of Companies is conclusive evidence that the requirements of the Companies Ordinance in respect of registration have been complied with. A company incorporated under the Companies Ordinance may be (i) a company limited by shares, (ii) a company limited by guarantee, (iii) a company limited by shares and by guarantee (a *hybrid*), or (iv) an unlimited company (whether or not having a share capital). Incorporation does not require disclosure of ultimate beneficial ownership. Pre-incorporated companies are available through lawyers and professional corporate administrators. Otherwise, the lender should note the following as the principal elements required for due incorporation:

- application to the Registrar of Companies for name approval (the use of names related to regulated activities such as 'Bank', 'Insurance' or 'Trust Company' will be dependent upon the appropriate licence or registration for such regulated activity);
- incorporation may only be made through Gibraltar lawyers, although pre-incorporated companies are available;
- the memorandum of association (to be submitted for registration) must contain (i) the name of the company (with 'Limited' as the last word in the case of companies limited by shares or guarantee), (ii) the situation of the company's registered office, (iii) the objects of the company, and (iv) the amount and division of the share capital (or, where the company is limited by guarantee, its terms, or in the case of a hybrid, the amount of division of the shares and the terms of the guarantee, or in the case of an unlimited company, the value of the share capital);
- the memorandum must be signed by the subscriber or subscribers, whose name and address must be given and whose signatures must be attested by a witness;
- registration also requires filing of a statement as to the registered office and the first appointment of directors by the subscriber or subscribers;
- private limited companies may now have a single subscriber and member;
- articles of association may be in the form set out in Table A to the Companies Ordinance, or may be specifically settled.

The Companies Ordinance draws a distinction between public companies and private companies. A company is a private company if by its articles it (i) restricts the right to transfer its shares, (ii) limits the number of members to less than 50 (not including the company's employees or former employees), and (iii) prohibits any invitation to the public to subscribe for any shares or debentures of the company. In relation to the continued standing of the company, and its valid existence, the lender will wish to know generally that the company borrower is not at risk of dissolution and has not committed offences under the Companies Ordinance so that, among other things, the following are relevant. (This is not intended to be an exhaustive list of such events or offences.)

- Has the company complied with an obligation to submit an annual return to the Registrar of Companies within 14 days of its annual general meeting, such annual return providing details of (i) the registered office of the company, (ii) the company's total indebtedness and security given for indebtedness, (iii) the names of the company's directors, (iv) details of the company's members (together with details of those members who have ceased to be members since the date of the last annual return), and (v) the annual return fee?
- Has the company held an annual general meeting in each calendar year and not later than 15 months following the last annual general meeting?
- Does the company have the minimum number of directors specified in the articles of association, or in any event at least one director (being either an individual or corporation) and who, unless the articles provide otherwise, holds a qualifying share? (It is also usual, but not necessary, to appoint a secretary.)
- Has the company appointed an auditor, being a qualified or approved accountant? (Audited accounts are presented to shareholders and to the tax authorities but, other than in the case of a public company, are not filed at the Companies Registry.)

14.8.2.2 Capacity

The Companies Ordinance allows that a company may pursue any lawful object and, otherwise, that the company has the capacity of a natural person, there being no application of the doctrine of *ultra vires.* Nevertheless, the company (acting through its directors) is required to act in accordance with the terms of its memorandum of association as a duty owed to its members such that a lack of capacity can be asserted against the company by a member.

14.8.2.3 Due authority

There are no general limitations on the borrowing powers of a Gibraltar company, although the lender should note that such restrictions may be contained within the articles of association and, in particular, of those relating to a collective investment scheme (see para 14.8.4 below). A company incorporated under the Companies Ordinance acts through its directors, who are bound by the terms of the articles of association and any objects set out in the company's memorandum of association. The Companies Ordinance provides that a company must have at least one director who can be a corporate director. Notwithstanding the general absence of a doctrine of *ultra vires* (see above, para 14.8.2.2) it is suggested that the lender should, in all cases, require sight of a minute or extract of a minute of the directors dealing with the following:

- confirming that the meeting was duly convened and quorate;
- evidencing consideration of the relevant aspects of the proposed transaction and in particular the commercial benefit to the company;
- considering the terms of the relevant transaction documents;
- approving the execution of the transaction documents substantially in the considered form (and as appropriate allowing for the negotiation or agreement of amendment to such documents);
- stating the manner in which such documents are to be executed, designating one or more persons to attest the common seal of the company or designating individuals as signatories to the documents; and
- disclosing the extent and nature of the directors' material conflicts of interest as necessary.

In the case of a company having a single director, the resolutions should be in a relevant 'minute of resolution' form. A Gibraltar company is required to keep minutes of all proceedings of directors and shareholders at its registered office and to make them available for inspection by a member. A register of directors and secretaries must be maintained at the registered office setting out residential addresses, nationality and business occupation. Where shareholder resolutions are required as an aspect of the authorisation for the transaction, the lender should note the following:

- Gibraltar companies may have a single member so that, in such cases, meetings will be constituted by a minute of resolution;
- notice of any general meeting at which a special resolution is to be considered requires 21 days' notice, provided that if all the members entitled to attend and vote at such meeting so agree, the time may be abridged.

The Companies Ordinance requires that a special resolution be passed by a majority of not less than three-quarters of those present (in person or by proxy) at a general meeting in respect of which the notice requirements have been complied with.

14.8.2.4 Due execution
The Companies Ordinance provides that contracts on behalf of the company may be made so that (i) a contract which if between private persons, would have to be under seal, may be made by the company under its seal, (ii) a contract which, if made between private persons, would be required to be made in writing and signed by the parties, may be signed on behalf of the company by any person acting under its expressed or implied authority, and (iii) a contract which if made between two private persons could be made by word of mouth, may be so made on behalf of the

company by any person acting under its expressed or implied authority. An attorney may be appointed to act for the company but must be appointed in writing and under the common seal of the company.

14.8.2.5 Issue of shares and circulation of a prospectus

A private limited company, limited by shares, must have at least one paid-up share and, as a requirement for *exempt company* status must have a minimum paid-up capital of £100.00, or for *qualifying company* status must have a paid-up capital of not less than £1000.00. Capital duty at the rate of 0.5% is payable on the authorised share capital of the company but not on any premium payable. Shares may only be issued in registrable form, but, in respect of shares issued and fully paid-up (and if permitted by the articles of association), a Gibraltar company may issue bearer warrants. Shares may be issued at a premium, in which case the premium paid must be reflected in a balance on a share premium account. Shares may be issued (subject to the provisions of the articles of association of the company) as redeemable shares, to be redeemed at the option of the company or of the shareholder. Shares may be issued with class rights, for example preferential and cumulative, or voting and non-voting. Subject to the provisions of the articles of association, a company may increase its share capital, with resolutions for such increase required to be filed with the Registrar of Companies. A capital reduction may be undertaken by special resolution, subject to confirmation by the court. The balance on share premium account and/or capital reserve account may be utilised in the manner provided for by the Companies Ordinance, effectively providing for a reduction in share capital without court sanction.

14.8.2.6 Licences and consents

If the activity of the company as borrower undertaken from or within Gibraltar is banking business, insurance business, investment business, or that of a collective investment scheme, the lender should note the requirements for the appropriate registrations and licences as set out at para 14.6 above.

14.8.2.7 Financial assistance

The Companies Ordinance restricts the giving of direct or indirect financial assistance for the purpose of a purchase by a company of its own shares, subject to exceptions in relation to money lent in the way of business, where money-lending is the ordinary course of the company's business and where the financial assistance forms part of an employee share scheme.

14.8.2.8 Disclosure of directors' interests

Directors must state any personal financial interest in contracts with the company.

14.8.2.9 Commercial benefit

The Companies Ordinance does not provide for specific statutory duties of directors, but the directors of Gibraltar companies are subject to a common law fiduciary obligation in relation to the company and its members to act in good faith and with the skill and care of a prudent man. A breach of such duty (arising if the directors resolve that the company should enter into a transaction for which there is no commercial benefit to the company) may give rise only to an action by the shareholders against the directors and may, if the lender has knowledge or is deemed to have knowledge of the breach, mean that the lender is unable to enforce the obligations against the company. The lender should seek to establish that the appropriate consideration has been given by the directors to the existence of commercial benefit to the company, or to ensure that an appropriate special resolution has been passed by shareholders, directing and requiring that the company enter into the transaction.

14.8.2.10 Tax and withholding

For Gibraltar tax purposes, Gibraltar companies may have the following status.

- *Exempt company:* being a company which has obtained a certificate under the *Companies (Taxation and Concessions) Ordinance*. The exemption certificate (which has a life of 25 years) exempts the company from income tax, withholding tax, estate duty and stamp duty (although a resident exempt company must pay stamp duty). An exempt company may not be beneficially owned by any resident of Gibraltar and must not carry on a trade or business from within Gibraltar. Exempt status is open to both resident and non-resident companies, where the distinction arises exclusively as a matter of the location of central management and control.
- *Qualifying company:* being a company registered under the *Income Tax Qualifying Company Rules*. A qualifying company elects to pay tax at rates between not less than 2% and not more than 35%. A qualifying company cannot be beneficially owned by a person resident in Gibraltar and cannot undertake any trade or business in or with Gibraltar, although it can have its central management and control in Gibraltar. A qualifying company pays a flat fee and must make a deposit as security for tax payable.
- *1992 holding company:* being a company incorporated so as to take advantage of EC Directive 435/90. Such a company (i) must be incorporated in Gibraltar after 1 January 1992 and must be ordinarily resident for tax purposes, (ii) must be an investment holding company, (iii) must have business premises and not less than two employees in Gibraltar, (iv) must not have any Gibraltar resident as a beneficial owner,

and (v) must otherwise satisfy such criteria as may, for the time being, be specified by the Financial and Development Secretary.

In the case of an exempt or qualifying company, there are no withholding taxes. In the case of a 1992 holding company, such a company holding more than 25% of the voting capital of a company incorporated in an EU Member State does not pay corporation tax on any income derived from such company and will pay only 1% withholding tax on dividends. Any company which is other than an exempt company, qualifying company or 1992 holding company (that is, an ordinarily resident trading company) is liable to Gibraltar company tax at a rate of 35% payable on profits whether retained or distributed. Tax is deducted at source from all dividends at the company rate. Importantly, investment holding companies will be considered ordinarily resident if they are controlled by persons domiciled in Gibraltar, and although they do not undertake business in Gibraltar or are not locally managed.

14.8.2.11 Redomiciliation
The *Companies (Redomiciliation) Regulations 1992* allow an EU company to redomicile in Gibraltar, pursuant to application accompanied by:

- the articles of association;
- a certificate of good standing issued by the authorities of the transferor domicile;
- evidence of consent to transfer given by the authorities of the transferor domicile; and
- evidence satisfactory to the Gibraltar Registry that the company is not insolvent and is not subject to legal proceedings.

Redomiciliation operates to transfer the place of registration to Gibraltar as a matter of Gibraltar law. The company otherwise maintains its legal personality so that its assets and undertaking continue to vest and it retains responsibility for its liabilities and obligations.

14.8.3 Lending to Gibraltar trusts

This paragraph sets out the issues relevant when lending to, or taking a grant of security from, a trust (through its trustee) which has as its proper law the law of Gibraltar. Gibraltar has adopted the Hague Convention to assist the proper law of trust doctrine. There is no consolidated trust law and the relevant statutory framework is, therefore, contained collectively within the following (which will be referred to collectively as the 'Trust Ordinances'):

- the *Trustee Ordinance* (which transposes into Gibraltar law the English *Trustee Act 1893*);

- the *Trustee Investment Ordinance* (which transposes into Gibraltar law the powers of investment of a trustee provided by the UK *Trustee Investments Act 1961*);
- the *English Law (Amendment) Ordinance 1970*, which transposes into Gibraltar law the UK *Variation of Trusts Act 1958*;
- the *Law of Property (Amendments) Ordinance 1983*, which transposes into Gibraltar law the restrictions on accumulations as enacted by section 164 of the UK *Law of Property Act* as amended;
- the *Perpetuities and Accumulations Ordinance 1986*, providing for a perpetuity period of up to 100 years and permitting the period of accumulation to extend from 40 to 100 years; and
- the *Bankruptcy Amendment Ordinance 1990* (as amended by the *Bankruptcy (No 2) Ordinance 1990*) intended to facilitate by express provision asset protection trusts.

References here to a trust mean a trust constituted in accordance with the Trust Ordinances and the proper law of which is that of Gibraltar. Gibraltar is a well established centre for the domicile of private trusts established through local accountants, lawyers and bankers operating professional trustee services. The most frequently encountered trust will be a family settlement, usually settled on either fully discretionary or partial discretionary terms. The *Bankruptcy Amendment Ordinance 1990* (as amended by the *Bankruptcy (No 2) Ordinance 1990*) provides a framework for the validity (as a matter of Gibraltar law) of *asset protection trusts* where:

- the settlor is non-resident;
- the property transferred into trust does not (if it is real property or tangible moveables) have a Gibraltar *situs*;
- the settlor was not insolvent when the transfer into trust was made and does not become insolvent as a result of the transfer; and
- the transfer of the trust property is registered pursuant to the *Bankruptcy (Register of Dispositions) Regulations 1990*.

In dealing with the trust as borrower and/or provider of security over property comprising the trust fund, the lender should note the following.

14.8.3.1 Legal personality
The trust does not, itself, have separate legal personality. The trust acts through its trustee or trustees who hold (or have held to their order) title to the trust fund.

14.8.3.2 Due constitution and validity of the trust
The following are the primary characteristics of a duly constituted valid trust pursuant to Gibraltar law:

- there are no requirements at general law that a trust be created in any specific form, with the law of Gibraltar applying equitable principles in that there must be certainty of intention to create a trust, certainty of objects and certainty of subject matter, but otherwise allowing for a trust to be constituted orally, in writing, or otherwise howsoever;
- the trustee of a trust is under a duty to act in the best interests of the beneficiaries and impartially and in good faith using the powers of the trust in furtherance only of the stated trust;
- pursuant to the *Perpetuities and Accumulations Ordinance 1986*, the trust may have a perpetuity period of one hundred years and may accumulate for the entirety of the perpetuity period; and
- pursuant to the *Trusts (Recognition) Ordinance 1990*, the title of trustee to property transferred into trust by a non-resident settlor during his lifetime is not (as a matter of the law of Gibraltar) invalidated by operation of *forced heirship rules*;
- the trust does not require registration on or following its setup (except for charitable purposes).

14.8.3.3 Capacity

The capacity of the trustee and the extent of the trustee's powers are of crucial importance to a lender contracting with the trustee and must be confirmed in accordance with the Trust Ordinances and the terms of the instrument constituting the trust. The lender should obtain and review the trust instrument (or ensure that the lawyers providing the Gibraltar law opinion have sight of it) to ensure that there are no restrictions on the trustee's powers.

14.8.3.4 Due authorisation

The lender should seek production of a trustees' minute pursuant to which:

- the trustees properly consider the terms of the proposed transaction and record the benefit to the trust and/or its beneficiaries;
- there are tabled and considered by the trustees the transaction documents;
- the trustees resolve to approve the transaction and execute the transaction documents; and
- the trustees authorise the execution of the transaction documents by their signature.

Provided that neither the settlor nor any beneficiary of a trust is a resident of Gibraltar, the trustee will not be assessed to tax on the income of the trust arising from a non-Gibraltar source, or on interest earned on Gibraltar bank deposits.

14.8.4 Lending to partnerships and limited partnerships

Gibraltar has not, to date, developed its partnership law with a view to generally facilitating the use of partnerships or limited partnerships in an offshore centre context. Partnerships are, as a matter of the law of Gibraltar, governed by either the *Partnerships Ordinance* (in the case of a general partnership), or the *Limited Partnerships Ordinance* (in the case of a limited partnership). Both the *Partnerships Ordinance* and the *Limited Partnerships Ordinance* are closely based on the UK *Partnership Act 1890* and *Limited Partnership Act 1909*. In any case involving either a general or limited partnership formed under the laws of Gibraltar, the lender should review the relevant partnership agreement to determine the identity of the partners and, in the case of a limited partnership, its general partner.

14.8.5 Lending to collective investment schemes

The description 'collective investment scheme' is a classification of investment activity under the law of Gibraltar which describes a regulated investment activity undertaken by a body corporate or unit trust falling within the scope of the *Financial Services Ordinance 1989* and the *Financial Services (Collective Investment Schemes) Regulations 1991*. The lender should be concerned with the issues of legal personality, capacity, due authorisation and due execution arising from the constitution of the body corporate or trustee of the unit trust and should ascertain that all regulatory licences and permissions have been obtained. As a particular issue arising in relation to capacity and due authority, the lender should ensure that there are no relevant *investment restrictions* which prevent either the borrowing or the application of the borrowed moneys, in the manner anticipated by the transaction documents. Where an open-ended investment company is the borrower or counter party, it will have a separate manager and custodian/trustee who may be required to grant, or join in, any disposition of property by way of security.

14.8.6 Taking security

There are no relevant restrictions on the capacity of a natural person, Gibraltar company (whether private or public), or trustee of a Gibraltar trust restricting their capacity as a matter of general law in the giving of a security pursuant to foreign law over immoveable, tangible moveable or intangible moveable property with a *situs* outside of Gibraltar. In its treatment of immoveable, tangible moveable and intangible moveable property, the law of Gibraltar follows, very closely, that of English private international law principles, with the consequent recognition of the obtaining of a security interest by way of registered mortgage/charge in respect of immoveable property, possessory assignment and/or mortgage or pledge in respect of tangible moveables, and charge/assignment in respect of intangible moveables.

14.8.7 Requirements for registration, filing and recording

The Companies Ordinance requires that a Gibraltar company should maintain a register of charges created by or against the property, including floating charges, if they are to provide the creditor with a secured position as against a liquidator of the company. In addition, the Gibraltar company must maintain a charges register at its registered office and all details of secured indebtedness are required to be given in its annual return.

14.9 Enforcement

The Supreme Court of Gibraltar will register a judgment in accordance with the provisions of the *Judgments (Reciprocal Enforcement) Ordinance* where the judgment is that of a superior court of the United Kingdom or another specified territory. On registration, the judgment will be enforceable as if it had been made by the Supreme Court of Gibraltar. If the judgment is obtained in a court other than that of a specified territory, it will be necessary to bring proceedings on the basis of the judgment evidencing a liquidated claim. For the future, the *Civil Jurisdiction and Judgments Ordinance* will allow registration of judgments given by the courts of those territories which are party to the Brussels and Lugano Conventions.

14.9.1 Interim relief

Where a lender is concerned to restrain the borrower from dissipating property pre or post a prospective judgment or other enforcement, the courts of Gibraltar will provide relief by way of *Mareva-type injunctions* and *tracing orders.*

14.9.2 Investigation and obtaining of evidence

At para 14.5 above, a general description has been given of the application of the common law duty of confidence owed by bankers and other professionals under the law of Gibraltar. The courts of Gibraltar have, in the past, shown a clear inclination to recognise and support the existence of a duty of confidence so as to restrain the obtaining of information by third parties, other than in cases covered by mutual assistance arrangements concerned with the combating of money laundering.

14.9.3 Winding-up and bankruptcy and dissolution

The Companies Ordinance provides for voluntary winding-up where:

- the period fixed for the life of the company has expired, or an event has occurred on the happening of which the articles provide that the company shall be dissolved; and
- where the members have resolved by special resolution that the company should be wound up.

The company may be subject to compulsory winding-up by order of court:

- where the company by special resolution has resolved that it should be wound up;
- on the petition of the company, its directors or creditors on the basis that it is insolvent;
- where default is made in delivering the annual report, or in holding an annual general meeting;
- where the company does not commence business within a year of incorporation, or suspends its business for a complete year; or
- where the court is of the opinion that it is just and equitable that the company should be wound up.

14.10 Recent and anticipated developments

It is anticipated that the required implementation of the EU Fourth Directive relating to companies will require substantial amendment to the Companies Ordinance, with particular emphasis on matters requiring disclosure through, for example, the filing of accounts.

Modifications of the *Companies Ordinance* and provisions for incorporation and administration of companies have been introduced which enables a Gibraltar company with a single member (*Ordinance 7/92*) to be incorporated and allows a single object company.

Following the enactment in 1991 of the enabling *section 295(A) in the Companies Ordinance* with regard to redomiciliation of European Union Companies in Gibraltar, the *Companies (Redomiciliation Regulations) 1992* were published on the 19 November 1992).

In 1993 the running of the Companies Registry was transferred to Companies House (Gibraltar) Limited. The company administers the Companies Registry and has introduced important reforms to the process of incorporation and filing of documents.

Amendment to the *Income Tax Ordinance* was introduced allowing the

'Qualifying Company' with exempt status to elect to pay income tax at concessionary rates as an alternative to seeking exempt status.

Under *Regulation 10 of the Bankruptcy (Registration of Disposition) Regulations 1990*, any person who gives incorrect information as regards registration is liable to a fine or imprisonment or both.

Gibraltar Bankruptcy Ordinance 1990 (as amended) has introduced legislation for creating protective settlements and their dispositions.

The Financial Services Ordinance 1990 (as amended) was introduced to regulate the financial services and aimed at controlling various licensed activities.

Legislation on money laundering in respect of money laundering and drug related activities has been passed into law in 1995.

Legislation has been drafted to clarify Gibraltar's position with regard to other countries' forced heirship rules.

Legislation relating to financial services generally, including the variety of *European Directives* concerning *Financial Services and Investment Services Directive* into Gibraltar Law is being drafted to bring it up to European Union Standards to allow Gibraltar companies to enjoy all European Union rights.

Amendments to the *Companies Ordinance* are to be introduced to regularise the position of public limited companies and to facilitate further incorporation of open ended investment companies.

15 | The British Virgin Islands

Introduction

The British Virgin Islands ('BVI') comprise a group of islands in the north-eastern Caribbean. The largest of the islands is Tortola, measuring some 21 square miles in area. The principal population centre (and the location of most of the financial institutions and professional support services) is Road Town. Tortola has a population of approximately 12 000. The BVI are English-speaking.

15.1 Currency and exchange control

The BVI have adopted the United States dollar, to which no exchange controls presently apply.

15.2 Constitution

The BVI are regarded as being politically stable, being a Crown dependency. A form of limited constitution was put in place in 1967, pursuant to which a United Kingdom-appointed Governor operates as a member of the Executive Council, which also has as members the Chief Minister and three further Ministers. The United Kingdom remains responsible for the external affairs and defence of the BVI. The Legislative Council is an elected body comprising nine elected officials capable of passing its own legislation. It is perhaps fair to say that the adoption of the United States dollar as the currency of the BVI has led to increasingly close ties to the United States.

15.3 Legal system

The BVI system of law is based on English common law. In addition to its own sourced legislation (which draws on the legislative experience of the United Kingdom), UK legislation has been extended to the BVI by Orders in Council. The practice and procedure of the BVI courts and judiciary follow, in large part, that of the United Kingdom.

15.4 Banking and professional confidentiality

There is no statutory bank secrecy framework in the BVI, and banking and other professional confidentiality arises as a matter of an express or implied contractual obligation.

15.4.1 BVI companies: disclosure of beneficial ownership

There is no requirement for disclosure of beneficial ownership on incorporation.

15.4.2 Disclosure to bankers by financial intermediaries

Disclosure required as part of the regulatory environment contained within the *Banks and Trust Companies Act 1990* and the *Company Management Act 1990* contain provisions expressly providing for the preservation of confidentiality and make it an offence for regulators or any other person to disclose any information obtained otherwise than pursuant to compulsion of law.

15.4.3 Disclosure under compulsion of law

Disclosure may be compelled pursuant to the *Drug Trafficking Offences Act 1992* and the *Drugs (Prevention and Misuse) (Amendment) Act 1992*, or the *Mutual Legal Assistance (United States of America) Act 1990* which enable the police and regulatory authorities to obtain information concerning drug trafficking, racketeering and insider trading, but do not extend to the investigation of fiscal offences.

15.5 Regulation in the financial sector

The primary responsibility for supervision of the provision of financial services and the finance sector in the BVI rests with the Chief Minister, who delegates responsibility to the Finance Minister, operating through a civil service executive in the form of the Financial Services Department of the BVI's Ministry of Finance. The Financial Services Department may presently call upon the assistance of a Foreign Office official based in Barbados as financial services adviser. The Financial Services Department operates as a primary regulator in accordance with the terms of the following key items of legislation:

- The *Banks and Trust Companies Act 1990* and the *Company Management Act 1990*, pursuant to which (i) general and restricted banking licences are granted and supervision conducted in respect of *general* and two classes of *restricted* banking licences, (ii) corporate trustee services are licensed (as *general* or *restricted* trust licences) and (iii) company administration and management services are licensed, in each case through the Inspector of Banks and Trust Companies, who has a supervisory role.
- The *Insurance Act 1994*, pursuant to which the conduct of insurance business both within and from the BVI is regulated.
- The *Companies Act 1885* and the *International Business Companies Ordinance 1984*, pursuant to which companies may be incorporated as 'international business companies' (IBCs), exempt from BVI income tax.

15.6 Anti-money laundering legislation and best practice

The BVI are members of the Caribbean Financial Action Task Force, the Offshore Group of Insurance Supervisors and the Offshore Group of Banking Supervisors, which commits to the recommendations of the Basle Committee (see Chapter 3 para 3.3 above). In the combating of the criminal misuse of its financial sector services, the BVI have adopted the following legislation.

15.6.1 Drug Trafficking Offences Act 1992 and Drugs (Prevention and Misuse) (Amendment) Act 1992

This legislation broadly follows the disclosure regime provided for by the UK *Drug Trafficking Offences Act 1986.*

15.6.2 Mutual Legal Assistance Treaty (United States of America) Act 1990

This treaty, entered into with the United States, allows for the mutual exchange of information between the investigating authorities of both jurisdictions concerning serious crime, including drug trafficking, racketeering and insider trading. The treaty does not allow for the obtaining and exchange of information relating to fiscal offences which do not involve other serious crime.

15.7 Lending with a British Virgin Islands foreign law connection

The text which follows will highlight those issues which may arise in connection with lending which has a BVI foreign law connection in that either the borrower is domiciled, resident and/or incorporated or constituted in the BVI, or because a transaction or security document has a proper or applicable law which is BVI law. The paragraphs below highlight, by reference to borrower type (building on the issues set out in Chapters 4, 5, 6 and 7), issues which arise for a lender where the borrower is domiciled, resident or incorporated in the BVI. For each borrower type, the issues considered are those which will, in the usual course, form the subject matter of a BVI foreign law legal opinion, being:

- legal personality (i.e. does the borrower have separate legal existence and if not, who may contract on behalf of the borrower?);
- capacity;
- due authorisation of the transaction;
- due execution of the transaction and/or security documents; and
- taxation, including withholding.

The remaining paragraphs will deal collectively with:

- the creation of security;
- enforcement and insolvency; and
- recent or anticipated developments in the relevant laws and practice of the BVI.

In dealing with the creation of security, it will be assumed that the law of the BVI is unlikely to be the proper or applicable law for the security agreements, in that the subject matter of the security does not have a BVI *situs*. The focus of attention is, therefore, the existence of any restriction on the capacity of the grantor to provide the security, and any formalities for due execution and perfection through registration or filing, etc. The lender will, however, need to consider adopting BVI law as the proper or applicable law if the security comprises bank deposits with a BVI bank and/or shares or securities deposited with a BVI bank or custodian or issued by a BVI incorporated company.

15.7.1 Lending to natural persons

The following issues are relevant when lending to, or taking a grant of security from, an individual domiciled and/or resident in the BVI.

15.7.1.1 Capacity

An individual is a minor and without legal capacity to contract (other than possibly for necessities) until attaining the age of 18 years.

15.7.1.2 Tax and withholding

An individual resident or ordinarily resident within the BVI is liable to assessment to tax on income wherever arising. An individual non-resident is liable to assessment on income having a BVI source. There is no withholding on interest payments to non-residents, and no capital gains tax, sales tax, or estate duty. The BVI has double taxation agreements with Japan and Switzerland and unilateral credit relief is, in addition, allowed in relation to other non-treaty countries.

15.7.2 Lending to companies

The legislative framework relating to a company incorporated under the law of the BVI is to be found in two distinct parts, being that which relates to international business companies and that which relates to *ordinary companies*. International business companies (popularly referred to as 'IBCs') are the best known and most frequently used of the BVI companies. The statutory framework for international business companies is contained within the *International Business Companies Ordinance (1984)* as amended ('CAP291'). The ordinary company is incorporated pursuant to the *Companies Act 1885* as amended, popularly referred to as 'CAP285'. CAP285 companies constitute fewer than 10% of all BVI incorporated companies; here, the focus will be on IBCs, such companies being the form most likely to be encountered by the lender. In relation to a company incorporated as an IBC under CAP291, the lender should note the following.

15.7.2.1 Legal personality, due incorporation and good standing

A company incorporated under CAP291 is from the date of its incorporation a body corporate having perpetual succession. Registration is a same-day process and the certificate issued by the Registrar of Companies under his hand and seal is conclusive as to due incorporation. A company incorporated as an IBC can have a variety of share-based capital structures, including (i) bearer shares, (ii) registered shares, and (iii) no par value shares. Incorporation does not require disclosure of ultimate beneficial ownership (but reliance is placed upon the due diligence undertaken by registered agents, who will maintain a stock of pre-incorporated companies). Otherwise the lender should note that the following are the principal elements required for incorporation:

- application to the Registrar of Companies for name approval (the use of names related to regulated activities such as 'Bank', 'Insurance' or 'Trust Company' will be dependent upon the appropriate licence or registration for such regulated activity);
- incorporation may only be achieved through an agent licensed pursuant to the *Banks and Trust Companies Act 1990* and the *Company Management Act 1990*;
- the memorandum of association to be submitted for registration must contain (i) the name of the company, (ii) the address of the registered office, (iii) the name and address of the registered agent, (iv) the objects, (v) the currency in which shares are denominated, the authorised share capital of the company and the number and classes and series of shares in issue, (vi) a statement of the conditions applicable to each of the classes of shares in issue, (vii) a statement of the number of shares to be issued as registered shares and a statement of the number of shares to be issued as bearer shares (unless such designation lies in the exercise of the directors' discretion), (viii) a statement of whether registered shares may be exchanged for bearer shares and vice versa, (ix) where bearer shares are permitted, the manner in which notices are to be given to members who are holders of bearer shares, and (x) a declaration that the company shall not undertake those activities prohibited by CAP291;
- the memorandum must be signed by the registered agent as subscriber, whose signature must be witnessed;
- the Registrar of Companies requires a written statement by the registered agent subscribing the memorandum of association that the requirements of CAP291 have been complied with;
- IBCs may have a single subscriber and member, who may be the holder of a single bearer share;
- the articles of association must be filed together with the memorandum of association as *regulations for the company* and when registered the articles bind the company and its members as if each member had subscribed his name and affixed his seal thereto.

IBCs are not subject to distinction between public and private companies. In relation to the continued standing of the company and its valid existence the lender will wish to know generally that the company borrower is not at risk of dissolution and has not committed offences under CAP291 so that, among other things, the following enquiries are relevant (this is not intended to be an exhaustive list of such matters):

- Does the company maintain a registered office in the BVI as stipulated in its memorandum of association (failure to comply will lead to the company being struck off the Companies Register)?
- Does the company stipulate the name and address of its registered agent (the identity of the original registered agent being required to be set out in the memorandum of association) and any subsequent change to be effected by resolution of members or directors?
- Does the company keep such accounts and records as the directors consider necessary or desirable in order to reflect the financial position of the company (but there is no audit requirement for an IBC)?
- Does the company minute all meetings of directors, members and committees of directors and maintain copies of all resolutions consented to by directors, members and committees of directors, officers or members at its registered office or at such other place as the directors may determine?
- Does the company maintain a register of members providing details of (i) the names and addresses of persons who hold registered shares in the company, (ii) the number of each class and series of registered shares held by each person, (iii) the date upon which any person ceased to be a member, (iv) the total number of each class of bearer shares, and (v) in relation to each bearer share, the identifying number, the number and class of each bearer share?

There is no requirement on an IBC to hold annual meetings, file audited or other financial statements or make any other form of annual return. The company has a discretion as to whether it maintains a register of directors, but if it does so maintain a register it must show (i) the names and addresses of the directors, (ii) the date on which the director was appointed and (iii) the date on which each person ceased to be a director. Such register, if kept, must be maintained at the registered office of the company. The company also has an option to maintain at its registered office a register of mortgages and charges. An IBC must pay an annual licence fee, which varies dependent on share capital (in default of payment the IBC may be struck off the Companies Register). An IBC may not (i) carry on business with persons resident in the BVI, (ii) own an interest in real property in the BVI other than a lease of property for office use, (iii) conduct banking, insurance or reinsurance, or provide registered office or agent facilities for BVI incorporated companies unless licensed to do so (see above, para 15.5), or undertake any other activity prohibited by BVI law.

15.7.2.2 Capacity

An IBC incorporated under CAP291 may pursue any lawful object; otherwise, the company has the capacity of a natural person, there being no application of the doctrine of *ultra vires*. Insofar as the memorandum of association contains any statement of objects or purpose, it may provide that the company be empowered to engage in any activity not prohibited under the laws of the BVI.

15.7.2.3 Due authority

There are no general limitations on the borrowing powers of an IBC incorporated under CAP291, although the lender should note that such restrictions may be contained within the articles of association. An IBC acts through its directors, who are bound by the terms of the articles of association and any objects set out in the company's memorandum of association, although no act of an IBC or transfer of real or personal property by or to a company is to be invalidated by reason of the fact that the company was without capacity. CAP291 provides that an IBC must have at least one director, who can be a corporate director. Notwithstanding the general absence of a doctrine of *ultra vires* it is suggested that the lender should, in all cases, require sight of a minute or extract of minute of the directors dealing with the following:

- confirming that the meeting was duly convened and quorate;
- evidencing consideration of the relevant aspects of the proposed transaction and in particular the commercial benefit to the company;
- considering the terms of the relevant transaction documents;
- approving the execution of the transaction documents substantially in the considered form (and, as appropriate, allowing for negotiation or agreement or amendment of such documents);
- stating the manner in which such documents are to be executed, designating one or more persons to attest the common seal of the company or designating individuals as signatories to the document; and
- disclosing the extent and nature of the directors' material conflicts of interest.

In the case of a company having a single director, the resolution should be in a relevant 'minute of resolution' form. An IBC is required to keep minutes of all proceedings of directors and shareholders at its registered office. Where shareholder resolutions are required as an aspect of the authorisation for the transaction the lender should note the following:

- an IBC may have a single member so that, in such cases, meetings will be constituted by a minute of resolution;

- the directors are required to give not less than seven days' notice of meetings of members (subject to anything in the memorandum and articles of association), provided that time for notice can be abridged if members holding a 90% majority have waived such requirement; and
- a resolution of members may be made by either a simple majority or such larger majority as may be specified in the articles of association.

There is no requirement that shareholder resolutions must be filed or otherwise recorded at the Companies Registry.

15.7.2.4 Due execution

The directors of an IBC have powers to bind the company in contract, or to appoint officers and agents to do so. A contract entered into by an IBC may be validly entered into by the company:

- if entered into between individuals and requiring to be made in writing under seal, then entered into on behalf of the company writing and under the common seal of the company;
- if entered into between individuals requiring by law to be in writing and under the hand of the parties, then entered into by or on behalf of the company in writing and signed by a person acting under the express or implied authority of the company; and
- if validly entered into between individuals orally and not requiring to be reduced to writing, then entered into by the company through a person acting under the express or implied authority of the company.

Notwithstanding a failure to apply the common seal of the company to a contract which is in form a deed, or otherwise requiring to be made under seal, CAP291 provides that such contract shall not be invalid as against the company. The directors of an IBC may by instrument in writing (whether or not under the company's common seal) appoint an attorney, either generally or in respect of specified matters, to act on behalf of the company and to execute contracts, agreements, deeds or other instruments by and for and on behalf of the company. The appointment can provide for sub-delegation by the appointed agent.

15.7.2.5 Issue of shares and circulation of a prospectus

There are no borrowing controls under the law of the BVI. An IBC can have an authorised share capital of any amount and, insofar as it may have a share capital comprising no par value shares, may have no share capital at all. Shares may be credited as paid-up against a promissory note or other debt security. An IBC may resolve to vary, increase or reduce its share capital by resolution of its members or (subject to the terms of the articles of association) of the directors. There is no duty payable on the authorised share capital, its issue or on its transfer. All issued share capital is required to be paid-up on issue, but, as noted above, may be credited as paid-up against a promissory note or binding debt obligation, in which case on insolvent winding-up the creditors of the company may require payment.

15.7.2.6 Licences and consents

If the activity of the IBC undertaken from or within the BVI is banking business, insurance business or that of an incorporation agent, then the licences referred to at para 15.5 above are required.

There are stamp duties and documentary taxes in BVI. Failure to pay does not affect the entry or performance of the documents, but in the event of legal proceedings to be enforced in BVI, stamp and documentary duties have to be paid. If the documents have been executed outside BVI, stamp duties may be paid within two months of when they first entered BVI. An IBC must renew licence with a payment of the appropriate fee by 31 May if it was incorporated within the first six months of a year, or by 30 November if incorporated in the later half of the year.

15.7.2.7 Financial assistance

There are no restrictions under CAP291 on the provisions of financial assistance by a company for the purchase of its own shares.

15.7.2.8 Disclosure of directors' interests

In order to avoid invalidity of a relevant contract, directors should disclose the nature and extent of any personal financial interest.

15.7.2.9 Commercial benefit

In accordance with the provisions of CAP291 and unless expressly varied by its memorandum of association, an IBC has express power to provide third-party guarantees and other security without the need for the company to have received tangible commercial benefit. Nevertheless, the directors remain subject to an obligation to act honestly and in good faith with a view to the best interests of the company such that there must remain a risk that knowledge of a breach of such fiduciary obligation might preclude enforcement of the obligation against the company. Best practice may therefore require that the lender establish that the directors have considered the best interests of the company (if not the existence of actual benefit), or that the lender ensures that an appropriate shareholder resolution has been passed, directing and requiring that the company enter into the transaction.

15.7.2.10 Tax and withholding

IBCs are exempt from local taxation in the BVI but pay an annual fee as follows:

- US$300.00 in respect of capital not exceeding US$50 000.00 or foreign currency equivalent;
- US$350.00, for a company with no capital, or a capital exceeding US$50 000.00 and where the company can issue shares with no par value; or
- US$1000.00 for capital exceeding US$50 000.00 or foreign currency equivalent.

There is no tax on interest arising on BVI bank deposits.

15.7.2.11 Redomiciliation

CAP291 allows for the redomiciliation of an IBC to another jurisdiction, or for a company from another jurisdiction to be redomiciled to the BVI. Where a company is to be redomiciled to the BVI there must be constituted *Articles of Continuation* in writing and in the English language, approved by a majority of the officers responsible for the affairs of the company, which contain (i) the name of the company and the name under which it is to be continued, (ii) the jurisdiction under which it is incorporated, (iii) the date on which it was incorporated, (iv) statements and other information complying with the requirements for the memorandum of association of an IBC, and (v) such amendments as may be necessary to ensure that its memorandum complies with CAP291. In addition, evidence of the company's prior good standing is required. On registration of the Articles of Continuation, the Registrar will issue a certificate of continuation under his hand and seal certifying that the company is incorporated under CAP291. Subject to the provisions of its memorandum and articles of association an IBC may seek to redomicile in a third country jurisdiction. Where allowed by its memorandum and articles of association, an IBC may, by resolution of directors or members, resolve to continue as a body corporate under the laws of a foreign jurisdiction. CAP291 requires that the company must be a company in respect of which the Registrar will issue a certificate of good standing and the IBC's registered agent must submit an affidavit to the Registrar of Companies within 30 days of the redomiciliation. The effect of registration is that (i) the company is struck off the register of companies in the BVI, (ii) the Registrar issues a certificate of discontinuance, and (iii) there is published, in the BVI official gazette, a notice of striking-off.

15.7.3 Lending to BVI trusts

The paragraphs which follow set out the issues relevant when lending to, or taking a grant of security from, a trust (through its trustee) which has as its proper law the law of the BVI. There is no consolidated trust law and the relevant statutory framework is contained within the *Trustee Act 1961* as amended by the *Trustee (Amendment) Act 1993* (together referred to as 'the Trust Acts'). Here, references to a 'trust' mean a BVI trust – one which, in accordance with the Trust Acts, has a proper law being that of the BVI. In dealing with a trust as a borrower and/or provider of security over property comprising the trust fund, the lender should note the following.

15.7.3.1 Legal personality

The trust does not, itself, have separate legal personality. The trust acts through its trustee or trustees who hold (or have held to their order) title to the trust fund.

15.7.3.2 Due constitution and validity of the trust

The following are the primary characteristics of a duly constituted and valid trust pursuant to the Trust Acts:

- there are no requirements as a matter of general law that a trust be created in any specific form, the law of the BVI applying common law principles in requiring that there be certainty of intention to create a trust, certainty of objects and certainty of subject matter, but otherwise allowing for a trust to be constituted orally, in writing, or otherwise howsoever;
- the proper law of the trust may be changed subject to the terms of the trust instrument;
- the trustee has a duty to act in the best interests of the beneficiaries and impartially and in good faith;
- the trust may have a protector;
- the title of the trustee to property transferred into trust by a non-resident settlor during his lifetime is not (as a matter of the law of the BVI) invalidated by operation of foreign law *forced heirship rules*;
- the trust may be established for any period not exceeding 100 years;
- income may be accumulated during the existence of the trust; and
- a trust may be established for a non-charitable purpose (i.e. as a 'purpose trust') which is particular, reasonable and possible and which is not immoral, contrary to public policy or unlawful and provided that the trust has, in addition to a 'designated trustee' a further named person empowered to enforce the trusts.

15.7.3.3 Capacity

The capacity of the trustee and the extent of the trustee's powers are of crucial importance to a lender contracting with the trustee and must be confirmed in accordance with the Trust Acts and the terms of the instrument constituting the trust. The Trust Acts contain a comprehensive schedule of powers of investment which can, nevertheless, be augmented. The lender should obtain and review the trust instrument (or ensure that the lawyers providing a relevant BVI law opinion have sight of it) to ensure that there are no restrictions on the trustee's powers and that exercise of the relevant trustee powers does not require the consent of a protector, if any.

15.7.3.4 Due authorisation

The lender should seek production of a trustees' minute pursuant to which:

- the trustees properly consider the terms of the proposed transaction and record the benefit to the trust and/or its beneficiaries;
- there are tabled and considered by the trustees the transaction documents;
- the trustees resolve to approve the transaction and execute the transaction documents; and
- the trustees authorise the execution of the transaction documents by their signature, or, if a corporate trustee, and so required, by the application of its common seal.

15.7.3.5 Taxation and withholding

In the case of a trust having a non-resident settlor and non-resident beneficiaries (and notwithstanding that it has a resident trustee or trustees) it will not be assessable to BVI income tax on income arising from a source outside of the BVI or on bank deposit interest arising within the BVI. The trust is subject to nominal 'trust duty' in respect of the stamping of the trust instrument.

15.7.4 Lending to partnerships and limited partnerships

The existing partnership law of the BVI makes no provision for limited partnerships and is contained in the *Partnership Act 1888*. The lender should obtain and review the partnership agreement of a general partnership. There are no registration requirements for general partnerships under BVI law. A company can be a partner in a general partnership.

15.7.5 Lending to collective investment schemes

At the present time, and although IBCs and BVI trusts are used to constitute open-ended investment scheme companies and unit trusts, there is no statutory regulation of collective investment or mutual funds under the law of the BVI. That is a position which it is intended to change with the introduction of a regulatory regime.

15.7.6 Taking security

It is assumed here that the lender will, in almost all cases, be concerned with the validity of security agreements governed by a proper or applicable law which is that other than the law of the BVI on the basis that the property which is the subject matter of the security agreement has a *situs* which is other than the BVI. Accordingly, the focus of concern will be the capacity of the grantor of the security (whether a natural person, body corporate or trustee of a trust), to grant the security.

15.7.6.1 Capacity to grant a foreign law security
There are no restrictions on capacity (or otherwise as a matter of public policy) which prevent the valid grant of foreign law security interests.

15.7.6.2 BVI law security interests
In its treatment of immoveable, tangible moveable and intangible moveable property the law of the BVI follows, closely, that of England with consequent recognition of the obtaining of security interests by way of registered mortgage/charge in respect of *immoveable property*, possessory assignment and/or mortgage or pledge in respect of *tangible moveables* and charge/assignment in respect of *intangible moveables*.

15.7.7 Requirements for registration, filing and recording

There is no register of charges maintained within the Companies Registry, but an IBC or ordinary company may maintain a register of mortgages and charges at its registered office which the lender should have inspected and on which the lender should ensure that the company enters details of the lender's security.

15.8 Enforcement

Reciprocal enforcement of judgments from designated territories including the United Kingdom and Commonwealth countries is provided for by the terms of the *Reciprocal Enforcement of Judgments Act* and the *Foreign Judgments (Reciprocal Enforcement) Act* which allow registration of judgments subject to conditions. The courts of the BVI will, without a retrial of the merits, give effect to a final and conclusive judgment rendered in any action or proceedings given by a superior court in a foreign territory as if the judgment was an action brought before the BVI courts, where the judgment is final and conclusive between the parties, is not in respect of a fine or penalty, is for a liquidated sum and where the original court had personal jurisdiction over the debtor.

15.8.1 Interim relief

Where the lender is concerned to restrain the borrower from dissipating property pre or post a prospective judgment or other enforcement, the courts of the BVI will provide relief by way of *Mareva-type injunctions* and/or *tracing orders.*

15.8.2 Investigation and obtaining of evidence

At para 15.4 above, a general description has been given of the application of the common law duty of confidence owed by bankers and other professionals under the law of the BVI. The courts of the BVI will, pursuant to the mutual assistance arrangements with the United States, make disclosure orders under legislation intended to combat drug money laundering, racketeering and other serious crime, but will not compel disclosure intended to facilitate enforcement of the fiscal laws of a foreign territory.

15.8.3 Winding-up and bankruptcy

CAP291 makes provision for voluntary winding-up of an IBC upon resolution passed by the members or the directors, or if the IBC has never issued shares, by resolution by the directors. A compulsory winding-up and dissolution will follow a resolution of the directors (i) on the expiration of the period of existence fixed for the company in its articles of association, or (ii) on the happening of an event which has been specified in the memorandum or articles of association as terminating the existence of the company. In any winding-up if the directors (or a liquidator if appointed) form the view that the company will not be able to discharge its liabilities in full, there is an obligation to give notice of such fact to the Registrar of Companies. A company may be compulsorily wound up under the supervision of the courts of the BVI in any case of a company's insolvency.

15.9 Recent and anticipated developments

It is anticipated that the BVI will shortly introduce legislation intended to provide for the regulation or enhanced regulation of mutual funds and insurance companies, allow the incorporation of hybrid companies, and the registration of limited partnerships. The BVI authorities may also introduce amendments to the Companies Acts to provide for an enhanced insolvency regime.

BVI has introduced its own Banking Policy and the Banking Licencing Guidelines based on the principles of International Banking Supervision in accordance with the *Basle Committees* requirements.

Trust legislation was enacted in 1993 and in 1994/1995 Financial Legislative programme relating to which duration companies, partnerships, limited partnerships, insolvency was declared by the Government.

Bank and Trust Companies Act, the *Companies Management Act* and *IBC Act* are expected to be introduced.

16 The Cayman Islands

Introduction

The Cayman Islands comprise three islands of a group situated in the western Caribbean, comprising Grand Cayman, Cayman Brac and Little Cayman. Of the three, Grand Cayman is the largest and is the focus of the financial services industry. The principal population centre of Grand Cayman (and the location of most of the financial institutions and the professional support services) is George Town. Grand Cayman has a population of approximately 28 000. The Cayman Islanders are English-speaking.

16.1 Currency and exchange control

The Cayman Islands have their own currency, the CI dollar, tied to the United States dollar at a fixed rate. There are presently no foreign currency exchange controls applicable to the Cayman Islands.

16.2 Constitution

The Cayman Islands are regarded as being politically stable. Their status is that of a British Crown dependent territory. They enjoy a right to internal self-governance through an elected Legislative Assembly, comprising 15 members. The government comprises an Executive Council established pursuant to a constitution first introduced in 1962 and subsequently amended. The Executive Council consists of three official members (selected by the Governor as the representative of the Crown), together with five members elected by the Legislative Assembly and the Governor. The United Kingdom government retains a residual right to legislate for the Cayman Islands and has authority for their external affairs, the civil service and law and order.

16.3 Legal system

The system of law followed in the Cayman Islands is English common law. The Cayman Islands have an autonomous court and judicial system, comprising the Grand Court, the Summary Court and the Court of Appeal. The Grand Court has principal jurisdiction for material civil matters and criminal matters. Appeals lie from the Grand Court to the Court of Appeal and from there, with leave, to the Judicial Committee of the Privy Council in the United Kingdom.

16.4 Banking and professional confidentiality

The Cayman Islands have supplemented the common law of duty of banking and professional confidentiality (as annunciated by the English courts in the case of *Tournier v National Provincial and Union Bank of England* [1924] 1 K.B. 461) through a series of statutory provisions:

- the *Banks and Trusts Companies Law 1989*, which imposes a duty on bank and trust company officers to maintain client confidentiality; and
- the *Confidential Relationships (Preservation) Law 1976*, as amended in 1979 and by the *Confidential Relationships (Preservation) 1995 Revision*.

The *Confidential Relationships (Preservation) Law 1976* makes it an offence for any person in possession of confidential information to divulge such information to any person who is not entitled to it. It is, further, an offence to make use of information which is confidential by the trading in, or misuse of, such information for personal gain. The 1979 amendments allow a party holding information which is confidential to seek direction from the courts of the Cayman Islands concerning requests for its disclosure. In the case *Matter of ABC Limited* [1985] F.L.R. 159, the courts of the Cayman Islands ruled that an apparent consent given by a relevant party could not be treated as properly consensual where it was given under the threat of contempt of a United States court. In the case *Re Bank of America Trust* 1992–93 C.I.L.R. 574, the courts of the Cayman Islands ruled that information concerning fund transfer records should not be produced, it being held that the value of the preservation of bank confidentiality to the economy of the Cayman Islands outweighed the interests of the United States IRS. Nevertheless, the application of the *Confidential Relationships (Preservation) Law 1976* is subject to the obligations of the Cayman Islands pursuant to the extension to it of the United Kingdom's *Evidence (Proceedings in Other Jurisdictions) Act 1975*, giving effect to the Hague Convention on Evidence, pursuant to which assistance is given to foreign courts in the taking of evidence in civil or commercial matters and, in relations with the United States, pursuant to the Treaty relating to the *Mutual Assistance in Criminal Matters of 3 July 1986*. The Treaty provides for mutual assistance to be provided to investigative authorities and to United States Grand Jury proceedings, where the offences under investigation are those punishable by more than one year's imprisonment, the crimes of racketeering, drug trafficking and failing to report transfer of illegally acquired money, insider dealing, and violations of the *Foreign Corrupt Practices Act*. The Treaty does not, however, extend to the enforcement of offences which are of an exclusively fiscal nature.

16.4.1 Cayman companies: disclosure of beneficial ownership

There is no requirement for disclosure of beneficial ownership on incorporation. The share register of a company does not reflect trusts affecting shares, which may be held through nominees.

16.4.2 Disclosure to bankers by financial intermediaries

Most, if not all, of the banks with a physical presence within the Cayman Islands are members of the Cayman Islands Bankers Association (CIBA) and subscribe to its Code of Ethics, containing a statement of best practice in relation to 'know your customer'. This is intended to translate to a best practice standard which requires that when opening a new account, a bank should seek to determine beneficial ownership of bodies corporate and the source of funds held, both for individuals and for bodies corporate.

16.4.3 Disclosure under compulsion of law

Disclosure may be compelled pursuant to the *Misuse of Drugs Law (1995 Revision)* and, as identified above, pursuant to the *Treaty* relating to the *Mutual Assistance in Criminal Matters*.

16.5 Regulation in the financial sector

The regulation of the Cayman Islands financial services sector rests with the Financial Services Supervision Commission. The Financial Services Supervision Commission operates as a primary regulator in accordance with the terms of the following key legislation:

1 The *Banks and Trusts Companies Law (1995 Revision)*, pursuant to which the conduct of a banking/deposit-taking business is licensed and supervised (by the Inspector of Banks) as (i) a general bank (entitled to conduct business onshore and offshore), (ii) an offshore bank, and (iii) a restricted offshore bank permitted only to conduct business with named approved persons.
2 The *Insurance Law 1979*, pursuant to which insurance companies, including captive insurance companies, are licensed in two categories as (i) local insurance business, or (ii) external insurance business (whether restricted or unrestricted).
3 The *Mutual Funds Law 1993*, pursuant to which a framework is provided for the licensing of mutual funds and those promoting and otherwise providing services to collective investment schemes or mutual funds.
4 The *Companies Management Law 1984*, pursuant to which the provision of corporate administration to Cayman Islands companies is licensed.

16.6 Anti-money laundering legislation and best practice

The Cayman Islands are members of the Caribbean Financial Action Task Force and have endorsed the 40 recommendations proposed for implementation by all participating countries. In combating the criminal misuse of its financial sector services, the Cayman Islands have adopted the following legislation.

16.6.1 Misuse of Drugs Law (1995 Revision)

The *Misuse of Drugs Law (1995 Revision)* provides a definition of drug trafficking as being where a person enters into or is otherwise concerned in an arrangement whereby the retention of control by or on behalf of another person of the other person's proceeds of drug trafficking is facilitated, or the proceeds of drug trafficking by another person are used to secure that funds are placed at such other person's disposal, or are used for the other person's benefit to acquire property by way of investment. A person is guilty of an offence under the *Misuse of Drugs Law* if knowingly or having reasonable grounds to believe that property is directly or indirectly another person's proceeds of drug trafficking, he (i) conceals or disguises the property, or (ii) converts or transfers the property or removes it from the jurisdiction to assist such a person to avoid prosecution for drug trafficking offences, or the making or enforcement of a confiscation order. Where a person discloses to the Constable of the Royal Cayman Islands Police a suspicion or belief that any funds or investments are derived from or used in connection with drug trafficking (or any matter on which such suspicion or belief is based) such disclosure is relieved from a breach of disclosure of information imposed by the *Confidential Relationships (Preservation) Law 1976.*

16.6.2 The Mutual Legal Assistance Treaty

As is set out at para 16.4 above, this Treaty provides for the mutual exchange of information in relation to serious crime between the investigating authorities of the Cayman Islands and the United States of America.

16.7 Lending with a Cayman Islands foreign law connection

The text which follows will highlight (building on the issues set out in Chapters 4, 5, 6 and 7) those issues which may arise in connection with lending which has a Cayman Islands foreign law connection in that either the borrower is domiciled, resident and/or incorporated or constituted in the Cayman Islands or because a transaction or security document has a proper or applicable law which is Cayman Islands law. For each borrower type, the issues considered are those which will, in the usual course, form the subject matter of a Cayman Islands foreign law legal opinion, being:

- the existence of and continuity of legal personality (i.e. does the borrower have and can the borrower maintain separate legal existence and if not, who may contract on behalf of the borrower?);
- capacity;
- due authorisation of the transaction;
- due execution of the transaction and/or security documents; and
- taxation, including withholding.

The remaining paragraphs will deal collectively with:

- the creation of securities; and
- enforcement and insolvency.

As in other chapters dealing with individual offshore centres, an assumption has been made that the proper or applicable law of security agreements will be a law other than that of the relevant offshore centre, on the basis that it is unlikely that the security will have a *situs* in such offshore centre. In common with the treatments given to this subject for Guernsey and Jersey, and because of the large banking presence in each of those jurisdictions and in the Cayman Islands (together with the existence of global custodial facilities in such jurisdictions), limited consideration will be given in this chapter to the taking of security under the law of the Cayman Islands.

16.7.1 Lending to natural persons

The following issues are relevant when lending to, or taking a grant of security from, an individual domiciled and/or resident in the Cayman Islands.

16.7.1.1 Capacity
An individual is a minor and without legal capacity to contract (other than possibly for necessities) until attaining the age of 18 years.

16.7.1.2 Tax and withholding
There are no direct taxes on income, capital gains, property transfers or on inheritance applicable in the Cayman Islands.

16.7.2 Lending to companies

The legislative framework relating to a company incorporated under the law of the Cayman Islands is to be found in the *Companies Law 1960* as amended.

16.7.2.1 Legal personality, due incorporation and good standing
A company (or corporation) is from the date of its incorporation under the *Companies Law (1995 Revision)* ('the Companies Law') a body corporate having a separate legal personality and the powers and responsibilities of a natural person. The issue of a certificate of incorporation by the Registrar of Companies is conclusive as to its due incorporation in accordance with the Companies Law. A company may be incorporated as (i) a company limited by shares, (ii) a company limited by guarantee with or without a share capital (a *hybrid*), or (iii) an unlimited liability company. Incorporation does not require disclosure of ultimate beneficial ownership. Otherwise, the lender should note the following as the principal elements required for incorporation:

- application to the Registrar of Companies for name approval (the use of names related to regulated activities such as 'Bank', 'Insurance' or 'Trust

Company' will be dependent upon the appropriate licence having been obtained for such regulated activity);

- incorporation may only be achieved through a professional agent, including an agent licensed pursuant to the *Companies Management Law 1984*, being those engaged in the management of companies;
- the memorandum of association to be submitted for registration must contain (i) the name of the company, (ii) details of the registered office, (iii) the objects of the company (if it is intended that the company has limited objects), (iv) a statement of the limitation of liabilities of members (unless the company is an unlimited company), and (v) the share capital of the company if limited by shares and the limit of liability of members, if limited by guarantee;
- the memorandum must be signed by each subscriber in the presence of, and be attested by, at least one witness;
- the company may have a single subscriber member who may be the holder of a single bearer share; and
- the articles of association must be filed together with the memorandum of association as the document regulating the manner in which the affairs of the company will be managed and, as a matter of form, is executed as a deed, the signatures of the subscribers being attested by at least one witness.

There is no distinction between public and private companies, companies being classified only for the purpose of determining the existence or otherwise of perpetual succession, and incorporation and annual fees, as being:

- an *ordinary company*, a company (not being an *ordinary resident company*, *exempted company*, or *exempted limited duration company*) having a perpetual succession and being entitled, from the issue of its certificate of incorporation, to carry on business within the Cayman Islands. An ordinary company must contain the word 'Limited' or 'Ltd'. It has a common seal, corporate legal personality and perpetual succession. An ordinary company intending to be designated non-resident under the *Local Companies (Control) Law* must show that it does not intend to conduct business;
- an *ordinary non-resident company*, a company which does not intend to carry on business within the Cayman Islands and in respect of which the Financial Secretary has provided a certificate designating it to be non-resident, and having perpetual succession;
- an *exempted company*, a company which may not conduct business in the Cayman Islands and in respect of which certain particular provisions apply in that (i) it does not have to file an annual return of its members and its share register is not open to public inspection, (ii) it does not have to hold an annual general meeting, (iii) it may have shares which

have no par value, or, in the alternative, a par value but not both classes of shares, (iv) it may have bearer shares (but only if fully paid) and a company owning bearer shares cannot own immoveable property in the Cayman Islands, (v) it may not make an invitation to the public in the Cayman Islands to subscribe for any of its shares or debentures, (vi) it may obtain an exemption from future taxes under the *Tax Concessions Law* for up to 20 years, and (vii) it may register as an exempted limited duration company, (viii) it may only operate in the Islands for the furtherance of its business carried on outside the Islands and for this purpose it may effect and conclude contracts in the Islands and exercise in the Islands all of its powers necessary for carrying on its business outside the Island, (ix) the directors of the company must file annually a declaration that the company has complied with the relevant provisions of the *Companies Law*, (x) it may deregister in the Islands and transfer to and continue in another jurisdiction. The companies incorporated in other jurisdictions than the Cayman Islands may transfer to and continue as exempted companies in the Islands;

• an *exempted limited duration company* – a company which must be dissolved within 30 years of incorporation – must have two or more members deemed to participate in the management of the company as directors, so that the company is treated for US tax purposes as a partnership. An amendment to the *Company Law* was passed in 1993 for the establishment of limited duration companies (LDCs). Limited duration companies are governed by the *Companies Law* regulating exempted companies with certain additions and exceptions. An LDC must include the words 'Limited Duration Company' or 'LDC' at the end of its name and must have at least two members. Its duration must be limited to 30 years or less and must have at least two share holders. Any transfer of shares or other memberships may require unanimous approval of all the other members. Its management may be vested in the members per capita or in accordance with the proportion of their shares or interest of provision of the Articles of Association. Management may be delegated to a Board of Directors in the usual manner.

In relation to the continued standing of the company and its valid existence, the lender will wish to know generally that the company borrower is not at risk of dissolution and has not committed offences under the Companies Law so that, among other things, the following enquiries are relevant. (This is not intended to be an exhaustive list of such matters.)

• Do all companies have a registered office in the Cayman Islands at which is maintained (other than in the case of exempt companies) a register of shareholders available for public inspection? In the case of an exempted company, the register of members may be kept at other than the registered office and is not available for public inspection.

- In the case of all companies, other than an exempted company, is an annual return of shareholders and their shareholdings made to the Registrar of Companies?
- Do all companies keep a register of charges at their registered office available for inspection by members or creditors?
- If an exempted company does it annually confirm that it has complied with the *Companies Law 1960*?
- Do all companies, other than exempted companies, hold an annual general meeting in each calendar year?
- Do exempted companies hold a meeting of directors in the Cayman Islands at least once in each year (such meetings can be convened and held by proxies or alternates)?
- Is there at least one director, with all changes to the directors and other officers registered with the Registrar of Companies within 30 days?

There is no obligation on companies to file accounts, although they are under an obligation to maintain accounts, which need not be audited.

16.7.2.2 Capacity

The Companies Law provides that no act of a company and no disposition of real or personal property to or by a company shall be invalidated by reason only of the fact that the company was without capacity or power to perform the act or to dispose of or receive the property, save that a member or director may bring proceedings against the company to prohibit the performance of any act, or the disposition of real or personal property and any such disposition in breach of a relevant restriction in the memorandum or articles of association will constitute a breach by the directors or former officers of the company, for which they may be liable in damages.

16.7.2.3 Due authority

There are no general limitations on the borrowing powers of a Cayman Islands company incorporated under the Companies Law, although the lender should note that such restrictions may be contained within the articles of association. It should be noted, however, that Table A standard form articles of association limit borrowing powers of the directors to the value of the issued and paid-up share capital. A Cayman Islands company acts through its directors, who are bound by the terms of the articles of association and any objects set out in the company's memorandum of association, although, as is set out at 16.7.2.2 above, no act of a Cayman Islands company, or transfer of real or personal property by or to the company is invalidated by reason of the fact that the company was without capacity. The *Companies Law* provides that a company must have at least one director, who can be a corporate director. Notwithstanding the general absence of the doctrine of *ultra vires* for companies incorporated after January 1988, it is suggested that the lender should, in all cases, require sight of a minute or extract of a minute of the directors dealing with the following:

- confirming that the meeting was duly convened and quorate;
- evidencing consideration of the relevant aspects of the proposed transaction;
- considering the terms of the relevant transaction documents;
- approving the execution of the transaction documents substantially in the considered form (and as appropriate allowing for negotiation or agreement of amendments to such documents);
- stating the manner in which such documents are to be executed, designating one or more persons to attest the common seal of the company or designating individuals as signatories to the documents.

In the case of a company having a single director, the resolution should be in a relevant 'minute of resolution' form. Subject to the articles of association, a Cayman Islands company may provide that proceedings of directors be undertaken by a committee to which powers of the directors have been delegated, or at meetings convened and held by telephone, or by resolution in writing signed by all of the directors. Where shareholder resolutions are required as an aspect of the authorisation for the transaction, the lender should note that the Companies Law:

- allows for the convening and conduct of general or class meetings of members in such manner as may be provided for by the articles of association and with only one such member being present, so that in the case of a single member company, a resolution will be constituted by a minute of resolution;
- does not make specific provision for the convening and/or conduct of meetings of members, but Table A requires that meetings be convened on not less than seven days' notice given in writing to members;
- provides that a resolution is a special resolution when it has been passed by a majority of not less than two-thirds (or such greater number as may be specified in the articles of association) of such members as, being entitled to do so, vote in person or, where proxies are allowed, by proxy at a general meeting of which notice specifying the intention to propose the resolution as a special resolution has been duly given, or (where authorised by the company's articles of association) it has been approved in writing by all of the members entitled to vote at a general meeting of the company in one or more instruments each signed by one or more of the members, in which case the effective date of the special resolution so adopted shall be the date on which the instrument or last of the instruments (if more than one) is executed;
- requires that a special resolution is filed with the Registrar of Companies within 15 days of it being passed or becoming effective and, where the

articles of association have been registered, a copy of every special resolution for the time being in force is required to be annexed to or embodied in every copy of the articles of association issued after the passing of the resolution.

16.7.2.4 Due execution

Subject to the articles of association, the directors of a company have power to bind the company in contract, or to appoint officers and agents to do so. It should be noted that an *exempted limited duration company* may be deemed to be managed and controlled by its members unless they delegate such management and control to a board of directors. In relation to a company generally, a contract may be validly entered into by the company:

- where, if entered into between individuals and requiring to be made in writing and under seal, when entered into on behalf of the company in writing and under the common seal of the company;
- where, if entered into between individuals requiring by law to be in writing and under the hand of the parties, when entered into by or on behalf of the company in writing and signed by a person acting under the express or implied authority of the company; and
- where, if entered into between individuals orally and not required to be reduced to writing, when entered into by the company through a person acting under the express or implied authority of the company.

Contracts validly entered into by a company in accordance with the Companies Law are deemed to be binding upon the company and its successors and all other parties thereto, their heirs, executors or administrators. A company may, by deed or instrument under seal, empower a person either generally or in respect of a specified matter to be its attorney to execute deeds or instruments under seal on its behalf and a deed or instrument under seal signed by a duly appointed attorney on behalf of the company shall bind the company and have effect as if it were executed by the company. A company may maintain a seal for use outside of the Cayman Islands as a duplicate seal and the company having a duplicate seal may authorise any person appointed for the purpose to affix the duplicate seal to any deed or other document to which the company is a party.

16.7.2.5 Issue of shares and circulation of a prospectus

The Companies Law and the law of the Cayman Islands generally provide no restriction on borrowing of general application. Shares may be issued by a company and paid-up at a premium, in which case the value of the premium must be reflected in the balance on a share premium account. Where allowed by the articles of association, a company may provide for the purchase or redemption of its own shares and may do so without the requirement for a formal court-sanctioned capital reduction if the source of the proceeds for purchase or redemption is as prescribed in the Companies Law, including the balance on a share premium account. Capital duty is payable on the authorised share capital of the company, and on any increase.

16.7.2.6 Licences and consents
If the activity of a company is that of banking business, insurance business, that of a mutual fund, or of a corporate managing agent, then the licences referred to at para 16.5 above are required.

16.7.2.7 Financial assistance
The Companies Law provides no specific restrictions on the provision of financial assistance by a company for the purchase of its own shares.

16.7.2.8 Disclosure of directors' interests
There are no specific provisions within the terms of the Companies Law making void or voidable transactions entered into by directors where conflict of interests exists. Nevertheless, it is clear that a director is, in relation to the company, in a fiduciary position and best practice may, therefore, be to insist on disclosure of interests in any material contract to which the company is a party.

16.7.2.9 Fraudulent preference/commercial benefit
The absence of commercial benefit does not, of itself, impact on the capacity of the company, and the validity of any act or transaction otherwise validly entered into. The Companies Law does, however, provide that any transaction which would, if undertaken by an individual trader pursuant to the *Bankruptcy Law*, be an undue or fraudulent preference of creditors, will represent undue or fraudulent preference undertaken by the company, such that the transaction will be invalid and, in determining the invalidity, the rules applicable on a personal bankruptcy will apply to the company.

16.7.2.10 Tax and withholding
Companies are not assessable to income or other taxes but are liable to pay the incorporation and annual fees applicable to them. Moreover, in the case of an exempted company, it may obtain a guarantee and undertaking providing that it shall not be liable for any possible Cayman Islands taxation imposed for up to 30 years.

16.7.2.11 Redomiciliation/continuation
The Companies Law provides in Part XII for transfer by way of continuation

by a foreign company to be continued as an exempted company in the Cayman Islands.

16.7.3 Lending to Cayman Islands trusts

The text below sets out the issues relevant when lending to, or taking a grant of security from, a trust (through its trustee) which has as its proper law the law of the Cayman Islands. The Cayman Islands trust law is based generically on English common law, varied by local legislation and case authority. The principal statutory provisions are contained within the *Trust Law (Revised) 1967* (based on the UK *Trustee Act 1925*), the *Trusts (Foreign Element) Law 1987, Fraudulent Dispositions Law 1989* and the *Perpetuities Law 1995* (together referred to as 'the Trust Laws'). References here to a 'trust' mean a Cayman Islands trust – one which, in accordance with the Trust Laws, has its proper law being that of the Cayman Islands.

The *Trusts (Foreign Element) Law 1987* (i) makes provision for a proper law doctrine for a trust, (ii) allows changes in the proper law of a trust, (iii) applies the law of the Cayman Islands to the determination of validity, form and administration of a trust, the proper law of which is expressed to be Cayman Islands law, and (iv) protects from attack dispositions into trust in breach of foreign law *forced heirship rules* affecting the non-Cayman Islands domiciled settlor. The *Fraudulent Dispositions Law 1989* makes Cayman Islands proper law trusts effective as asset protection trusts.

In dealing with a trust as a borrower and/or provider of security over property comprising the trust fund, the lender should note the following.

16.7.3.1 Legal personality
The trust does not, itself, have separate legal personality. The trust acts through its trustee or trustees who hold (or have held to their order) title to the trust fund.

16.7.3.2 Due constitution and validity of the trust
The following are characteristics of a duly constituted and valid trust pursuant to the Trust Laws:

- there are no requirements as a matter of general law that a trust be created in any specific form (the Trust Laws allow for those (i) created by statute, (ii) created intentionally by the act of the parties, (iii) arising from the presumed intention of the parties, and (iv) arising by operation of law, for example constructive or resulting trusts) but it is usual for creation to be by a deed notarised or witnessed before a consular official on which stamp duty is payable;
- the perpetuity period for a Cayman Islands trust is, pursuant to the *Perpetuities Law 1995*, a period of 150 years;

- the trust may have a protector; and
- the title of the trustee to property transferred into trust by a non-resident settlor during his lifetime is not (as a matter of the law of the Cayman Islands) invalidated by operation of foreign law *forced heirship rules.*

16.7.3.3 Capacity

The capacity of the trustee and the extent of the trustee's powers are of crucial importance to a lender contracting with the trustee and must be confirmed to be in accordance with the Trust Laws and the terms of the instrument constituting the trust. It is usual practice to give the trustee full and extensive powers to invest the trust fund, including power to acquire and hold companies as a trust investment and to accumulate trust income during the perpetuity period.

16.7.3.4 Due authorisation

The lender should seek production of a trustees' minute pursuant to which:

- the trustees properly consider the terms of the proposed transaction and record the benefit to the trust and/or its beneficiaries;
- there are tabled and considered by the trustees the transaction documents;
- the trustees resolve to approve the transaction and execute the transaction documents; and
- the trustees authorise the execution of the transaction documents by their signature, or, if a corporate trustee, and so required, by the application of its common seal.

16.7.3.5 Taxation and withholding

Where a Cayman Islands trust (i) is a discretionary trust, (ii) has no beneficiaries that are Cayman Islands residents, and (iii) has a trust instrument in a form first approved by the Registrar of Trusts, it may apply for *exempted trust* status. An exempted trust may obtain a certificate guaranteeing and undertaking that the trust will not be subject to any tax of an income or capital nature introduced in the Cayman Islands for a period of up to 50 years from the date of its creation. There are nominal fees and stamp duties payable on the registration and otherwise on an annual basis.

16.7.4 Lending to partnerships and limited partnerships

The law of the Cayman Islands draws a distinction between a *general partnership* (being the relationship which subsists between persons carrying on a business in common with a view to profit and regulated pursuant to the *Partnership Law 1983*, a law which is materially similar to the UK *Partnership Act 1890*) and *limited partnerships* which may be of two types, being:

- an *ordinary limited partnership*, registered under the *Partnership Law 1983*; or
- an *exempted limited partnership*, registered under the *Exempted Limited Partnership Law 1991* pursuant to the *Exempted Limited Partnership Regulations 1991* ('the Regulations').

Here, a reference to a limited partnership means an exempted limited partnership. Where the lender is dealing with a limited partnership as a prospective borrower and/or grantor of security, the following is relevant as a matter of the law of the Cayman Islands.

16.7.4.1 Legal personality, constitution and valid existence

A limited partnership does not have a separate legal personality (*cf* an *exempted limited duration company*). The Regulations do, however, provide, at regulation 4(1), that an exempted partnership may be formed 'with the rights and powers, and subject to the conditions, limitations, restrictions and liabilities' provided for by the Regulations. The Regulations provide that a certificate issued by the Registrar of Exempted Limited Partnerships shall be conclusive evidence that compliance has been made with all the requirements of the law in respect of formation and registration, such certificate being issued when the Registrar has received the fee payable on registration, together with a statement signed by or on behalf of a general partner setting out details of:

- the name of the exempted limited partnership;
- the general nature of the business of the exempted limited partnership;
- the address in the Cayman Islands of the registered office of the exempted limited partnership;
- the term, if any, for which the exempted limited partnership is entered into, or, for an unlimited duration, a statement to that effect and the date of its commencement;
- the full name and address of each general partner (accompanied in the case of a corporate general partner by a certificate of incorporation, certificate of good standing or similar document); and
- a declaration that the exempted limited partnership shall not undertake business with the public in the Cayman Islands, other than so far as may be necessary for the carrying on of the business of the exempted limited partnership outside of the Cayman Islands.

A certificate issued by the Registrar of Limited Partnerships is conclusive as to delivery of the statement and declaration and of the establishment of the limited partnership. Otherwise, the following are the relevant features of a duly constituted and validly existing exempted limited partnership:

- an exempted limited partnership is constituted by an association of one or more general partners and one or more limited partners (either of whom may be a body corporate);
- the exempted limited partnership should have (but the Regulations do not make it mandatory) a 'partnership agreement', being an agreement of the partners which provides for the establishment of and regulates the affairs of the exempted limited partnership, the conduct of its business and the rights and obligations of the partners amongst themselves;
- the exempted limited partnership must maintain at its registered office a register in writing setting out the name and address, amount and date of the contribution or contributions of each partner and the amount and date of any payment representing a return of any part of the contribution of any partner, it being the obligation of the exempted limited partnership to amend the register to reflect relevant transactions within 21 business days of any change in particulars;
- a limited partner is not liable for the debts or obligations of the exempted limited partnership unless such partner participates in the management of the exempted limited partnership (the Regulations exclude certain activities from being a participation in management);
- a general partner shall, in the event that the assets of the exempted limited partnership are inadequate, be liable for all the debts and obligations of the exempted limited partnership;
- the death, insanity, retirement, bankruptcy, commencement of liquidation proceedings, resignation, insolvency or dissolution of the sole or last remaining general partner will cause the immediate dissolution of the exempted limited partnership which is required forthwith to be wound up in accordance with the provisions of the partnership agreement or orders of the court, unless within 90 days of the date of such dissolution the limited partners unanimously elect one or more new general partners, in which case the exempted limited partnership is deemed to have continued as provided for in the partnership agreement;
- there is no limitation on the number of limited partners; and
- both a general partner and a limited partner may be a body corporate.

16.7.4.2 Capacity
The Regulations provide that the rules of equity and of the common law applicable to partnerships as modified by the *Partnership Law 1983* (but excluding ss. 46–56 thereof) apply to an exempted limited partnership, otherwise than as modified by the Regulations and the Exempted Partnership Law. In relation to the capacity of the general partner to act on behalf of, and contract for, the exempted limited partnership the lender should have regard to the following:

- any property of the exempted limited partnership which is conveyed to or vested in or held on behalf of any one or more of the general partners or which is conveyed into or vested in the name of the exempted limited partnership is held or deemed to be held by the general partner (and if more than one of them, by the general partners jointly), upon trust as an asset for the exempted limited partnership in accordance with the terms of the partnership agreement;
- any debt or obligation incurred by a general partner in the conduct of the business of an exempted limited partnership is deemed to be the debt or obligation of the exempted limited partnership; and
- an 'insolvency' of the exempted limited partnership arises when the general partner is unable to pay the debts and obligations of the exempted limited partnership (otherwise than in respect of liabilities to partners on account of their partnership interest) in the ordinary course of business as they fall due and out of the assets of the exempted limited partnership (without recourse to the separate assets of the general partner), so that references to being 'solvent' are construed accordingly.

16.7.4.3 Due authorisation and execution

Due authorisation of a transaction on behalf of the exempted limited partnership should be resolved upon by the general partners and the lender should obtain and have reviewed, in the context of a Cayman Islands foreign law opinion, a minute of resolution of the general partners. It may be necessary to consider further foreign law connections if one or more of the corporate general partners is incorporated outside of the Cayman Islands. Although the Regulations do not expressly so provide, the application of the rules of equity and common law applicable to partnerships means that a person dealing with the general partner in that capacity is entitled to deal with the general partner as having ostensible authority to contract for and on behalf of the limited partnership.

16.7.4.4 Tax and withholding

The exempted partnership may, on the application of a general partner, obtain a certificate issued by the Governor of the Cayman Islands undertaking that in respect of the exempted limited partnership no taxes imposed by the Cayman Islands in a period not exceeding 50 years from the date of approval shall be payable.

16.7.5 Lending to collective or mutual investment funds

The Cayman Islands have enacted the *Mutual Funds Law 1993* as a framework pursuant to which a definition of a mutual fund has been provided which excludes closed-ended funds, and provides for the licensing of mutual funds constituted in the Cayman Islands and the licensing of those who provide management, administration and custodial services to such mutual funds in and from within the Cayman Islands. The *Mutual Funds Law 1993* does not, itself, extend to the operation of licensed mutual funds and does not, in particular, contain restrictions on investment. As is the case with any collective investment fund or mutual fund, the lender should be concerned with the issue of legal personality, capacity, due authorisation and due execution arising from the constitution of the body corporate, trustee of the unit trust or general partner of the limited partnership which is the issuer of shares, units or limited partnerships interests respectively and should ascertain that all regulatory licences and permissions have been obtained. Notwithstanding the absence of a statutorily imposed regime of investment restrictions, the lender should ensure that no such restrictions are applicable so as to prohibit the borrowing proposed and/or the application of the funds and that, to the extent that there is a separate manager and/or custodian or trustee holding assets, they are joined in the transaction documents as appropriate.

16.7.6 Taking security

Where the property comprising the subject matter of the proposed security interest has a *situs* outside of the Cayman Islands and where, otherwise, the proper or applicable law (selected in accordance with the application of private international law principles to the transfer, assignment or other creation of security interest in the underlying property) is other than the law of the Cayman Islands, the lender will be concerned exclusively with:

- the capacity of the Cayman Islands domiciled, resident or incorporated entity as party to the relevant security agreement;
- that there is no supervening issue of public interest which will make the security unenforceable as a matter of Cayman Islands law; and
- that the foreign law security is otherwise properly perfected (by for example execution and registration), so that the courts of the Cayman Islands will enforce such security.

There is no presently existing issue of capacity or public interest arising in relation to grantors of foreign law security likely to affect the valid grant of title to property (or the grant of a floating or general business charge) by a Cayman domiciled resident or incorporated grantor.

16.7.7 Property with a Cayman Islands *situs*

Title to immoveable property in the Cayman Islands is determined through a registered land system, pursuant to which the Register of Titles gives a complete picture of the title, a prospective purchaser (or mortgagee) is not affected by trusts and/or equities which are not shown on the Register and the registered title operates as a 'guarantee' in favour of the registered proprietor. A security interest in immoveable property may be obtained by way of charge or mortgage, the existence of which can be registered in the 'encumbrances section' of the Registry and pursuant to which no disposition or dealing with the land affected is permitted without the consent of the registered charge holder. Otherwise, and in the case of intangible moveable property comprising a chose in action represented by a bank deposit placed by the depositor (as debtor) with a bank as secured party, the Cayman Islands have, through the enactment of the *Law of Property (Miscellaneous Provisions) Act 1994*, provided for the express recognition of a charge given by the depositor (as debtor) in favour of the deposit-holding bank (as secured party).

16.7.8 Requirement for registration, filing and recording

The *Companies Law (1995) Revision* requires that every limited company shall keep at its registered office a register of all mortgages and charges specifically affecting property of the company, and shall enter into such register in respect of each mortgage or charge a short description of the property mortgaged or charged, the amount of the charge created and the names of the mortgagees or persons entitled to such charge. The register of mortgages is required to be open for inspection by any creditor or member of the company at all reasonable times. A failure to maintain the register, or to allow access to it, is an offence. There is, however, no requirement to register, file or otherwise record mortgages and charges affecting a company's property at the Register of Companies, and a failure to record the mortgage or charge in the company's own register does not, in accordance with the terms of the Companies Law, invalidate the mortgage or charge.

16.8 Enforcement

Although the *Foreign Judgment Reciprocal Enforcement Law* provides for the registration of judgments made by the courts of designated territories, it is of extremely limited application. For practical purposes the lender is likely to require to bring proceedings on the judgment as a liquidated debt claim. In such an action, and provided that the court making the original judgment had jurisdiction on the basis of residence or submission to jurisdiction, the judgment is for a liquidated sum not in respect of a finance or a penalty and was final and conclusive between the parties, there is no retrial on the merits.

16.8.1 Investigation and obtaining of evidence

At para 16.4 above, a general description has been given of the application of the statutory framework for the duty of confidence owed by bankers and other professionals under the law of the Cayman Islands. The courts of the Cayman Islands will, pursuant to mutual assistance arrangements with the United States, make disclosure orders under legislation intended to combat drug money laundering, racketeering and other serious crime, but will not compel disclosure intended to facilitate enforcement of the fiscal laws of a foreign territory.

16.8.2 Winding-up and bankruptcy

The *Companies Law (1995 Revision)* makes provision for the winding-up of a company as follows. A company may be wound up voluntarily:

- when the period, if any, fixed for the duration of the company by the articles of association expires, or whenever the event, if any, occurs upon the occurrence of which it is provided by the articles of association that the company is to be dissolved, and the company has by resolution of its members adopted a resolution requiring the company to be wound up voluntarily; or
- if the company has passed a special resolution requiring the company to be wound up voluntarily.

On the commencement of a voluntary winding-up, the company is required to cease business. A voluntary winding-up of a company does not operate as a bar to the right of any creditor of such company to have the company wound up by the court, if the court is of the opinion that the rights of such creditor would be prejudiced by a voluntary winding-up. The *Companies Law (1995 Revision)* makes further provision for the conversion of a voluntary winding-up into a court-supervised winding-up pursuant to a petition presented by a creditor or contributory.

17 | Bermuda

Introduction

Bermuda consists of a chain of narrow islands, the principal ten of which are connected by bridges or causeways and which are located in the Atlantic Ocean some 750 miles south-east of New York. The principal population centre of Bermuda (and the location of most of the financial institutions and professional support services) is the city of Hamilton. Bermuda has a population of approximately 60 000. The principal business language is English.

17.1 Currency and exchange control

The currency of Bermuda is the Bermuda dollar, which has parity with the United States dollar. A residual exchange control regime applies to residents of Bermuda pursuant to the *Exchange Control Act 1972*. The lender is unlikely to be concerned with its operation as, in most cases (but this must not be assumed), the borrower or obligor will be an *exempted* entity, entitled to operate outside of the Act's application, free to make payments of capital and interest distributions and to operate foreign currency bank accounts within Bermuda.

17.2 Constitution

Bermuda is politically stable. It is a self-governing dependent territory of the English Crown and a member of the British Commonwealth. Bermuda adopted a written constitution in 1968 (made pursuant to the UK *Bermuda Constitution Act 1967* extended to Bermuda by Order in Council) providing for government through a legislature made up of the House of Assembly (consisting of 40 elected members) and the Senate (consisting of 11 senators appointed by members of the House of Assembly and, as to three senators, appointed at the Governor's discretion). The Governor is the representative of the English Crown in Bermuda, which has through that office residual responsibility for the defence, external affairs and internal security of Bermuda.

17.3 Legal system

The system of law followed in Bermuda is English common law. Bermuda has an autonomous court and judicial system consisting of a Magistrates' Court, a Supreme Court and a Court of Appeal, with the highest appellate court being the Privy Council in the United Kingdom.

17.4 Banking and professional confidentiality

Bermuda does not have a statutory framework for bank or professional secrecy. Banking and other professional confidentiality arises as a matter of common law, and as an express or implied contractual obligation. Consequently, the Supreme Court in Bermuda will have regard to the principles set out in the English decision of *Tournier v National Provincial and Union Bank of England* [1924] 1 K.B. 461.

17.4.1 Bermuda companies: disclosure of beneficial ownership

It is a requirement on incorporation of a Bermuda company that the names, addresses and occupations of all beneficial owners be disclosed to the Bermuda Monetary Authority ('the BMA'). It is, likewise, a requirement that in the case of an *exempted company* incorporated with objects which restrict its activity to that of administering a single trust or settlement, details of the family forming the class of beneficiaries are disclosed. This information is not available on public files and is held as confidential by the BMA. It is an offence for employees of the BMA to disclose information which is confidential to the government of Bermuda or of a person concerned: *Bermuda Monetary Authority Act 1969,* s.31.

17.4.2 Disclosure under compulsion of law

Disclosure of otherwise confidential information may be required, *inter alia*, pursuant to a notice issued by the Minister of Finance under the provisions of the *USA–Bermuda Tax Convention Act 1986*. This Act provides for the implementation in the domestic law of Bermuda of a Convention providing for mutual assistance in combating tax fraud and evasion. The Minister of Finance will issue a notice only on receipt of a request relating to information, documents, copy documents, or an examination or deposition of a taxpayer in respect of tax evasion or fraud. Information produced pursuant to a notice may be disclosed to the United States tax authorities.

17.5 Regulation in the financial sector

The regulation of the financial services sector in Bermuda rests with the Bermuda Monetary Authority constituted pursuant to the *Bermuda Monetary Authority Act 1969*. Save in the case of insurance business (where the principal regulator is the Registrar of Companies) the BMA operates as a primary regulator in accordance with the terms of the following key legislation.

- The *Banks Act 1969* as amended in 1990, pursuant to which the conduct of banking business in Bermuda is (i) restricted to companies incorporated under the *Companies Act 1981* and beneficially owned by Bermudian residents holding not less than 60% of the voting equity capital, and (ii) to companies licensed by the Minister of Finance. In consequence, there are only three banks licensed to conduct banking business in Bermuda and no foreign banks.
- The *Companies Act 1981* as amended (including the *Companies Amendment Act 1986* and the *Companies Amendment Act 1994*), pursuant to which the incorporation of *local, exempted, permit/overseas, mutual fund* and *limited duration* companies is regulated.
- The *Insurance Law 1978* as amended (by the *Insurance Amendment Act 1981*, the *Insurance Amendment Act 1983*, the *Insurance Amendment Act 1985* and the *Insurance Amendment Act 1996*), pursuant to which insurance companies, including captive insurance companies, are licensed and regulated. It is relevant for lenders to .note that 'captive insurance' and 'reinsurance' constitute a substantial part of the finance sector activity in Bermuda. Demand for banking facilities from this sector includes global custody, foreign exchange lines and investment management.

- The *Code of Conduct 1994*, pursuant to which a framework is provided for the conduct of mutual funds and those providing services to collective investment schemes or mutual funds.
- The *Trust Companies Act 1981*, pursuant to which the provision of trust administration to Bermuda trusts is licensed.
- The *Bermuda Stock Exchange Company Act 1992*, pursuant to which listing on the Bermuda exchange is regulated.

Regulation of the finance sector in Bermuda also involves consensual regulation through codes of conduct agreed between the relevant professionals and the BMA, an example of which is the code of conduct first introduced in 1994 to introduce agreed minimum standards for those providing management and custodial services to collective investment funds. Other codes of conduct provide for the prevention of money laundering and the conduct of professional investment advisers. Bermuda is:

- a party to the Convention of the Organisation for Economic Co-operation and Development;
- a member of the Offshore Group of Banking Supervisors; and
- has designated territory status under the United Kingdom *Financial Services Act 1986*, s.87.

17.6 Anti-money laundering legislation and best practice

Bermuda is a member of the Caribbean Financial Action Task Force (although geographically it is not in the Caribbean) and has endorsed the 40 recommendations proposed for implementation by all participating territories. In combating the criminal misuse of its financial sector services, Bermuda has hitherto relied upon its voluntary codes of conduct in relation to the prevention of money laundering and *know-your-customer* compliance. This regime is to be replaced by a statutory regime when the presently proposed *Proceeds of Crime Bill* becomes law.

17.7 Lending with a Bermuda foreign law connection

The text which follows highlights those issues which may arise in connection with lending which has a Bermuda foreign law connection in that either the borrower is domiciled, resident and/or incorporated or constituted in Bermuda, or because a transaction or security document has a proper or applicable law which is Bermuda law. The issues are first dealt with by reference to borrower type in relation to issues which will, in the usual course, form the subject matter of a Bermuda foreign law legal opinion, being:

- the existence of and continuity of legal personality (i.e. does the borrower have and can the borrower maintain separate legal existence, and if not, who may contract on behalf of the borrower?);
- capacity;
- due authorisation of the transaction;
- due execution of the transaction and/or security documents; and
- taxation, including withholding.

The remaining paragraphs then deal collectively with:

- the creation of securities; and
- enforcement and insolvency.

As in other chapters dealing with individual offshore centres, an assumption has been made that the proper or applicable law of security agreements will be a law other than that of the relevant offshore centre, on the basis that it is unlikely that the security will have a *situs* in such offshore centre.

17.7.1 Lending to natural persons

The following issues are relevant when lending to, or taking a grant of security from, an individual domiciled and/or resident in Bermuda.

17.7.1.1 Capacity
An individual is a minor and without legal capacity to contract (other than possibly for necessities) until attaining the age of 18 years.

17.7.1.2 Tax and withholding
There are no direct taxes on income, capital gains, property transfers or on inheritance applicable to non-resident or exempted persons under the law of Bermuda.

17.7.2 Lending to companies

The legislative framework relating to a company incorporated under the law of Bermuda is to be found in the *Companies Act 1981* as amended by the *Companies Amendment Act 1986, Companies Amendment Act 1993* and the *Companies Amendment Act 1994* ('the Companies Acts').

17.7.2.1 Legal personality, due incorporation and good standing
A company (which for this purpose means an exempted company) may, under the Companies Acts, be incorporated either by registration (a *registered company*) or by Private Act (a *statutory company*). A company is, from the date of its incorporation by registration under the *Companies Act 1981*, a body corporate having a separate legal personality and, if it is not a limited duration company, will have perpetual succession. The issue of a certificate of incorporation by the Registrar of Companies is conclusive as to its due incorporation in accordance with the Companies Acts. A company may only be incorporated:

- as a company incorporated by shares;
- as a company incorporated by guarantee; or
- as an unlimited liability company.

The lender should note the following as the principal steps for and elements of due incorporation:

- there is no opportunity to apply for name approval prior to incorporation but it may be possible to 'reserve' a name in advance of incorporation (the use of names related to regulated activities such as 'Bank', 'Insurance' or 'Trust Company' will be dependent upon the appropriate licence having been obtained for such regulated activity);
- incorporation may only be achieved through local lawyers – pre-incorporated or shelf companies are not permitted;
- application must be made to the BMA and, in the case of a private company, bank reference(s) are required in respect of the ultimate beneficial owner (whose identity must be disclosed to the BMA), or, in the case of a public company, audited accounts must be produced;
- the incorporation of the company must be advertised stating the name of the company and its objects;
- the memorandum of association (setting out (i) the name of the company, (ii) the objects of the company, (iii) a statement of the limitation of liabilities of members (if appropriate), (iv) the share capital of the company and its division into shares of a specified par value, or, if appropriate, a statement that it is limited by guarantee, and (v) the powers of the company if different than those set out in the Companies Acts) must be submitted for registration; and
- the company may have a single subscriber member: *Companies Amendment Act 1993*.

No express distinction between *public* and *private* companies is made in the Companies Acts, but provision is made regarding the issue of shares to the public. A company which has its shares listed on a recognised stock exchange may, pursuant to the *Companies Amendment Act 1996*, enjoy the same alternatives to having a quorum of Bermudian resident directors as are available for a private company. The Companies Acts distinguish between:

- *mutual fund companies:* the Companies Acts provide separately for the flexible redemption or repurchase of its shares by a *mutual fund company,* defined as a company (i) limited by shares, (ii) having the power to redeem or purchase its shares (without thereby reducing its authorised share capital), and (iii) being incorporated for to invest the subscriptions of members for their mutual benefit;
- *limited duration companies:* a limited duration company is a company incorporated under the Companies Acts which provides in its memorandum of association that it is deemed to be subject to the commencement of a voluntary winding-up at the expiry of the period stated for its existence or on the happening of a prescribed event, where at least one such 'trigger' must be stated in the memorandum of association;
- *overseas or permit companies:* being a company incorporated outside of Bermuda which wishes to carry on business in the same way as an exempted company (that is, to carry on business external to Bermuda within or from within Bermuda) may do so subject to application for a permit issued by the Minister of Finance. Generally, an overseas company will require a permit if it occupies premises in Bermuda or purports to operate from an address in Bermuda. For practical purposes the process of application for a permit is similar to that of incorporation of an exempted company (including disclosure to the BMA of beneficial ownership with bank references etc), and an overseas company is subject to the application of provisions of the Companies Acts relating to, for example, the raising of moneys through the circulation of a prospectus; and
- *exempted companies:* being a company incorporated in Bermuda which is exempted from the requirement to have majority local beneficial ownership.

A lender will most frequently encounter exempted companies. The following are the principal characteristics of and formalities associated with an exempted company:

- it must have a registered office in Bermuda at which is maintained a register of shareholders and of directors;
- it must have liability limited by shares;
- it must have a minimum authorised capital of B$12 000 (or equivalent) which must be subscribed and allotted but which need not be paid-up (in which case the shareholders will be liable for such unpaid amount on insolvent winding-up);
- it may have a single subscriber/member;

- its officers must include two individuals resident in Bermuda serving (i) one as secretary and one as a 'resident representative', or (ii) one as secretary and one as director, or (iii) both as directors; if the company is a listed company it must have a 'resident representative';
- it must adopt by-laws, first through the provisional directors and subsequently by the statutory meeting, which provide for the internal governance of the company, regulating, for example, the holding of an annual general meeting, an audit of accounts, a quorum for transmission of shares, the allotment of shares and the distribution policy of the company;
- it must hold an initial general meeting (the 'statutory meeting') at which (i) the by-laws are confirmed, (ii) the first directors are appointed, and (iii) auditors are appointed;
- it must hold an annual general meeting in each year (which may be held outside Bermuda and may be substituted by a written resolution);
- it must elect directors at the statutory meeting (there is no share qualification required) who are charged with the management of the company;
- it must maintain accounts at its register or principal office address, although the requirement for audited accounts may be waived;
- it must, in January of each year, make a return to the Registrar of Companies declaring (i) the company's principal business and (ii) the amount of its share capital for the purpose of assessment of its annual fee, such return being signed by two directors or one director and the secretary;
- although incorporated in Bermuda, it may generally only carry on business in respect of transactions and activities outside Bermuda;
- it is restricted by the 1981 Act from carrying on business in Bermuda except where it is so authorised by its constitutional documents and has been granted a licence by the Minister of Finance;
- for carrying on activities for example, doing business with other 'exempted companies, permit companies, exempted partnerships and exempted unit trust schemes, dealing in securities of other exempted undertakings and carrying on business' as manager or agent for, or consultant or advisors to the business of an exempted undertaking a licence is not required. As the *Companies Amendment Act 1993* makes provision for the incorporation of Single Member Companies, references to shareholders also include the sole shareholder of such a company;
- it must apply to the Registrar of Companies to be registered as an exempted company and submit to the Registrar, followed by the advertisement of a legal notice in a local paper announcing the intention to incorporate an exempted company with the selected name and specified objects;

(i)   a declaration signed by the proposed directors confirming that the operations of the proposed exempted company will be conducted mainly from outside Bermuda;

(ii)   the name of the proposed company, the nature of its intended business and the proposed beneficial ownership (details of which are confidential), together with bank references on ownership unless the owners are well known to the authority in which case the latest annual report will be required.

(iii) it must file within six months after the date of the grant of consent of the Minister, the memorandum (signed by three persons who are normally nominees resident in Bermuda) and articles of the company with the required non refundable fee;

- it must reserve the proposed name with the Registrar and advertise the proposed incorporation;
- it must pay the required annual government fee within 30 days of incorporation;
- it must advertise its change of objects and a change of name in a local paper and obtain consent of the Minister and a resolution of the Members passed at general meeting of the Company;
- it may, provided it is authorised by its bylaws and the members in general meeting divide and subdivide its shares; make provision for the issue and allotment of non voting shares; cancel authorised but unissued shares; and change its currency denomination; issue preference shares and redeem them; and
- it must appoint an independent representative of the members as its auditors and place the audited financial statements before the membership at each annual general meeting.

References to a *resident representative* mean the term as it is defined in the *Companies Amendment Act 1996*, which requires that a *resident representative*: (i) be entitled to attend at and participate in (other than by voting) all meetings of directors and shareholders or any committee of directors, (ii) be entitled to receive notice of all meetings of directors and shareholders, and (iii) be appointed to act as agent for service of process in Bermuda. The *resident representative* is under an obligation to report to the Registrar of Companies any material breach of the Companies Acts by the company or any breach of an Act governing the issue or transfer of shares. Where the exempted company is a listed company (i.e. a public exempted company) the *resident representative* (i) is under an obligation to report to the Registrar of Companies any de-listing, (ii) must have authority to file all documents and do all acts required by the company in compliance with the Companies Laws, and (iii) must maintain at an office in Bermuda originals or copies of the minutes and financial statements required to be maintained in compliance with the Companies Acts. For the lender to an exempted company, the following are of particular note.

17.7.2.2 Capacity

The company's capacity is limited to its objects as set out in its memorandum (standard objects are set out in the Companies Acts, which may be adopted and supplemented as appropriate). The powers of the company are also set out in its memorandum (the standard powers as set out in the First Schedule to the Companies Acts will apply unless expressly excluded) and such powers must be exercised consistently with the stated objects. The company may only alter its objects pursuant to (i) consent of the Minister of Finance, (ii) a resolution of members, and (iii) a notice published in a local newspaper. The powers of the directors are set out in the by-laws and are exercisable by the directors subject to a duty to act honestly, in good faith and with a view to the best interests of the company. The lender must, in respect of a company, ensure that the intended borrowing is within the objects of the company, although, generally, the stated objects will be broadly drawn so as to avoid problems of an exercise of powers *ultra vires* the company, but will not, in any event, allow the company (i) to own land in Bermuda, (ii) to take security over land in Bermuda, (iii) to acquire shares in a local company, or (iv) to carry on business in Bermuda. The lender should note that a company incorporated by Private Act may have special objects and/or powers as set out in the Act.

17.7.2.3 Due authority

The lender should note that restrictions on directors' powers may be contained within the by-laws of the company. A Bermuda company acts through its directors, who are bound by the terms of the by-laws and any objects and corporate powers set out in the company's memorandum of association. The by-laws are not a public document but the lender should insist on their production and review the by-laws as part of its due diligence and, where a foreign law legal opinion is sought, they will form part of the confirmation of due authority. The Companies Acts provide that a company must have at least two directors (a president and vice president); corporate directors are not permitted. Only another director may act as a director's alternate at a board meeting. The lender should, in all cases, require sight of a minute or extract of minute of the directors dealing with the following:

- confirming that the meeting was duly convened and quorate (notice of directors' meetings is required to be given);
- evidencing consideration of the relevant aspects of the proposed transaction;
- considering the terms of the relevant transaction documents;
- approving the execution of the transaction documents substantially in the considered form (and as appropriate allowing for negotiation or agreement of amendments to such documents);
- stating the manner in which such documents are to be executed,

designating one or more persons to attest the common seal of the company or designating individuals as signatories to the documents.

Subject to the by-laws, a Bermuda company may provide that proceedings of directors be convened and held by telephone, or by resolution in writing signed by all of the directors. The directors may act through committee. Where shareholder resolutions are required as an aspect of the authorisation for the transaction, the lender should note that the Companies Acts:

- allow for the convening and conduct of general or class meetings of members in such manner as may be provided for by the by-laws and with only one such member being present, so that in the case of a single member company, a resolution will be constituted by a 'minute of resolution'; and
- require a minimum notice period of a general meeting of five days (which may be extended by the by-laws), although time for notice may be abridged by agreement of all members attending and entitled to vote at the meeting.

17.7.2.4 Due execution
Subject to the by-laws, the directors of an exempted company have power to exercise all of the powers of the company set out in its Memorandum of Association. A company must have a common seal retained at its registered office. The directors may authorise execution of contracts by the affixing of the common seal attested by two directors or by one director and the secretary. A third party dealing with the company in the ordinary course of its business is entitled to assume due execution on behalf of a company where the agreement is executed by two directors or by the president (the Companies Acts impose an obligation to appoint a president and vice president), who can be assumed to have ostensible authority. A company may, by deed or instrument under seal, empower a person either generally or in respect of a specified matter to be its attorney to execute deeds or instruments under seal on its behalf and a deed or instrument under seal signed by a duly appointed attorney on behalf of the company binds the company as if it were executed by the company. A company may maintain a seal for use outside of Bermuda as a duplicate seal and the company having a duplicate seal may authorise any person appointed for the purpose to affix the duplicate seal to any deed or other document to which the company is a party.

17.7.2.5 Issue of shares and circulation of a prospectus
An exempted company must have an authorised and subscribed capital of not less than B$12 000, which need not be paid-up. If the exempted company writes insurance it must have a share capital of not less than

B$120 000 subscribed and paid-up. Bearer shares are not permitted. A company which offers shares to the public must publish a prospectus which (i) is signed by or on behalf of the directors, (ii) is filed with the Registrar of Companies, and (iii) is certified by a lawyer as complying with the provisions of the Companies Acts or with those of an 'appointed stock exchange'. Members are required to pay-up any unpaid share capital on an insolvent winding-up. Shares may be issued in classes including non-voting, preference and redeemable shares (redeemable at the option both of the company or of the member) and may be issued at a premium. An annual fee is payable in relation to the 'assessable capital', that is its authorised share capital and value of its share premium account.

17.7.2.6 Licences and consents
If the activity of a company is that of banking business, insurance business, or of a corporate trustee (being a public trustee) managing agent, the licences and permissions are required under the statutes referred to at para 17.5 above.

17.7.2.7 Financial assistance
The Companies Acts prohibit the provision by a company of direct or indirect financial assistance for the purchase of the company's shares. Provision is made to allow such assistance if (i) the assistance is provided out of distributable profits or does not, after it has been given, reduce the net asset value of the company, (ii) the directors provide an affidavit confirming the solvency of the company, and (iii) the giving of the assistance is confirmed by the members.

17.7.2.8 Disclosure of directors' interests
The directors are required to disclose interests in any contract with the company.

17.7.2.9 Commercial benefit
This issue arises for the lender as a consequence of the duty of the directors of a Bermuda exempted company to exercise the powers of the company in the best interests of the company, usually requiring that the transaction confer some benefit on the company. The absence of tangible benefit is most likely to occur in the case of guarantees given for the liability of third parties (and, in particular, *upstream guarantees*). If there is an element of doubt as to the existence of benefit, the lender should:

• take the contractual undertakings in the form of a deed;
• require a shareholder resolution authorising and directing the grant of security; and

- ensure that to avoid the risk of a voidable transaction on insolvency, the directors resolve to enter into the transaction (i) having regard to the authority and direction of the shareholders, and (ii) having noted that, on reasonable evidence, the company is solvent at the time of the giving of the security and will not become insolvent as a consequence of giving it. See further reference to the application of the *Bankruptcy Act 1989*, para 17.8.2 below.

17.7.2.10 Tax and withholding

Exempted companies are not assessable to income or other taxes but are liable to pay the incorporation and annual fees applicable to them. Pursuant to the *Exempted Undertakings Tax Protection Act 1966* an exempted company may apply for a certificate of undertaking confirming that any tax introduced on profits or gains will not apply to an exempted company.

17.7.2.11 Redomiciliation/continuation

The Companies Acts provide for transfer by way of continuation by a foreign company to be continued as an exempted company in Bermuda. The formalities are broadly similar to those required on incorporation of an exempted company.

17.7.3 Lending to Bermuda trusts

The following text sets out the issues relevant when lending to, or taking a grant of security from, a trust (through its trustee) which has as its proper law the law of Bermuda. Pursuant to extension to Bermuda of the UK *Recognition of Trusts Act 1987* the law of Bermuda recognises foreign trusts based on the criteria set out in the *Hague Convention* on the *Law Applicable to Trusts and on their Recognition*. Bermuda trust law is based generically on the English common law and varied by local legislation and case authority. The principal statutory provisions are contained within the *Trustee Act 1975* (based on the UK *Trustee Act 1925*), the *Trusts (Special Provisions) Act 1989* and the *Conveyancing Act 1983* as amended by the *Conveyancing Amendment Act 1994* (together referred to as 'the Trust Laws'). References here to a 'trust' mean a Bermuda trust which, in accordance with the Trust Laws, has a proper law being that of Bermuda. The application of the law of Bermuda to a trust allows for, or particularly facilitates, their use in relation to the following:

- *Private, discretionary and/or fixed interest trusts,* in which connection the validity of trusts is determined in accordance with the provisions of the *Trusts (Special Provisions) Act 1989* which (i) establishes a doctrine of choice of proper law for a trust, (ii) allows for a change in the proper law of a trust, and (iii) provides for all matters of validity concerning transfers of property (other than real property) made *inter vivos* in accordance with the law of Bermuda, thereby facilitating the defeat (as a matter of Bermuda law) of foreign *forced heirship* provisions.

- *Private trusts constituted under a private trust company,* in which advantage is taken of the opportunity to constitute a trustee of a family trust (as an exception to the requirement that an exempted company conduct no business in Bermuda) through which (as shareholders) the family can retain a degree of control over the trust assets.
- *Non-charitable purpose trusts* (sometimes referred to as *special purpose trusts*), in which a trust is constituted which has no beneficiaries but which has a stated purpose. Again this form of trust is used together with a private exempted trust company to provide flexibility, not least in asset financing and leasing structures.
- *Asset protection trusts,* which are usually a classification by use of a private trust where the predominant purpose is to preserve assets transferred into trust from the claims of future creditors of the settlor. The *Conveyancing Amendment Act 1994* amended the *Conveyancing Act 1983* repealing section 37 of the 1983 Act, providing for a regime which, in summary, is intended to provide a regime under which a party seeking to set aside a transfer into trust does not have the benefit of any presumption arising from a transfer at an undervalue and requiring proof by the creditor of a requisite intention to put assets beyond the reach of an existing or reasonably foreseeable contingent creditor. This regime works in conjunction with a framework of fixed limitation periods requiring that a creditor be an eligible creditor (as a person owed an obligation on or within two years of the transfer of assets into trust) and requiring a claim to be brought within six years of transfer into trust.

In dealing with a trust as a borrower and/or provider of security over property comprising the trust fund, the lender should note the following.

17.7.3.1 Legal personality

The trust does not, itself, have separate legal personality. The trust acts through its trustee or trustees who hold (or have held to their order) title to the trust fund.

17.7.3.2 Due constitution and validity of the trust

The following are characteristics of a duly constituted and valid trust pursuant to the Trust Laws:

- there are no requirements as a matter of general law that a trust be created in any specific form and the Trust Laws allow for those (i) created by statute, (ii) created intentionally by the act of the parties, (iii) arising pursuant to will, (iv) arising from the presumed intention of the parties, and (v) arising by operation of law, for example constructive or resulting trusts;

- the perpetuity period for a Bermuda trust is a period of 100 years;
- accumulation is permitted for the whole of the perpetuity period; and
- the trust may have a protector.

17.7.3.3 Capacity

The capacity of the trustee and the extent of the trustee's powers are of crucial importance to a lender contracting with a trustee and must be confirmed in accordance with the Trust Laws and the terms of the instrument constituting the trust. It is normal to give the trustee full and extensive powers to invest the trust fund, including the power to acquire and hold interests in companies. The lender should obtain and review the trust instrument (or ensure that lawyers providing a relevant Bermuda law opinion have sight of it) to ensure that there are no restrictions on the trustee's powers and that the exercise of the relevant trustee powers does not require the consent of the protector, if any.

17.7.3.4 Due authorisation

The lender should seek production of a trustees' minute pursuant to which:

- the trustees properly consider the terms of the proposed transaction and record the benefit to the trust and/or its beneficiaries;
- there are tabled and considered by the trustees the transaction documents;
- the trustees resolve to approve the transaction and execute the transaction documents; and
- the trustees authorise the execution of the transaction documents by their signature, or, if a corporate trustee, and so required, by the application of its common seal.

17.7.3.5 Taxation and withholding

There is no tax on income or gains and no withholding tax payable in respect of the income or gains of a Bermuda trust.

17.7.4 Lending to partnerships and limited partnerships

The law of Bermuda draws a distinction between a *general partnership* (being the relationship which subsists between two or more persons carrying on a business in common with a view to profit and regulated pursuant to the *Partnership Law 1902*, a law which is materially similar to the English *Partnership Act 1890*) and *limited partnerships* constituted pursuant to the *Limited Partnerships Act 1883*. A general partnership may be either:

- an *ordinary general partnership*, under the *Partnership Law 1902*; or
- an exempted general partnership, registered under the *Exempted*

Partnership Law 1992 which requires that (i) one or more of the partners is non-Bermudian, (ii) if a partner is a company, it is not a local company, (iii) one or more partners is not in any way connected with Bermuda, (iv) is formed by first obtaining written approval of the Minister of Labour and Immigration who must approve its articles before it is registered with the Registrar General, (v) it must keep in accordance with the *Exempted Partnership Act 1992* an office and a resident manager in Bermuda and keep at its office audited accounts and records, (vi) it must file a certificate, signed by all the partners, with the Registry containing the name of the firm which must consist of the surnames of the general partners only; the names and addresses of the partners, indicating whether general or special; the general nature of the proposed business to be transacted, the amount of capital contributed by each partner, and the commencement date and the termination date, (vii) it may obtain an undertaking from the Government exempting them from future taxation;

17.7.4.1 Legal personality, constitution and valid existence
Neither a general partnership nor a limited partnership has separate legal personality.

17.7.4.2 Capacity
In the case of a general partnership, capacity will be determined as that of each of the partners (whether as natural persons or companies) in accordance with the law of their domicile. In the case of a limited partnership, capacity is that of the general partner exercising powers contained in the partnership agreement.

17.7.4.3 Due authorisation and execution
Due authorisation on behalf of a general partnership is by each partner where joint and several liability is sought. Due authorisation of a transaction on behalf of the limited partnership should be resolved upon by the general partner(s) and the lender should obtain and have reviewed, in the context of a Bermuda foreign law opinion, a minute of resolution of the general partner(s). It may be necessary to consider further foreign law connections if one or more of the corporate general partners is incorporated outside of Bermuda. The application of the rules of equity and common law applicable to partnerships, means that a person dealing with the general partner in that capacity is entitled to deal with the general partner as having ostensible authority to contract for and on behalf of the limited partnership.

17.7.4.4 Tax and withholding
The exempted partnership may, on the application of a general partner, obtain a certificate issued by the Governor of Bermuda undertaking that in respect of the exempted limited partnership, no taxes imposed by Bermuda

in a period not exceeding 50 years from the date of approval shall be payable.

17.7.5 Lending to collective or mutual investment funds

As is the case with any mutual or collective fund, the lender should be concerned with the issues of legal personality, capacity, due authorisation and due execution arising from the constitution of the body corporate (regulated in the case of a Bermuda company as a mutual fund company pursuant to the *Companies Act 1981* as amended), trustee of the unit trust or general partner of the limited partnership. The lender should, however, be particularly mindful of the need to join any 'custodian' or 'manager' into transaction documents and have regard to any relevant investment restrictions.

17.7.6 Taking security

Where the property comprising the subject matter of the proposed security interest has a *situs* outside of Bermuda and where, otherwise, the proper or applicable law (selected in accordance with the application of private international law principles to the transfer, assignment or other creation of security interest in the underlying property) is other than the law of Bermuda, the lender will be concerned exclusively with:

- the capacity of the Bermuda domiciled, resident or incorporated entity as party to the relevant security agreement;
- that there is no supervening issue of public interest which will make the security unenforceable as a matter of Bermuda law; and
- that the foreign law security is otherwise properly perfected by execution and registration, so that the courts of Bermuda will enforce.

There is no presently existing issue of capacity or public interest arising in relation to grantors of foreign law security likely to affect the valid grant of title to property (or the grant of a floating or general business charge) by a Bermuda domiciled resident or incorporated grantor.

17.7.7 Requirement for registration, filing and recording

The *Companies Act 1981* provides for registration of charges (i) created by a company incorporated under the Act, or (ii) created by a foreign company over Bermuda *situs* real property. The Registrar of Companies maintains the Register of Charges. Registration is not compulsory but the lender should in all cases register, as registration determines priority and a registered charge (irrespective of its date of creation) will have priority over a non-registered charge.

17.8 Enforcement

The courts of Bermuda will register or otherwise give effect to any final and conclusive judgment rendered in any action or proceedings given by a superior court in England without re-examination of the merits. The courts of Bermuda apply general principles of private international law in allowing proceedings to be brought on a judgment which is for a liquidated sum, is final and conclusive between the parties, is not in respect of a fine or penalty and will not require a retrial on the merits where the original court had in personam jurisdiction.

17.8.1 Investigation and obtaining of evidence

At para 17.4 above, a general description has been given of the application of the statutory framework for the duty of confidence owed by bankers and other professionals under the law of Bermuda. The courts of Bermuda will, pursuant to mutual assistance arrangements with the United States, make disclosure of information obtained pursuant to a notice issued under the *USA–Bermuda Tax Convention Act 1986* (para 17.4.2 above).

17.8.2 Winding-up and bankruptcy

The *Companies Act 1981* makes provision for the winding-up of a company as follows. A company may be wound up voluntarily:

- in the case of a limited duration company, when the period, if any, fixed for the duration of the company by the articles of association expires, or whenever the event, if any, takes place upon the occurrence of which it is provided by the articles of association that the company is to be dissolved, and the company has by resolution of its members adopted a resolution requiring the company to be wound up voluntarily; or
- if the company has passed a special resolution requiring the company to be wound up voluntarily.

On the commencement of a voluntary winding-up, the company is required to cease business. A voluntary winding-up of a company does not operate as a bar to the right of any creditor of such company to have the company wound up by the court, if the court is of the opinion that the rights of such creditor would be prejudiced by a voluntary winding-up. The *Companies Act 1981* makes further provision for the conversion of a voluntary winding-up into a court-supervised winding-up pursuant to a petition presented by a creditor or contributory.

Where the Bermuda courts have jurisdiction in a bankruptcy so that the *Bankruptcy Act 1989* applies, the lender should note that the trustee in bankruptcy has the right to treat as void a transfer of property made by the debtor at a time when he was insolvent and made in the five years preceding the bankruptcy, or at a time when the debtor was solvent but made for no consideration (but excluding transfers or dispositions made in consideration of marriage or made in favour of a purchaser or mortgagee in good faith). Likewise, transactions that are made with the intention of giving a preference to a creditor (where such preference is given within the six months preceding the bankruptcy) may be deemed void subject to court order.

Index